Prais ... es:

"The: ... packed full of infor ... nough to slip insid

"Dit ... n het 'n groot opvc

"Handy travel companions … these guides may be small but they're literally jam-packed with information … making these guides holiday must-haves for an informed and more enjoyable trip."
—***Longevity Magazine***

"These handy books are accessible to everyone from the lay person to geologists and scientists, answering all your questions regarding these sites."—***Saturday Dispatch***

"… compact pocket guides packed with info, maps and colourful pictures." —***50/50***

"They are a celebration of various aspects of South African culture, including our historical inheritance and the land on which we live."—**Diane de Beer, *The Pretoria News***

"There's this marvellous new collection of pocket guides by Southbound, each highlighting a specific World Heritage Site in South Africa … Easy to use and fun to read, the pocket guides are a must for anyone remotely interested in our country's heritage."
—***The Independent on Saturday***

"These books reveal fascinating parts of our country that many of us aren't properly aware of. They'd make excellent gifts, singly or collectively, and are great primers for planning a holiday."
—**Bruce Dennill, *The Citizen***

"All [eight] of South Africa's World Heritage Sites are covered, each in a manageable pocket guide which provides a remarkable amount of information for the edification of the serious ecotourist … comprehensive contents … an extensive amount of information …"
—**Carol Knoll, *Environmental Management***

"… intensely practical … fantastic series to buy …"
—**Jenny Crwys-Williams, *Talk Radio 702***

"… these are among the best we have—opinionated and full of personality."—**Patricia McCracken, *Farmers Weekly***

Published in 2008 by Southbound
An imprint of 30° South Publishers (Pty) Ltd.
28, 9th Street, Newlands,
Johannesburg, South Africa 2092
www.30degreessouth.co.za

Design, origination & maps by 30° South Publishers (Pty) Ltd.

Printed and bound by Pinetown Printers (Pty) Ltd.

ISBN 978-190143-25-1

Southbound Pocket Guides
to South Africa's
World Heritage Sites

David Fleminger

Richtersveld
Cultural and Botanical landscape

---

including
Namaqualand

South Africa's Eight World Heritage Sites

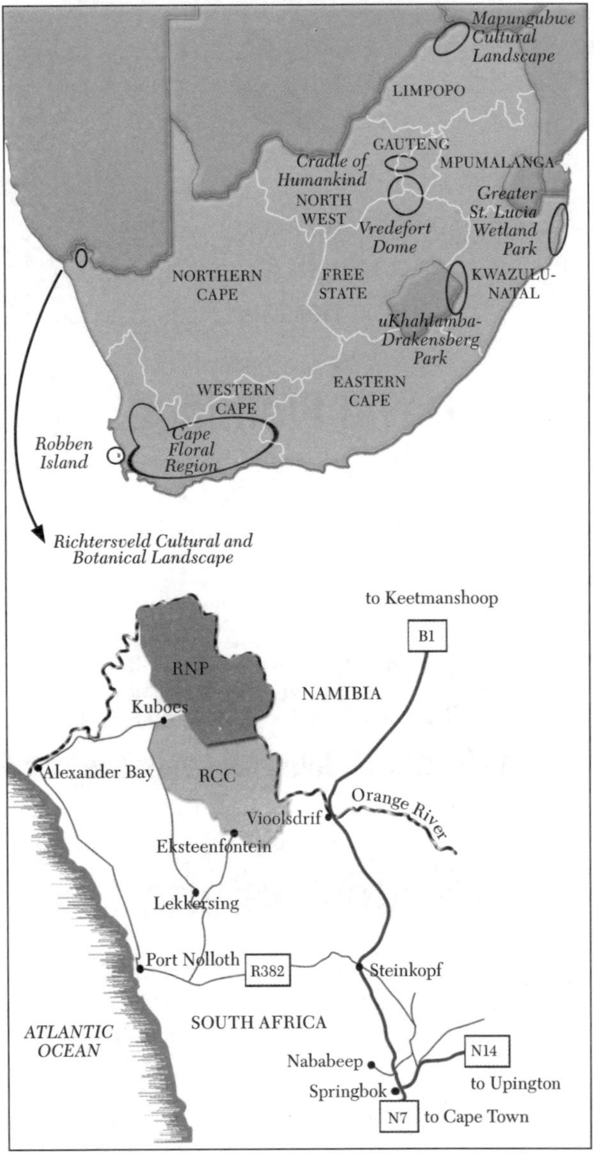

Contents

Contents

What is UNESCO and the World Heritage List?

UNESCO (United Nations Economic, Scientific and Cultural Organization) was formed shortly after World War II, when it was realized that, as a species, we don't really get along. The newly formed United Nations therefore set up an organization that would encourage co-operation between nations by sharing knowledge and promoting culture. But, after the horror of two world wars in which millions of lives and many irreplaceable global resources were lost, it became apparent that building classrooms, mounting festivals and publishing scientific papers that no one would read was not enough. So, the UN tasked this specialized agency with a very ambitious goal: to build peace in the minds of men (and presumably women too).

But that's not all. To quote from UNESCO's most recent manifesto, the organization "is working to create the conditions for genuine dialogue based upon respect for shared values and the dignity of each civilization and culture. This role is critical, particularly in the face of terrorism, which constitutes an attack against humanity. The world urgently requires global visions of sustainable development based upon observance of human rights, mutual respect and the alleviation of poverty, all of which lie at the heart of UNESCO's mission and activities."

In 1972, UNESCO's mandate was significantly enlarged at the *Convention Concerning the Protection and Preservation of World Cultural and Natural Sites*. The original impetus for this worthy endeavour came about several decades earlier because, as is often the case, a valuable site was about to be destroyed in the name of progress. In this instance, it was the Abu Simbel temples in Egypt, which were going to be flooded by the soon-to-be-completed Aswan Dam. The year was 1959 and, thanks to international pressure and funding, the threatened temples were quickly dismantled and re-assembled out of harm's way before the damn dam was built.

Soon, authorities in charge of other endangered sites applied to the UN for protection and assistance and, in 1965, the United States proposed a 'World Heritage Trust' that would identify, promote and protect "the world's superb natural and scenic areas and historic sites for the present and the future of the entire world citizenry". In 1968, the International Union for Conservation of Nature (IUCN) developed similar proposals for its members and, eventually, a single text was agreed upon by all parties concerned, which resulted in the adoption of the above-mentioned convention of 1972.

So, if bird flu, global warming and nuclear Armageddon don't get us, UNESCO is working, along with its 190 member states, to make sure that our precious heritage resources are maintained for future generations. As UNESCO acutely points out: "By regarding heritage as both cultural and natural, the Convention reminds us of the ways in which people interact with nature, and of the fundamental need to preserve the balance between the two."

That's good thinking, and the World Heritage List continues to grow. Every year, additional sites are proposed by local stakeholders to the central committee. A team of investigators is then sent out to write up a report on each nominated site. After studying these independent reports, the committee finally selects several lucky applicants to be inducted onto the list. Since South Africa ratified the World Heritage Convention in 1997, we have become particularly well endowed in this regard. We already have eight sites on the list, which is quite a large number considering the relatively small size of our country and the short time we have been back in the UN fold since the dark days of international isolation.

Furthermore, our sites are biologically diverse and historically significant, reminding us of the vast power of the universe and our fragile place within it.

UNESCO and the Richtersveld cultural and botanical landscape

The Richtersveld is a remote region; hot, dry and seemingly lifeless. It has a certain esoteric beauty, sure, but why should such a barren place be worthy of World Heritage status? Well, according to the documents prepared by the nominating party, the site has both natural and cultural criteria that make it unique. In other words, there's much more to the Richtersveld than first meets the eye.

In terms of cultural significance, the Richtersveld is the home of the last remaining members of the Nama tribe of Khoikhoi who still practise their traditional semi-nomadic way of life. This special form of 'transhumance' entails small family groups who move with their herds of sheep and goats from one seasonal grazing area to another. Significantly, some of them still live in their traditional dome-shaped *matjieshuise* (reed huts), known as *|haru oms* in the Nama language. This unbroken cultural and architectural tradition stretches back over 2,000 years.

The natural criteria are equally impressive. Despite the low annual rainfall, several climatic conditions are present in the Richtersveld that allow an amazing diversity of botanical life to proliferate. Three hundred and fifty species are endemic to the region and it contains the world's most diverse lichen fields (found near Alexander Bay). Furthermore, the Richtersveld is part of the Succulent Karoo biome, which covers the western coastal regions of South Africa and southern

Namibia. This wider region contains over 5,000 plant species and around 40 per cent of these are endemic, including many rare succulents, making it one of only two arid bio-diversity hotspots in the world (the other is on the Horn of Africa).

Nevertheless, it was the cultural significance of the Nama stock farmers and their ancient lifestyle that most impressed UNESCO and its investigating committee. In their report, they found that the site has a high degree of integrity and authenticity in this regard. The traditional system of seasonal migration is still functional, the stock-posts and *|haru oms* are being used as part of daily life, and the nomadic form of herding practised by the Nama is testimony to an ancient form of land management that has helped maintain the fragile Succulent Karoo ecosystem.

In light of these findings, the Richtersveld cultural and botanical landscape was admitted onto the World Heritage list in terms of cultural criteria iv and v, viz.:

Criterion iv. *to be an outstanding example of a type of building, architectural or technological ensemble or landscape which illustrates (a) significant stage(s) in human history.*

Criterion v. *to be an outstanding example of a traditional human settlement, land-use, or sea-use which is representative of a culture (or cultures), or human interaction with the environment, especially when it has become vulnerable under the impact of irreversible change.*

These have been interpreted by UNESCO as follows:

Criterion iv. *The rich diverse botanical landscape of the Richtersveld, shaped by the pastoral grazing of the Nama represents and demonstrates a way of life that persisted for many millennia over a considerable part of southern Africa and was a significant stage in the history of this area.*

Criterion v. *The Richtersveld is one the few areas in southern Africa where transhumance pastoralism is still practised: as a cultural landscape [implying a significant interaction between humans and their physical environment] it reflects long-standing and persistent traditions of the Nama, the indigenous community. Their seasonal pastoral grazing regimes, which sustain the extensive bio-diversity of the area, were once much more widespread and are now vulnerable.*

As is indicated above, however, the integrity of the site is under threat. There are currently only around 300 individuals who still practise the traditional form of stock farming, and most of these people are elderly. The area has also become overgrazed, mainly because private land ownership has encroached on the Nama over the last couple of hundred years and this has limited the wider migration patterns of the stock farmers. Mining activities along the Orange River and in the Richtersveld National Park are also potentially damaging, as this destroys both the physical environment and the cultural traditions of the Nama, who often leave their villages to work on the mines and in the nearby towns.

In view of this, the actual World Heritage Site has been limited in size to what is called the Richtersveld Community Conservancy (RCC). This is an area of 160,000 hectares of grazing land, which is controlled by the Sida !hub Community Property Association (CPA). To be more specific, the declared area is bounded in the north by the Vandersterr mountains, and by the Orange River and Nababeep mountains in the east. To the south and west, the area is buffered by additional tracts of grazing land.

At this stage, the spectacular Richtersveld National Park (located north of the Vandersterr mountains) is excluded from the World Heritage Site because there is still mining activity going on within the park's boundaries. There is a possibility, however, that World Heritage status will be extended to the park once the mines are shut down and the land has been rehabilitated. This may happen sooner rather than later because the mines are nearly exhausted, and there are already agreements in place which allow the Nama stock farmers to graze within the park's boundaries.

Overview

An unlikely Eden

The Richtersveld is located in the extreme north-west of South Africa. As such, it is far away from everything, isolated by the Atlantic Ocean to the west, the Namib Desert in the north and the arid savannah of the Kalahari to the east. This is a dry region, technically a desert, with an average rainfall below 220mm. Mountains of bare rock slash across the hot plains. Succulent plants with thick leaves cling to the boulders and hide in the shadows. Summer temperatures can soar to over 50°C and winter nights can be freezing. The only perennial water source is the mighty Orange River, which flows obliviously through the barren landscape. And yet, for all this, the Richtersveld is one of the most biologically diverse deserts in the world.

It also has a long and valuable cultural tradition,

characterized by the traditional Nama stock farmers, who have been grazing their goats here for over 2,000 years. The natural and cultural integrity of the region is therefore priceless and it is probably the geographical isolation of the region that has ensured its relatively pristine condition. In other words, it is so hard to reach that the various colonizing forces (who generally mucked things up in the rest of the country) simply couldn't find a way to profitably exploit the Richtersveld.

So, what does all this mean for someone who wants to explore the Richtersveld today? Well, in terms of human development, there are few roads and fewer people. Only a handful of small towns offer any form of social and tourism infrastructure. Economic activities are very limited. There's a little bit of commercial agriculture on the banks of the Orange River, but the main activity in the area is diamond mining (which seems to be controlled by all-powerful companies who operate under an impenetrable veil of secrecy). But don't let me overstate the case. The Richtersveld is quite accessible and it is not difficult to plan a trip to this unique piece of Africa.

The purpose of this book, then, is to give the reader a compact overview of this beautiful and complicated region. It also contains practical travel information which will help you plan your itinerary to the Richtersveld Community Conservancy and the Richtersveld National Park. If you aren't actively planning a trip, it is hoped that the pages that follow will encourage you to experience this little-known and seldom-visited gem for yourself.

But, before we continue, I should mention that the Richtersveld cannot be understood out of context. This region is like an onion; a series of concentric circles with various botanical biomes, political districts and cultural groups existing within one another. Most significantly, the Richtersveld is part of the wider Namaqualand region, and the one cannot be profitably discussed without the other.

Like the Richtersveld, Namaqualand is a dry and somewhat remote region. Some sources say that its population density is a mere one person per square kilometre, and the first tarred road in the region was only constructed in the 1960s. Accordingly, the towns are small and spread out, isolated from one another by vast tracts of inhospitable land. But, as is the case with the Richtersveld, it is a beguiling place to visit and very accessible to travellers.

For most people, the first association with Namaqualand is the 'daisies'. This is shorthand for an annual wild flower spectacle in which millions of plants burst into bloom for a few short weeks each spring. This annual display is a must-see, and the normally sleepy Namaqualand district pumps with tourists during flower season. Unfortunately, the flowers do not keep to a timetable and getting to the right place at the right time can be tricky.

The second component of this book, therefore, covers the whys, whens and wheres of Namaqualand. Ideally, you should try to combine a Namaqualand trip with a Richtersveld itinerary. It'll be an unforgettable journey through a remarkable landscape.

Orientation

Before we begin in earnest, let's take a moment to familiarize ourselves with the geography of the area. In terms of location, the greater Richtersveld region can be said to form a rough square in the top left hand corner of South Africa. The borders of this square are as follows: the western boundary is the Atlantic coast, from Alexander Bay to Port Nolloth; in the south, it's the R382 road that runs from Port Nolloth to Steinkopf (a former mission station about 90km inland); in the east, it's the N7 highway from Steinkopf up to the Namibian border post at Vioolsdrif; and in the north, it's the Orange River (or *!Gariep*, meaning 'great river' in the Nama language). This major watercourse also marks the international boundary between South Africa and Namibia.

Politically speaking, southern Namibia is not part of the Richtersveld, but ecologically speaking, it is very similar. On the South African side of the border, the closest major town is the dusty oasis of Springbok, about 60km to the south of Steinkopf on the N7 highway.

The Richtersveld Community Conservancy is located in the middle of this square, bounded by grazing lands to the south and west, by the N7 highway and the Nababeep Nature Reserve in the east, and by the Vandersterr mountains to the north. Beyond the Vandersterr mountains lies the Richtersveld National Park, which extends to the banks of the Orange River. The land between the coast and these two conservation areas is held in private hands and is mainly utilized for mining activities.

If we widen out a bit, we will see that the Richtersveld is located in the top-left corner of the wider Namaqualand region, a maddeningly imprecise term that can be defined in different ways. As Willem Steenkamp recounts in his memoirs, *Land of the Thirst King*, "The place is like a concertina. If you want to live inside its borders you stretch it out all the way to Vredendal. But if you don't fancy being called a Namaqualander you squeeze it flat till it ends at Garies, and that's that."

Botanically speaking, however, Namaqualand is roughly defined as "the part of the Succulent Karoo that is strongly influenced by winter rainfall and fog". Following this description, the southern boundary of Namaqualand extends from the mouth of the Olifants River, near Vredendal, to the edge of the Matsikamma mountains at

Vanrhynsdorp. The eastern boundary then follows the Bokkeveld escarpment, running between Nieuwoudtville and Loeriesfontein, and thence into the north-west, all the way to the coast at Lüderitz in Namibia.

From a political point of view, however, the Namaqua District Municipality includes several environmental units that are quite distinct from the Succulent Karoo. Thus, in the north, it runs along the course of the trusty Orange River from Alexander Bay to Pofadder (in Bushmanland). In the west, it follows the Atlantic shore to a point some 35km south of Garies. From here, it extends eastwards and somewhat south into the Hantam Karoo (including the towns of Loeriesfontein, Nieuwoudtville, Calvinia, Sutherland and Fraserberg).

Finally, in terms of the wild flowers, these occur throughout the Namaqualand region, including the seemingly barren Richtersveld. You also get wild flowers south of Vanrhynsdorp, in what is technically the Cape Floral (or Fynbos) biome. Although they are several hundred kilometres apart, the towns of Springbok and Nieuwoudtville usually act as the de-facto centres of the spring flower experience. The emerging Namaqua National Park, near the town of Kamieskroon, is another good flower-spotting area. The most notable flower destinations outside of Namaqualand can be found in the Cederberg mountains, along the coast around Elands Bay and in the West Coast National Park at Langebaan (the closest destination to Cape Town).

The rocks of the Richtersveld

By its nature, geology is an intricate and rather painstaking business. Moreover, the Richtersveld and Namaqualand boast a particularly long and convoluted geological timeline which, quite frankly, sets my mind a-boggle. Nevertheless, the peculiar landscape, plant life, mineral deposits and cultural riches of the region are directly connected to the rocks on which they rest. So, here's a quick overview of the story …

The earliest identifiable rock layers in the Namaqualand region date to around two billion years ago. Known as the Orange River Group, these are mainly igneous rocks that are volcanic in origin. The lavas of the Orange River Group were then overlain by some sedimentary rocks (sandstone and shale). These can still be seen in the Rosyntjieberg Formation, located in the Richtersveld National Park.

There followed a long period of intrusion events during which molten rock from the mantle was pushed up through cracks in the crust and cooled close to the surface. This resulted in the formation of several granitic suites that formed a granite 'basement', which stretches from the Knersvlakte (north of Vanrhynsdorp) to Steinkopf. In the Richtersveld, these intrusions include the Vioolsdrif Suite (emplaced 1.9–1.75 billion years ago), the Richtersveld Igneous Suite (dating back one billion years) and the Gannakouriep Suite (a series of north–south tending black dykes that were emplaced between 870 and 540 million years ago).

This area is now known as the Namaqualand Metamorphic Complex or Province, as the heat from these subterranean intrusions transformed (metamorphosed) the surrounding rocks. Thus, volcanic rocks changed into schist, shale turned into slate and sandstone became quartzite.

Another important element of these intrusion events is the presence of a series of discontinuous 'mafic bodies', which contain deposits of copper and other valuable minerals. These isolated bodies of ore are found in distinctive 'steep structures' and are known collectively as the Koperberg Suite. The erratic copper deposits of Namaqualand would later play an important role in the development of the region.

Then, around 850 million years ago, the vast landmass of Pangaea began to split apart (or rift) into the continents that we know today. This caused an ocean trough to form in a north–south orientation across much of present-day Namaqualand. Material was subsequently eroded from the hinterland and deposited into this trough, consolidating into the various formations of the Gariep Group.

In the Richtersveld, some of these sediments are thought to have collected at the foot of an ancient mountain range. This caused calcium carbonate to precipitate, forming limestone and dolomite. These rocks were subsequently subjected to heat and pressure, causing them to metamorphose into the erosion-resistant quartzites and marbles of the Stinkfontein Group.

The Vandersterr and Stinkfontein mountains (the so-called backbone of the Richtersveld) are part of this group and contain some of the highest peaks in the area. Ecologically, these two ranges are important because they act as a barrier that prevents the moisture-bearing clouds that roll in from the Atlantic Ocean from reaching the interior. This creates several distinct micro-climates within the Richtersveld, which is one of the factors that contribute to its high botanical diversity.

Another element of the Stinkfontein Group is the Kaigas Formation, a collection of tillite rock, deposited by glaciers that once crept through the region. This is the oldest known glacial deposit in the world.

Next, around 570 million years ago, there was a period of sedimentation that created the Nama and Numees groups, which consist of dolomite, limestone (the Hilda Suite), shale and sandstones. Five hundred and forty million years ago, this group of flat-lying rocks was intruded by the Kuboos–Bremen suite of granites, which occur in a rough line that runs northwest–southeast. The Ploegberg Mountain (near the village of Kuboes) and the granitic Tatasberg pluton (located in the Richtersveld National Park) are part of this suite. These plutons are large domes of rock that are created when volcanic material rises up from the mantle and cools in underground chambers, only to be exposed when the rocks above it are eroded away. Another example of a pluton is the famous Paarl (Pearl) Rock, located in the south-western Cape.

Around 450 million years ago, continued continental rifting caused a large basin to open up in the vicinity of what is now the south-western Cape. This caused the erosive forces that were eating away at the Namaqualand plateau to shift to the south. The sediments that were thus transported into the new basin would eventually form the great Cape Fold mountain ranges and the nutrient-poor soil of the Cape Floral Kingdom (also known as Fynbos).

Skipping forward 100 million years, the supercontinent of Gondwanaland was now drifting slowly across the southern polar region and the land was covered with thick ice sheets. The grooves scoured out by these glaciers can still be seen at Grasdrif, close to the Richtersveld National Park, and at Nieuwoudtville.

By 270 million years ago, however, the land had moved out of the polar region and things were starting to heat up. Accordingly, the glaciers began melting, leaving behind glacial deposits that became the Dwyka Group of tillites. This marks the start of the Karoo Supergroup, which extends over much of South Africa's current interior. These deposits are distributed unevenly in the Namaqualand region, lying on top of the Nama Group of rocks.

Around the same time as the Dwyka deposition, the entire region was subject to an extended period of geological turbulence, when Gondwanaland started splitting apart into what are now the South American and

African continental landmasses. This caused dramatic folding of the rock layers and considerable orogenic (mountain-building) activity across the region. As part of this upheaval, a large basin was formed across the Karoo region and the south-eastern parts of Namaqualand. The Ecca and Beaufort groups were subsequently deposited into this basin, forming the basement of much of the Nama–Karoo biome.

As part of this process, the sea level also receded to expose the coastal plains, and rivers running down to the new coastline proceeded to erode the uplifted plains. This caused, amongst other things, the formation of the Fish River Canyon (second largest on Earth, after the Grand Canyon in North America). By this time, the Namaqualand region was already quite dry and the newly exposed marine terraces began to get covered by sandy deposits.

The next important phase occurred around 120 million years ago, when a series of volcanic pipes pushed their way up from the mantle towards the surface. These funnel-shaped pipes carried with them considerable quantities of diamonds, formed at a depth of up to 250km below the surface. The gems were encased in a special kind of crumbly rock called Kimberlite. Over the millennia that followed, these diamondiferous pipes were subsequently eroded by rivers (most notably the Orange River) and the glittering wealth was washed away towards the Atlantic. The diamonds were thus deposited along the banks of the Orange and at the river's mouth, with the thickest layer of diamondiferous gravel being laid down between 20 and 15 million years ago.

By 100 million years ago, South America and Antarctica had separated from the African landmass and the African sub-continent (which had once been in the centre of the Gondwana supercontinent) was surrounded by water. This caused the rim of the subcontinent to 'buckle', resulting in the creation of a low-lying coastal plain that was separated from the high interior plateau by a sharp 'escarpment'.

By now, the river that would become the Orange (or *!Gariep*) was already the major watercourse in the region. It originated in the highlands of Lesotho and flowed in a westerly direction to enter the Atlantic Ocean near present-day Alexander Bay. Then, around 65 million years ago, a little geological hiccup caused the Orange to change its course. It subsequently shifted to the south and ran through the Koa valley to reach the Atlantic near the mouth of the present-day Olifants River. This meant that millions of tons of diamond-bearing gravel were now getting washed into the sea, only to be transported up the coast by the nascent, north-flowing Benguela Current. Fifty million years later, however, another subterranean glitch caused the Orange to revert to its original course through the Richtersveld to Alexander Bay. The result of all this to-ing and fro-ing is that the entire north-western coast of South Africa, as well as the southern coast of Namibia, is laden with diamonds.

Moving right along, the western coast of South Africa grew steadily drier over the next couple of million years. The Namib Desert, one of the world's oldest, was thus established between 40 million and 25 million years ago. Finally, by five million years ago, the cold Benguela Current (which originates in the Antarctic) had become the dominant climatic factor in this arid region. This coincides with a climatic change which saw Namaqualand shift from a summer rainfall area to a winter rainfall area.

The last major geological development started around five million years ago, when the Namaqualand coastal plain was uplifted. This exposed several marine terraces that were gradually covered by a variety of sand types.

Mixed in with the sand, however, were millions of those gem-quality diamonds we mentioned above, and these gravel beds are being voraciously mined today. We should also note that the marine deposits which remain underwater also contain diamonds, and these are being exploited by diamond boats which suck up the valuable sand and transport it to on-shore sorting facilities.

One last thing to mention: the most recent rocks in the region are found along the banks of the Orange River where thick layers of silt have accumulated as a result of flooding. Some of these banks are 30m higher than the current water level, signifying the biggest floods in southern Africa. Dating of these rocks has shown that some of these floods took place a mere 700 years ago, which suggests that they could occur again!

And so we come to the end of this part of the story, and the final result is the landscape we see today: a rugged, cold shoreline with a wide, sandy coastal plain separated from a hot, dry interior by several ranges of jagged mountains. It is indeed a strange land of contrasts, resting on a jumble of volcanic, igneous, sedimentary and metamorphic rock formations. As Francois Odendaal and Helen Suich write in their book on the Richtersveld, "There are few places in South Africa where such a large number of geological units are visible, and it is partly this diverse range of rock types, as well as their varied elevations, that creates the variety of habitats in the Richtersveld, which in turn makes it possible for such a high plant diversity to evolve."

How does the garden grow?

I have already mentioned the remarkable bio-diversity of the Richtersveld and Namaqualand. But this is an arid region with an average annual rainfall of around 150mm, making it technically a desert. It's also very hot, with summer temperatures often climbing to around 50°C.

So, how can such an inhospitable place succour such a rich botanical heritage?

Well, there are several climatic conditions that have conspired to create this unlikely Eden. The first important element to consider is the cold Benguela Current, which flows in a northerly direction up the west coast of the sub-continent. The Benguela originates in the Antarctic region, where the warmer water of the Atlantic mixes with the icy Southern Ocean. This meeting causes the warm water to cool and sink, causing an 'upwelling' of cold, nutrient-rich water from the bottom of the southern oceans. Powerful winds from the South Atlantic anticyclone system drive this stream of cold water up to the Cape of Good Hope and along the west coast. It finally peters out along the shores of Angola, when it meets with warmer equatorial currents.

The Benguela Current has a major impact on the environment of the sub-continent. The nutrient-rich waters support a large stock of pelagic fish, which in turn support seals, water birds and other marine life. The cold surface water, which is about five degrees cooler than the off-shore waters at equivalent latitudes, also limits the amount of evaporation that can occur. As a result, the rainfall along the west coast is low and the current has a generally 'aridifying' effect on the region.

But the Benguela Current has its upside in that it has a stabilizing effect on the region. The cool winds that blow in off the sea moderate the temperature of the coastal belt, so the summers aren't too hot and the winters aren't too cold. However, because of the mountains, these sea breezes do not penetrate into the interior, and summer temperatures in the Richtersveld can soar well above 40°C.

The Benguela Current is also the source of thick, moisture-laden fogs that regularly roll in from the coast. These heavy mists, known as *malmokkies* or *!hurries* by the locals, are created when humid air blows in from the west and is cooled down by the cold surface water. This forces the warm air to condense into a thick fog that creeps over the coastal plains, covering the plants with a fine haze of moisture. Occurring mainly in the autumn months, when the wind speeds are low, these *malmokkies* are a regular occurrence and a crucial component of the region's relative fertility.

The reliability of the *malmokkies* is supplemented by a surprisingly regular rainfall pattern. Unlike other desert regions, Namaqualand does not suffer prolonged periods of drought. So, while rainfall is low, it is reasonably constant and this allows plants to perpetuate their life cycles. The reasons for this regular precipitation cycle are not well understood.

The last important climatic condition which sustains the Namaqualand ecosystem is the Berg winds, which blow down from the South African interior every winter. This phenomenon is caused by a high-pressure cell of dry air that descends on the high plateau. The air is then drawn towards the low pressure systems along the coast, causing it to rush down the mountain slopes of the steep escarpment. As it descends through the valleys, the air heats up and becomes turbulent. The result is hot, dry winds that blow across the coastal plains. In Namaqualand and the Richtersveld, these Berg winds create warm winter temperatures that allow the plants and animals to develop and reproduce.

Zooming in on Namaqualand

So, there are several environmental conditions that allow life to thrive in Namaqualand. But we still have some way to go before we can understand the full botanical context of this remarkable region. To do this, however, we have to widen our perspective to get the big picture. We will then zoom in, step by step, to understand the various components that come into play. Bear with me now …

The Richtersveld is a small part of the much larger Karoo–Namib botanical region, which extends from southern Angola all the way to the western Free State and the Eastern Cape midlands. This large 'province' is made of three sub-regions. Briefly put, these break down as follows, and I'm quoting here:

Sub-region	Rainfall type	Average annual rainfall	Characteristic vegetation
Namib Desert	Summer; unpredictable	Less than 100mm inland; less than 25mm at the coast	'Sand-sea' with sparse vegetation, mostly ephemerals (short-lived herbs and grasses) and a few perennials (e.g. *Welwitschia mirabilis*)
Nama-Karoo	Summer; sporadic	100mm to 300mm	'*Karoobossies*' —hardy, low shrubs adapted to extreme temperatures
Succulent Karoo	Winter; regular	Around 150mm per year	Dwarf shrubs with succulent leaves (i.e. they store water)

Okay. Zoom into the Succulent Karoo. This region has a very high bio-diversity, containing over 5,000 plant species, 2,400 (48 per cent) of which are endemic. A total of 18 per cent of the plant species found here are endangered, thanks to their limited habitats. The defining characteristic of succulents is that they can store water, either in their thick leaves, swollen stems or other 'organs'. Here's a brief overview of the dominant plant types found in the Succulent Karoo:

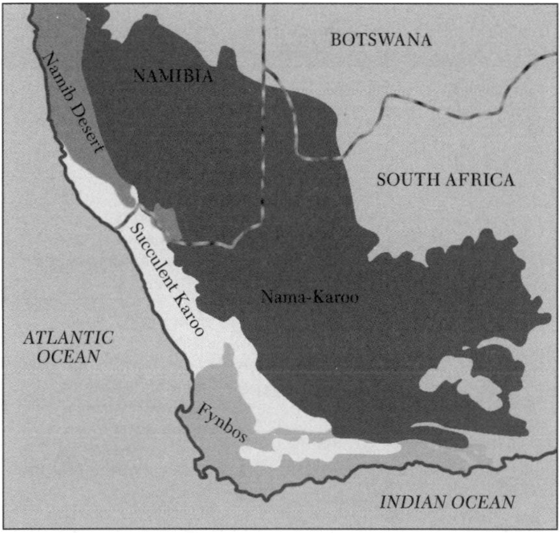

Plant type	Approx. no. of species	Characterized by
Leaf succulents	1,700	"Shallow rooted, compact shrubs with relatively small, succulent, evergreen leaves." Most common are the Mesembryanthemum family (known as 'vygies' or 'mesembs', for short); also includes crassulas and haworthias. Seven hundred of these species are considered compact or miniature forms, such as the many endemic lithops or stone plants—the smallest perennial plants in the world.
Stem succulents	130	Succulents with thick stems, common to many desert areas. Includes euphorbias (over 30 species), pelargoniums, stapeliads and tylecodons (such as the botterboom).

Plant type	Approx. no. of species	Characterized by
Geophytes (bulbs, tubers etc.)	630	Seasonal plants that store water in an underground 'organ'; includes lachenalias, moraeas, romuleas and 'exquisite amaryllids'. Proportionately, a very high number of species when compared to other desert areas.
Annuals	390	Seasonal plants, such as daisies (part of the Astraceae family). Largely responsible for famous 'spring flower' displays. Proportionately, quite a low number of species when compared to other desert areas.
Trees	35	Low number of tree species, usually found along watercourses and in rocky landscapes where there is water runoff. Several species are remnants from the ancient summer rainfall regime.

Right, got all that? Good, because we're now going to zoom in some more. The Succulent Karoo can be split into four regions. Running from north-west to south-east, these are: Namaqualand, the Western Mountain Karoo, Tanqwa Karoo and the Little Karoo. Now, forget about the others and zoom in on Namaqualand for a quick overview of some its more exciting specifics:

OVERVIEW

Plant type	Description
Succulents	About 1,000 species, which equates to around one-third of the total flora and represents ten per cent of all known succulent species. There are 60 species of stem succulents, including the iconic 'halfmens' and the various aloe tree species (also known as kokerbooms or quiver trees). There are at least 250 'compact' species, but these rare miniatures are hard to find (some only poke a couple of millimetres out of the ground). Needless to say, they drive botanists wild!
Geophytes	About 480 species (which is a lot) comprising about 16 per cent of the total flora. Known informally as 'bulbs', these plants flower from March to September. Nieuwoudtville, on the south-eastern edge of Namaqualand, is the self-proclaimed 'bulb capital of the world'.
Annuals	About 330 species. Most flower over a short period in spring, creating the 'carpets' of flowers that tourists want to see.
Shrubs	About 650 species; most of them are evergreen. Includes a number of Fynbos shrubs, found mainly along the coast and on the high mountain slopes.
Grasses	About 200 species; some veld types can support extensive grazing.
Trees	About 35 species. Most are evergreen, with hard leaves.

We have one more zoom-in to make, because Namaqualand can now be split into five distinct geographical and environmental units:

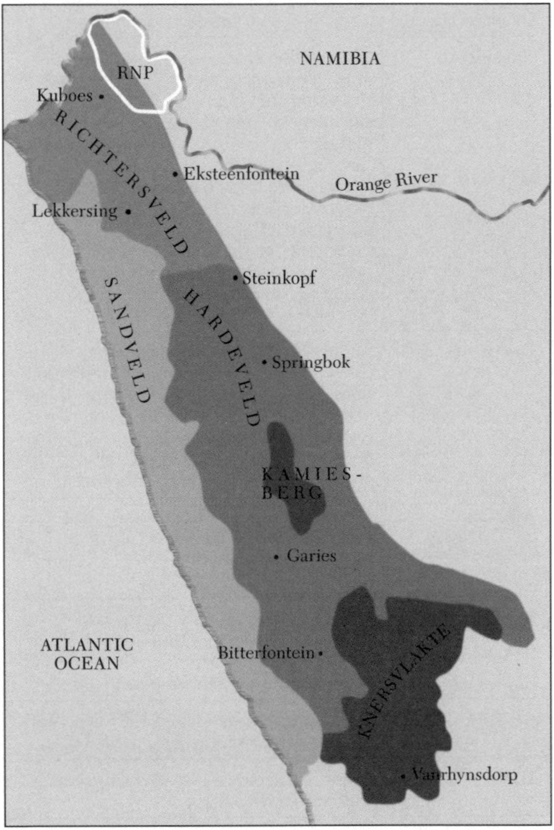

Area	Description	Average rainfall	Location
Knersvlakte	Flat plains with white, quartz gravel	150mm	Begins north of the Olifants River
Hardeveld	Granite hills and mountains	200mm	Part of the Great Escarpment that extends around southern Africa

Area	Description	Average rainfall	Location
Kamiesberg	Huge granite domes (up to 1,700m high)	400mm	Highest, wettest and coldest part of Namaqualand
Sandveld	Sandy coastal strip	150mm in south; 100mm in the north	Northern boundary is the Holgat River
Richtersveld	Transitional zone with several ecosystems	50mm on valley floors; 300mm on west-facing mountain slopes	'Starved' of sand by ridges that stop sand blowing in from the coast

And now, finally, it's time to zoom in to the Richtersveld—the titular hero of this book—to take a closer look at some of its botanical treasures.

Plants of the Richtersveld

The Richtersveld is an environmental marvel that fires the imagination, and its unusual plants attract succulent-spotters from around the world. When I was in the area, I met two amateur botanists from Germany who had been planning their trip for years. Needless to say, they were thoroughly prepared for their expedition and could hardly contain their excitement.

And I'm sure they weren't disappointed. In the Richtersveld, 360 flowering plant species have been counted in an area of one square kilometre. The Mesemb, or Vygie, family is particularly well represented, with 50 out a total of 160 genera being present in the region. That's pretty good for a desert.

One of the reasons for this incongruous bio-diversity is that the Richtersveld is located in a transition zone between the winter rainfall zone of Namaqualand and the summer rainfall zone of the Nama-Karoo. In some places this zone is only ten or 20km wide, which makes for some interesting intermingling of plant types.

Additionally, there are three main biomes in the Richtersveld: the predominant Succulent Karoo biome, the smaller 'Desert' biome (in the north and east) and isolated bits of Fynbos biome (on the high mountain slopes). It's also worth nothing that the mountain ranges, which tend to run in a north–south direction, stop the *malmokkies* and rain clouds from penetrating into the interior. So, seaward-facing slopes get lots of precipitation, while inland-facing slopes (especially in the eastern section) are drier and contain species more usually associated with the Nama-Karoo (such as euphorbias).

All of these conditions create dozens of microclimates in the Richtersveld, and each valley or ridge has a subtly specific combination of rain, wind, soil, heat and exposure. These isolated habitats encourage 'speciation'—the evolutionary process whereby a species adapts to its environmental conditions until it is biologically distinct from its parent population. In the Richtersveld, some of the endemic plant species have become so finely adapted to their specific environments, they are only found in a single valley or a 'narrow' location.

Still, no matter how big or small, the theme common to all the plants of the Richtersveld is survival. As described above, many of the plants store water, either in their leaves, stems or in underground organs, but the ingenuity of these determined life forms goes further than that. Some plants are almost entirely subterranean, with only a few tiny tendrils poking out of the sand. Others grow flat on the ground to avoid the wind, with broad leaves that trap moisture from the ground. Some grow fine hairs or spikes to catch the drops of dew. Some are able to close their pores to prevent evaporation. A few are psammophorous, which means that they exude a sticky substance which catches and secures a layer of sand to their surface, in order to protect themselves against sand storms.

Although most plants in the Richtersveld are evergreen (which is unusual for a winter-rainfall desert) there are a few that drop their leaves in summer to reduce water loss. Others deflect the sun with tiny scales, or by growing a waxy bark, or by retaining old leaves. Some have become miniature, to reduce their need for scarce resources. Some only grow in the nooks and crannies of the rocks, keeping to the cool shadows. In other words, the plants of the Richtersveld are endlessly creative in their survival strategies.

All in all, the Richtersveld is said to contain 4,849 succulent plants, 40 per cent of which are found nowhere else. Many of these plants also have practical applications and are effectively utilized by the native people. Seventy species are used for food (or *veldkos*—bush food), 40 have medicinal applications and 54 have other functional purposes, such as rope-making, soap-making and firewood. There are also several hallucinogenic plants, which are sometimes used for religious purposes. But don't go around licking the succulents—many of them are toxic!

In addition to all the strange and rare plants that haunt the fever dreams of ambitious botanists, the Richtersveld is also characterized by a number of more common plants that have become icons of the region.

The halfmens

The amazing halfmens *(Pachydodium namaquanum)* is a much-photographed pin-up plant that has come to symbolize the Richtersveld. A large stem succulent, or tree succulent, the enigmatic and endangered halfmens (meaning half human) is a cactus-like plant with a sprout of leaves on top of its 'head' and couple of curved appendages that bend out from the central stem. The 'head' of the plant always leans towards the north and this inclination is explained by an ancient legend.

Many years ago, there was a warlike tribe who lived in the north. One day, during a battle, they were driven from their lands and chased over the Orange River, into the Richtersveld. Here, God turned them into strange creatures; half-human, half-plant. With their feet literally rooted to the spot, the tribe was stranded and, to this day, they stand in the Richtersveld, always looking north to gaze longingly at their former home.

It's a nice story, but the botanical reality is far more prosaic. The waxy rosette of leaves on the plant's 'head' is actually its energy source, absorbing water and the sun's energy. Thus, they incline to the north in order to harness the sun more effectively.

Growing up to five metres tall, the halfmens develops mainly in the winter months, when it sprouts nectar-rich, trumpet-shaped flowers. In summer, it drops its leaves and relies on a thick, spiny covering to protect it from the burning sun. The spines also help ward off hungry animals and aid in the collection of rain water and moisture from the *malmokkies*.

The halfmens is endemic to the Richtersveld and it is quite rare. I must confess that during my visit, I totally failed to spot one. Nevertheless, it is one of the most famous plants of the region. Its closest relative *(P. lamerei)* is found only in Madagascar.

Kokerbooms

The aloe trees are another staple of the Richtersveld landscape. Also called kokerbooms, or quiver trees, these attractive stem succulents can live up to 400 years and they come in a variety of shapes and sizes. They are fairly common and can be seen sticking out of rocky ridges and, occasionally, along the roadside. The name 'quiver tree' refers to the Bushmen and Khoikhoi hunters, who used to carry their arrows in hollowed-out kokerboom branches.

In the Richtersveld, three of the five species of kokerboom can be found. These are:

Quiver tree/Kokerboom ***(Aloe dichotoma)***

It grows up to nine metres high and is characterized by a large central stem with a broad spray of branches and leaves growing out of the upper reaches. It's found east of the Stinkfontein mountains and in the arid northern Richtersveld, where it tends to grow taller with simpler branch structures. The kokerboom forest (more correctly called a colony) in the Richtersveld National Park is the best place to check out these ancient aloes.

PLANTS

Pillan's quiver tree, also called the Bastard quiver tree or Basterkokerboom ***(A. pillansii)***

It grows up to ten metres tall with a thick stem. It has fewer, thicker branches and larger leaves than its cousin, *A. dichotoma.* They remind me a little of Sideshow Bob's hair, from *The Simpsons*, if that helps. They grow on mountain slopes close to the Orange River, from Baken to the Tatasberg, with a southern extension on the Dragon's Back Mountain near Eksteenfontein. In the Richtersveld National Park, they can be seen in Helskloof and on Cornell's Kop.

The Maiden's quiver tree or Nooienskokerboom ***(A. ramosissima)***

Less common than the other kokerbooms, this aloe resembles a shrub rather than a tree. It has many branches that spread out from low down on the central structure. It can grow up to several metres high and blooms with bright-yellow flowers, usually in May. Found in the higher mountain slopes and occasionally in riverbeds.

Pearson's aloe ***(Aloe pearsonii)***

A rather rare shrub, the Pearson's aloe is endemic to Helskloof in the Richtersveld National Park and adjacent mountains across the Orange River in Namibia. It has many low branches with triangular leaves that grow in dense layers, with four leaves per layer. These layers curve downwards in an attractive geometric pattern. The colony at Helskloof is extensive and the plants literally cover the mountains on either side of the rocky road pass. The plant is named after Dr H. H. W. Pearson, the first director of Kirstenbosch Botanical Gardens, who first collected the plant in 1910.

Vygies/mesembs

As mentioned above, there are many species of vygies in Namaqualand and the Richtersveld, contributing a great deal to the region's bio-diversity. Despite their ubiquity, they only start to appear on the fossil record a relatively recent 12,000 years ago. However, this may be because desert environments are not conducive to the creation of plant fossils.

Vygies are succulents, with special bladder cells contained in their leaves. Their flowers are also very bright, even luminous, with lots of petals. This eye-catching 'inflorescence' is designed to attract the attention of pollinating insects. Mesembs are sometimes called 'midday flowers' because they usually open their flowers when the sun is at its brightest. Their leaves are not palatable and are rarely eaten by grazing animals or insects. The Rosyntjieberg Mountain in the Richtersveld National Park contains a large number of vygie species.

Other interesting plants

Botterboom *(Tylecodon paniculatus)*
Translated as 'butter tree', this is a chubby dwarf succulent with a thick stem. It is found in many parts of the Richtersveld Community Conservancy and in the Richtersveld National Park.

Ghaap *(Hoodia Gordonii)*
Hoodia has been used as an appetite suppressant by Bushmen and Khoikhoi people for hundreds of years. The plant's active ingredient has been isolated by the South African Council for Scientific and Industrial Research (CSIR). This is licensed to pharmaceutical companies who market it as a diet pill. Following a legal challenge, the CSIR concluded negotiations with Bushmen representatives in 2002 and now pays a royalty to San Hoodia Benefit Sharing Trust for the indigenous knowledge that led to the development of the pill. The money goes towards the upliftment of San communities across southern Africa.

Bushman's Candle *(Sarcocaulon patersonii)*
This plant has a thick, waxy bark to protect it from sand storms. The bark burns quite easily, albeit with a lot of smoke, giving the plant its common name.

Animals of the Richtersveld

The Richtersveld is not the place to go if you want to do some game spotting. Big Five country, it ain't. And yet, despite the arid climate, there is an impressive range of smaller mammals, reptiles, insects and bird life that will appeal to people with these acquired tastes. But before we look at the modern animals you can find, let's take a look at the creatures that used to live here.

The fossil record demonstrates that, in wetter times, the region contained prehistoric horses, elephants, giant shrews, enormous tortoises, short-snouted crocodiles, predatory 'bear-dogs', large proto-ostriches and other arcane species. These traces of ancient life forms are supplemented by fossilized footprints, burrows and impressions of trees (called dendrites) that indicate a fertile land covered with forests. The sea was also warmer in those days, and fossilized shark teeth and unusual oyster shells have been described by various explorers (dating as far back as William Paterson in 1779).

In more recent times, Bushmen carved petroglyphs into the rocks of the region (see below). These petrified 'snapshots' indicate that lion, giraffe, rhino, hippo and even elephant used to roam through the area. Today, however, large animals are rare and it is the smaller life forms that proliferate.

There is also verbal and written evidence that the plains of Namaqualand and the Richtersveld used to be heavily populated by large herds of springbok and other antelope species. In 1892, the magistrate based at Springbokfontein (now simply called Springbok) writes that he witnessed a migration of 'millions' of these graceful creatures.

These flocks of game are now, sadly, a thing of the past; hastened into local extinction through hunting, livestock disease (such as the Rinderpest epidemic of 1896) and human interference with the landscape. Nevertheless, you can still find gemsbok (oryx), klipspringer, duiker, vaalribbok and steenbok in the region, although these animals are more common in the restricted mining areas on the Namibian side of the border, where human activity is limited. The rare Hartmann's mountain zebra is also present.

In terms of mammalian predators, the Richtersveld

contains Brown hyaenas, aardwolfs, caracals and leopards (although these are very rare). You also get Black-backed jackals, the Cape fox, the Bat-eared fox, the African wild cat and Striped polecats (also called the Zorilla). Other mammals include meercats (suricates), Small-spotted genets and several species of mongoose. Primates are represented by Chacma baboons and Vervet monkeys (found mainly along the banks of the Orange River).

Bats, shrews, rats, mice, rabbits and gerbils are reasonably common in the Richtersveld. These include the Striped field mouse, Karoo bush rat, Brant's whistling rat (!), Round-eared elephant shrew, Striped mouse, Long-tailed pygmy mouse, Namaqua rock mouse, tree rats, Cape hare, Smith's red rock rabbit, ground squirrels, Namaqua dune molerat, Common molerat, Rock dassie (hyrax), Dassie rat (which is not related to the dassie) and porcupines. Gerbils include the Namaqua short-tailed gerbil and the Hairy-footed gerbil. There is also a large number of bat species.

In terms of reptiles (scaly) and amphibians (slimy), herpetologists will be delighted with the variety of species that slither and crawl through the Richtersveld. These include the world's smallest tortoise, the Namaqua or Speckled padloper (adults measure around 100mm long). You also get the Angulate (or geometric) tortoise and the Namaqua tent tortoise. Lizards include the large Nile monitor (or waterlikkewaan), Karoo girdled lizard, Armadillo girdled lizard, Smith's desert lizard and the rare Cape flat lizard.

In terms of chameleons and geckos, you get the unusual Namaqua chameleon (which prowls the gravel plains, instead of living in trees), Namib web-footed gecko, Giant ground gecko, Smith's desert gecko, Austin's dune gecko, the recently discovered Leaf-toed gecko, as well as a couple of skinks. For its size, this area represents one of the richest gecko faunas in the world.

Snakes are relatively rare, but those that are present are pretty potent. These include the Black spitting cobra and a variety of desert adders (Puff adder, Horned adder, Desert mountain adder and Namaqua dwarf adder).

There are not many amphibious species in the Richtersveld, as these animals usually require water for breeding. Nevertheless, there are eight species of frog, most of which are known to bury themselves under the sand and emerge only after good rains. These include the Karoo toad, the endangered Namaqua rain frog and the recently discovered Paradise toad. The sudden appearance of frogs after a heavy rainfall has given rise to a local legend that the frogs are actually transported into the region by the clouds that drift in from the sea.

The Orange River is the only perennial water source in the Richtersveld and it supports a fairly traditional assortment of freshwater species. Fish include Yellow fish, Sharptooth catfish (barbel), sardine, Banded bream and the endemic Namaqua barb. The Cape clawless otter can be seen around the mouth of the river, at Alexander Bay, and large numbers of Cape fur seals (now called the South African fur seal) can be found along the coast.

The wide Orange River mouth (or estuary) is one of the most fertile places in the region. With its mud flats, marshes, flood plains and islands, it supports an amazing diversity of birds—up to 10,000 of them, representing over 60 species. These include flamingos (many hundreds of which can be seen perching precariously in the water), Cape cormorants, Chestnut-banded plovers, Egyptian geese, Cape teal, Great white pelican, South African shelduck and the African sacred ibis. There are also about 14 species that are listed in the IUCN Red List of Threatened Species. These include the Damara tern, African purple swamphen, Barlow's lark and the Cape long-billed lark.

In light of this, the Orange River mouth has been declared a RAMSAR wetland of international importance. Unfortunately, the site has been severely degraded by all the mining activity that takes place along both banks; its plight being barely noticed by environmental watchdogs because of its isolated location within the formerly restricted diamond mining town of Alexander Bay. Now, thankfully, the various Namibian and South African authorities are trying to rehabilitate this wetland and restore it to its former glory.

Additionally, various bird species (197) have also been identified within the |Ai-|Ais/Richtersveld Transfrontier Conservation Area. These are found mainly on the banks of the Orange, along dry riverbeds and in the mountain ranges. They include the Lanner falcon, Black eagle, Southern pale chanting goshawk, Spotted eagle-owl, Black-chested snake-eagle, African fish eagle, Cape eagle-owl, Jackal buzzard, Rock kestrel, Cape spurfowl, Bokmakierie, Namaqua sandgrouse, Cape bunting, Diedrich cuckoo, Red-chested cuckoo, African hoopoe, Cape bulbul, Red-eyed bulbul, Tractrac chat, Mountain chat, Long-billed lark, Dusky sunbird, Swallow-tailed bee-eater, Red-knobbed coot (which sounds like a dirty old man), Fiery-necked nightjar, Pied kingfisher, various swifts, a couple of swallows and several incongruous ostriches (which are now part of a large-scale agricultural breeding project).

Finally, we come down to the insects. These little buggers play an important role in the Richtersveld ecosystem as they contribute to the diet of larger species, and they are also responsible for pollinating many of the plants. As is usually the case, insects are the most numerous animals in terms of numbers, as well as species. Like the other animals that live here, the insects have developed several ways to thrive in the desert environment.

These survival strategies include: waxy body coatings

that retain water, special chemical processes that produce internal moisture, and ingenious forms of camouflage that help them blend into the rocks. Some termite species are even known to bury up to 20 metres under the sand to find the water table. Several narrowly endemic species have also evolved hand-in-hand with specific endemic plants and are uniquely adapted to 'fit' these flowers.

There are several groups of insects: the primary feeders (which eat plants and/or nectar), secondary feeders (which eat the primary feeders) and detritus feeders (which chase after organic bits and pieces blown around by the wind). Pollination is done largely by bees (notably Carpenter bees), bee flies and pollen wasps (the variety of pollen wasps in the western part of southern Africa is among the highest in the world). Other insect species include: Milkweed locusts, Tortoise beetles, Blister beetles, Monkey beetles, Mouldy beetles, crickets, ground grasshoppers, stone grasshoppers, Praying mantises, millipedes, centipedes, cicadas, flies and the like.

Several unique butterfly species are also found here, including the Namaqua arrowhead, the Warrior silverspotted copper, the Roseate emperor (actually a day-flying moth) and a subspecies of the Boland tholly. Silverfish (also known as fishmoths) are present in the Richtersveld and the region is home to the largest diversity of these bugs in the world, including many endemic species. Silverfish are interesting little critters: they are nocturnal, shed their skins, grow tiny scales, do not have a pupal or larval stage (so emerge fully formed from their eggs) and they absorb moisture through glands in their anus—which is quite a good trick, when you think about it. By the way, the common fishmoth (the one that eats your clothes) is not indigenous to South Africa.

Arachnids, the eight-legged bogeymen of the insect

world, are well represented in the Richtersveld. These include the Trapdoor spider, Buckspoor spider, Sicarus spider, the very toxic Black button spider and Sun spiders or Romans (including four species endemic to the Richtersveld). Three families of scorpion are also found here, including ground scorpions, rock scorpions and thick-tailed scorpions (several species of which are among South Africa's most poisonous). So, if you're camping in the area, don't forget to check your shoes in the morning!

The human experience

Early humans

The first evidence of human beings in Namaqualand and the Richtersveld is represented by crude stone tools, such as choppers and hand axes fashioned from a stone pebble or core. These Early Stone Age implements are associated with various *Homo* species who lived between 2.5 million and 200,000 years ago, such as *Homo habilis, Homo erectus* and archaic *Homo sapiens*. Thus far, however, no human fossils have been found in this part of the world.

The Middle Stone Age is said to range between 200,000 and 35,000 years ago. This era marks a transition from core-based tools to flake-based tools, a more sophisticated tool-making technology in which slivers of rock are struck off a stone core to create scrapers, blades or points. Many examples of these smaller stone tools are found in Namaqualand, with several archaeological sites in the Richtersveld containing a large number of flakes and rock fragments, which suggests that they were tool 'factories'. The West Coast National Park, near Langebaan, also contains a remarkably tangible fossil footprint made by one of our *Homo sapiens* ancestors during this era.

The Later Stone Age coincides with the emergence of *Homo sapiens sapiens*, anatomically modern human beings just like you and me. The tools associated with this period are more refined and task-specific. They include blades, borers and points, many of which were attached to wooden shafts to form spears or knives. Bone and ivory were also used to create blades, needles and even fishing hooks.

Several archaeological sites in the Richtersveld (dating back to over 3,000 years ago) offer evidence of this kind of technology. Further testament to human habitation is also found in the form of processed animal bones, blackened hearths and a number of middens (prehistoric rubbish tips) containing human detritus, which have been found along the coast.

So, according to the archaeological evidence, nomadic hunter-gatherers have been living in Namaqualand and the Richtersveld for well over 200,000 years. It could not have been an easy life. Water would have been scarce (there is evidence of ostrich egg shells being used as storage containers) and there was always a risk of over-hunting. But, for once, humans seemed to understand that their survival depended on collaborating with the environment in a sustainable manner.

The Bushmen

It's hard to say when the Bushmen (or San) developed as a distinct cultural group—some say it was as long as 40,000 or 30,000 years ago, when a prolonged dry period separated people in the south-western part of the subcontinent from the more Negroid tribes to the north. In any case, the Bushmen utilized and refined the Later Stone Age technology described above.

The Bushmen also developed a social structure that revolved around their traditional hunter-gatherer lifestyles. As a rule, it was the men who did the hunting, while the women gathered bulbs, berries and other plants. Their tacit grasp of nature saw these small family groups moving around the land in harmony with the game and the seasons.

In terms of religion, the Bushmen enjoyed a sophisticated ideology that combined the natural world with the spiritual realm. This belief system is expressed in their numerous rock paintings, which often illustrate shamanistic trance dances. In the Richtersveld, however, no cave paintings have been identified.

Instead, we find petroglyphs—engravings made by cutting into the surface of a rock with a sharp stylus or rock hammer. These enigmatic and beautiful petroglyphs depict a variety of subjects, ranging from abstract geometric patterns to more realistic depictions of animals, such as zebra and eland. The study of these petroglyphs is still in its infancy and, sadly, many of the sites have been damaged by mining and/or careless visitors. Access to most of these sites is now restricted to prevent further damage.

The number of Bushmen living in Namaqualand and the Richtersveld would have, of necessity, been relatively low. This was, after all, a thirstland with only a few reliable water sources. The coast was a much better proposition, however, and there are a number of archaeological sites that demonstrate significant interaction between the Bushmen and marine resources such as seals and shellfish. These coastal populations have been called 'strandlopers' (beach walkers) and evidence of their habitation is found at various locations along the shores of Namaqualand and, indeed, most of southern Africa.

The Khoikhoi

About 2,000 years ago, a new group of people entered the picture. They were closely related to the Bushmen, with one major difference. They were pastoralists; nomadic farmers who schlepped around the countryside with herds of domesticated fat-tailed sheep. Later, they would also cultivate crops, keep cattle and, in colonial times, incorporate goats into their menageries. They still hunted wild game, preferring to keep their livestock for ceremonial purposes, but the arrival of the Khoikhoi nevertheless heralded the dawn of a new era.

The origin of the Khoikhoi is somewhat uncertain. Early colonial writers claimed that they came from Asia, moving south around the time of the great flood. Some even said they had Hamitic or Jewish origins. At the turn of the century, the historians Stow and Cooke hypothesized that they came from the Great Lakes region in central Africa before migrating down the west coast of the subcontinent. But modern historians, such as Richard Elphick, have made more reliable linguistic studies of the Khoikhoi and it is now accepted that they originated in the Zambezi valley of northern Botswana.

Here, they made the transition from a hunter-gatherer society to a culture that kept domesticated animals. This kind of farming 'technology' originated in the Middle East about 10,000 years ago. It reached the northern Sahara around 7,000 years ago and continued to spread down the African continent, where it was adopted by the Bantu tribes of West Africa. These people, in turn, carried the pastoral tradition with them when they began to migrate south, reaching East Africa around 4,000 years ago and southern Africa some time later.

It is thought that the Khoikhoi picked up the pastoralism habit from these Bantu tribes. However, there are some theorists who claim that the Khoikhoi developed a pastoral tradition all on their own, but this is still being debated by those feisty academics.

In any case, once the Khoikhoi had embraced this new concept of farming, they took their sheep and migrated south, crossing the Orange River near its confluence with the Vaal between 2,000 and 1,600 years ago. From this point, they began spreading out into the eastern, southern and western Cape. The Negroid Bantu tribes, for their part, arrived in southern Africa a short time later and settled along the eastern seaboard and on the interior plateau.

In time, the Khoikhoi would establish themselves as a number of distinct tribes, each with their own territories and dialects. These political units were organized around a hierarchical system, based on chieftains, headmen and family clans. So, for example, you had the Cochoqua and Guriqua in the south-west, the Chainoqua, Hessequa, Gouriqua, Attaqua and Houteniqua in the east and the Goringhaiqua, Gorachouqua and Goringhaikona around the Cape Peninsula.

At the mouth of the Orange River, the Khoikhoi spilt into two groups. The Great Namaqua settled north of the river in what became Namibia. The Little Namaqua populated the area to the south, establishing five clans between the Orange River and present-day Vanrhynsdorp. These people gave the region its modern name and are the antecedents of the present-day Nama people, who are still resident in the Richtersveld.

Although the Khoikhoi and the Bushmen are related, both genetically and linguistically, there must have been a culture clash when the two groups first encountered each other. The Khoikhoi, for their part, held their herds in very high esteem, considering them a sign of status and wealth. The animals were viewed as private property, so families with lots of animals were considered 'rich', while those with few animals often had to take up positions as servants for more powerful clans. This was a significant move away from the more socialist structure of the Bushman groups, whom the Khoikhoi considered inferior.

Even the name 'Khoikhoi' (meaning 'men of men') served to distinguish them from the lowly Bushmen, whom they called 'Sonqua' or 'San' (meaning 'men with nothing'). For this reason, many modern Bushmen reject the term 'San' as an insult, which is why I stubbornly refer to them as 'Bushmen' throughout this book.

So, the Khoikhoi and the Bushmen led different lifestyles, based on divergent economic models. As such, conflict over water, resources and territory were inevitable. Also, the Khoikhoi were still active hunters and competition over the wild game must have been reasonably intense. For the most part, however, the two groups seemed to find a way to get along and they co-existed as distinct cultural entities for at least 1,500 years—until the Europeans came along and muddied the waters. There are even cases where Bushmen took jobs with Khoikhoi families, looking after their herds, supplying them with honey or providing rain-making skills in exchange for food.

In the Richtersveld, however, the Bushmen seem to have dissipated soon after the arrival of the Khoikhoi (apart from a few Strandloper clans who continued to live along the coast). This may have been a result of migration from or integration with the Namaqua. After all, it is not a region that can support a large population.

Richard Elphick, on the other hand, has a theory that the division between herders and hunters was much more fluid, depending as much on luck as it did on economics. For Elphick, the Khoikhoi and the Bushmen were essentially the same people.

Thus, a Khoikhoi tribe could easily lose their herds through drought, theft or disease, causing them to revert to the hunter-gatherer economy of the Bushmen. As this was considered an inferior way of life, the ambitious Khoikhoi clan would then try to re-build its herds through theft, barter or service. This created a cyclical model of pastoralism vs hunting.

Based on archaeological evidence, however, it seems that there were indeed two distinct groups within the Khoi-San nation. But Elphick's model is still useful if applied to the colonial era, when Europeans were putting pressure on the traditional lifestyles of indigenous people at the Cape.

Archaeological digs have also pointed to a connection between domesticated herds and pottery. This is because farmers need to store surplus goods, whereas hunters tend to consume things on the spot. The presence of heavy pottery also implies that the Khoikhoi did not move around as much as the peripatetic Bushmen. This makes sense as the Khoikhoi herds provided them with some food security, so they didn't have to travel around as much and were able to sustain higher population densities. Nevertheless, they still practised a nomadic lifestyle, moving with the seasons in search of good grazing land.

Each Khoikhoi clan, therefore, controlled a rather vaguely defined territory and members of the clan moved across their lands in a regular, seasonal pattern of transhumance. This led to the development of portable *matjieshuise* or *|haru oms* that could be assembled at the various stock-posts and watering holes, which were inhabited periodically throughout the year. Occasionally, outsiders were allowed to use the clan's land in exchange for a tribute or payment to the chief. At no stage, however, was land allowed to be owned by any private individual. It is this ancient form of nomadic farming that is still practised in the Richtersveld World Heritage Site.

PEOPLE

The *|haru oms*

The basic housing unit of the Khoikhoi was a dome-shaped hut called a *|haru oms*. These were created by building a circular framework of green branches that were stuck into the ground, bent over and tied together with thin strips of leather. This structure was then covered by handmade mats made of reeds that were woven together. It was the man's job to build the frame, while the women made the reed mats.

The |*haru oms* were eminently practical. The raw materials for construction were freely available across the region. In summer, the reed mats allowed air to circulate and offered shade from the hot sun. In winter, skins or extra mats were attached to the frame to keep the huts warm. Furthermore, when it rained, the reeds swelled up to keep the water out of the huts and the round shape of the huts provided protection against strong winds. All in all, it was a rare example of form meeting function.

The |*haru oms* were also portable. So, when it was time to leave, the mats were simply rolled up and carried to the next location. The frames were usually left behind to be re-used the following season. However, not every member of the family was able to participate in the annual migrations. The very young and the elderly often stayed in permanent villages, which could include well over 100 people. These settlements also utilized |*haru oms* as housing, although the huts were not taken down unless they were in disrepair. In fact, the |*haru oms* were so suited to the environment that they were even adopted by the first white settlers who moved into the area, and remained the most common form of housing in Namaqualand until well into the 1900s.

Today, the Richtersveld is the only place in the world where you still find the |*haru oms*. They are used by the nomadic stock farmers who live in the Richtersveld Community Conservancy, and you can even spot a couple in the modern villages, sitting incongruously in the yard next to neat brick houses. Admittedly, these modern examples are often supplemented by contemporary materials, such as plastic sheeting, but it is still testament to a continuous architectural tradition that stretches back a couple of thousand years.

Sadly, however, the art of building the *|haru oms* is in danger of being forgotten, and only a handful of Nama people living in the Richtersveld retain the necessary skills. But this is a form of indigenous knowledge that must be conserved and there is an ongoing effort to transfer this knowledge to new generations. For example, recently, a group of Nama from the Richtersveld went across the border into the //Gamaseb community in Namibia to re-teach their brethren how to build these traditional reed huts. Young people in the Richtersveld are also being encouraged to learn the technique, and it is hoped that the advent of tourism and the bestowal of World Heritage status (partly because of the *|haru oms*) will give this programme extra impetus.

History of the area

First impressions

By the late 1400s, southern Africa was home to a number of indigenous people who can be grouped together into three cultural units. The Khoikhoi lived mainly in the coastal regions, ranging from the Orange River to the Eastern Cape. The Bushmen were found throughout the country, with large populations living along the Drakensberg mountains. The Bantu were found on the East Coast (Xhosa, Swazi and the group that would become the Zulu) and in the interior (Sotho, Tswana, Pedi etc.).

Although there were undoubtedly a number of conflicts between these different people, each with their own agendas and priorities, it seems that things were pretty stable in the sub-continent. Then, like a spark to gunpowder, came the whiteys.

The first Europeans had started sailing down the west coast of Africa in the late 15th century, seeking a sea route to the riches of the East. Then, in 1488, Bartolomeu Dias successfully rounded the Cape of Good Hope and Vasco da Gama followed in 1497. This opened the floodgates and, from the 1500s onwards, a succession of merchant ships from Portugal, Spain, France, England, Holland and other European nations began sailing around the tip of the continent en route to the spice fields of Asia.

It was a long journey for ships under sail. Crews required fresh water, vegetables, fruit and meat to keep their health up, and this necessitated landing on the unknown shores of southern Africa. At first, ships did not stop on the Namaqualand coast as the seas were rough and the anchorages were poor. Instead, they followed the lead of Bartolomeu Dias and Vasco da Gama, who had identified a freshwater spring close to the coast, near to what is today Mossel Bay.

But getting water was not as simple as the Europeans would have liked. The Khoikhoi people (who would bear the brunt of dealing with the early white seafarers) believed that water sources belonged to the clan who controlled the area. As such, they did not take kindly to the brazen Europeans who simply helped themselves without asking permission or offering payment. And so, the very first meeting of white and black people in South Africa was characterized by a fight.

This incident is recounted by the diarist of Vasco da Gama, who was writing about the previous voyage of Bartolomeu Dias: "One day, as he [Dias] was taking water from a very good watering-place that lies at the edge of the sea here, they [the Khoikhoi] defended this watering-place with stones thrown from the top of a hillock which is above it; and Bartolomeu Dias fired a crossbow at them, killing one of them."

Clearly, things were not off to a good start and as the number of ships sailing around the Cape increased, so did the tensions between the indigenous people and the Europeans. Apart from disputes over water rights, the Khoikhoi were reluctant to trade away their cattle or sheep, as these animals were kept for ceremonial occasions. This infuriated the hungry Europeans, who soon developed a nasty habit of raiding Khoikhoi homesteads to steal their livestock. Sometimes, the white men even kidnapped a couple of Khoikhoi to ensure favourable trading terms. This resulted in a number of skirmishes, including one memorable incident where a Portuguese viceroy and a bunch of high-ranking officers were trampled to death by the Khoikhoi's trained war-cattle!

This event, in 1510, consolidated the European opinion that the Khoikhoi were savage, primitive, heathen and treacherous (although how the raiders could presume to call their victims 'treacherous' is beyond me). Nevertheless, this perception of the Khoikhoi was repeated so many times over the next few hundred years that eventually it came to be considered a sociological fact. The Europeans even coined a new name for the group, calling them 'Hottentots'—a pejorative term apparently derived from a popular chant the Khoikhoi liked to sing in their 'weird', clicking language.

Accordingly, contemporary European descriptions of the 'Hottentots' were scathing. One observer wrote that they were "entirely naked but for an ox-hide around them like a cloak … always stank greatly, since they besmeared themselves with fat and grease … begged for entrails, which they ate quite raw after scraping out most of the dung … they speak very clumsily". Another simply stated that they were the "most savage and beastly people as ever I thinke God created". A third account described the Cape coast as a "shore so evill that nothing could take land, and the land itselfe so full of tigers, and people that are savage and killers of all strangers".

Even the respected Swedish scientist, Carl Peter Thunberg, thought they were horrible, writing as late as 1775 that: "In a people so plunged in sloth, and so overwhelmed with filth, as the Hottentots actually are, one would not expect to find the least trace of vanity. It is however to be found even among these, the most wretched of the human race; for … amongst their ointments they mix the powder of a strong smelling herb which they called 'bucku', and which gives them so disagreeable, so fetid, and at the same time so rank an odour, that I sometimes could not bear the smell of the Hottentots that drove my wagon. The language, which frequently is almost the only thing that distinguishes the indolent Hottentots from the brute creation, is poor, unlike any other in the world, is pronounced with a clack of the tongue, and is never written. Idleness is so predominant amongst the greatest part of the Hottentots that few of the animals without souls surpass them in that vice. In arts and sciences they are as rude and uncultivated as they are in every other aspect."

Of course, the idea that the Khoikhoi lived "without law or religion, like animals" is both insulting and inaccurate. They did have a comprehensive system of political, economic and spiritual controls, but these were different and thus invisible to the narrow-minded Europeans. For example, the fat and grease that they smeared over their bodies had both an aesthetic purpose (it made their skins glisten) and a practical function (it protected them both from the sun and various bugs and parasites).

Nevertheless, the disdain with which the Europeans beheld the Khoikhoi was perpetuated, perhaps because it enabled them to deny the Khoikhoi any basic human rights. This dismissive attitude is amply illustrated by the sad story of Saartjie Baartman. She was a Khoikhoi woman who was taken to Europe in 1810 and exhibited to curious onlookers because she had an unusually big bum (a condition known as steatopygia).

As such, she became known as the 'Hottentot Venus' and was toured through England and France (where gawping customers could touch her posterior for an additional charge). Although there is no evidence that Saartjie was taken against her will, or ill-treated by her exploiters, it is telling that she died only five years later in France.

Her skeleton, brain and preserved genitals (which were elongated, a relatively common condition among Khoi–San women, creating what was termed the 'Hottentot Apron') were subsequently put on display in Paris's Musée de l'Homme. They remained in public view until 1974, after which she was packed away into storage. Saartjie's remains were only returned home to South Africa in 2002, after an appeal from Nelson Mandela. She has now been given a proper burial close to her home in the Gamtoos valley of the Eastern Cape.

Into the north

After 150 years of rather unregulated sea-faring, one European nation decided that the time had come to establish a permanent trading station at the Cape. This effort was spearheaded by the Dutch East India Company (VOC) on behalf of the nation of Holland. And so, in the fateful year of 1652, Jan van Riebeeck and a group of Company employees landed at Table Bay with instructions to build a garrison and plant a vegetable garden. The new commander was also responsible for establishing trading ties with the Khoikhoi in order to secure a reliable supply of cattle and sheep.

At first, it didn't go well. The Dutch had no idea how

to grow plants in the strange soil and the Khoikhoi were very reluctant to barter with the long-hairs, who were already building a suspiciously permanent-looking fort. Van Riebeeck also had trouble communicating with the Khoikhoi, having to rely on the services of the unreliable Autshumao (called Herrie by the Dutch) and his unfortunate niece Krotoa (called Eva).

The stories of Van Riebeeck, Herrie, Eva and the other Peninsula Khoikhoi are poignant and fascinating, but they are too long to be narrated here. Instead, allow me to summarize by saying that the Dutch and the Khoikhoi endured several stormy decades of conflict and a couple of armed uprisings, usually concerning land ownership and grazing rights. Ultimately, a series of smallpox epidemics, starting in 1713, wiped out large numbers of Khoikhoi across the country and effectively ended the independence of the Khoikhoi nation.

But that lay in the future. What concerns us now is the interaction between the Europeans and the Namaqua people, far to the north of Cape Town.

Initially, Van Riebeeck and the VOC had little interest in the country beyond the Cape Peninsula. They had their hands more than full in trying to deal with the intransigent Khoikhoi who lived in the vicinity of the fort. However, the growing settlement at the Cape soon needed more meat, and explorers were sent out to make contact with more distant (and hopefully more co-operative) tribes.

There was also another, more romantic reason for this exploratory urge. For many years, there had been rumours swirling around Europe; stories of a mythical city, located somewhere in the African interior, that was rich in ivory and gold. Some said it was called Vigiti Magna, located on the banks of the mighty Rio do Infanta. Others called it Cortado, Cammissa or Vallenta. Whatever its name, this was proclaimed to be the fabled

Ophir of the Bible (the place where King Solomon had his mines). It was even accepted that this city was ruled by an apocryphal white Christian emperor named Prester John.

All in all, it was a crazy story, concocted to explain the source of the gold ornaments that kept coming out of Africa. Then, in 1512, a Portuguese explorer named Antonio Fernandez set out from the east coast and came across a grand stone city called Monomatapa somewhere in the interior (this settlement was one of the successors of Mapungubwe and Great Zimbabwe). Even though maps were very vague at this time, this didn't stop cartographers from marking the city on their charts and Monomatapa became embroiled with the legend of Vigiti Magna.

So, by the 1650s, Van Riebeeck had in his possession several tantalizing (if hypothetical) maps that clearly showed the location of a great city which lay north and east of his new post at the Cape. He had also heard some local stories that told of a wealthy tribe called the Namaqua who lived in the north. The Namaqua were even said to be white! Clearly, he had to find out more.

The first expedition to the north thus began as early as 1655, under the command of Jan Wintervogel, but the sandy plains, river valleys and high mountains soon forced these pathfinders to turn back back somewhere in the Malmesbury/Darling area. Then, in late 1660, Jan Dankaert set out with several men including two Khoikhoi interpreters and one Pieter van Meerhof (who was to participate in no less than six expeditions to the north). The going was tough but Dankaert persevered until he found himself at the foot of some mighty mountains about 150km north of Cape Town, at what became the town of Piketberg.

Luckily, Dankaert met up with some Bushmen who showed him a path over the mountains and, from the summit, Dankaert looked out across a wide river valley and into the north. He descended the mountains near present-day Citrusdal and explored the banks of the fertile river, which he called 'Olifants' because he saw several hundred of these majestic creatures wandering along the watercourse. This pass (Piekenierskloof) quickly became an essential component of the route to the north, and it is still part of the N7 highway from Cape Town to Springbok.

The next expedition left only ten days after Dankaert returned to the fort in early 1661. This one was led by Pieter Cruijthoff, with Van Meerhof acting as second in command. Once again, they travelled with a couple of Khoikhoi interpreters. As they journeyed, however, they met up with several groups of Bushmen who all warned them against the Namaqua, saying that the travellers would be killed by this fearsome tribe. Undeterred, the plucky Europeans continued on their way, crossing the mountains and venturing north towards the Cederberg. Then, the party came across some deserted kraals which showed evidence of cattle and sheep herding.

According to Van Meerhof's journal, that evening they saw a fire burning in the hills, a short distance away. Eager to find out more, Van Meerhof and his two 'hottentoos' climbed a hill.

"When halfway up Donckeman [one of the Khoikhoi interpreters] began to shout, 'Mr Pieter, Namaqua,' and I saw above me some three-and-twenty figures standing on the rocks gazing towards us ... my Hottentoos were so affrighted that they made to take the shoes from off their feet, the better to run back. They cried, 'Namaqua! Shields of ox-hide! Danger!' I used my glass to see if it were so. I saw that they were armed with dry hides and had [prepared] skins hanging from their left arms, bow and arrows upon their shoulders, and in each hand a spear. On reaching the heights we could not perceive them [the Namaqua] whence they had disappeared amongst the boulders. I directed our Hottentoos to call out that if they would come to us we would give them tobacco and beads and copper, but they gave no reply. I waited an half-hour upon the mountain side, hoping they would return. Longer I durst not wait, for the night fell and it became very dark, ere I returned to our people. We hope they will return upon the morrow and come amongst us."

The next day, the fearless Van Meerhof waited and, sure enough, the Namaqua re-appeared, keeping their distance. He then instructed his 'Hottentoos' to call out to them, promising that they would come to no harm. Eventually, they approached the strange white-faced visitors and tobacco was passed around, even though most of the Namaqua didn't know how to smoke properly. With diplomatic channels thus opened, Van Meerhof asked which one was their 'king'. A suitably large chief, named Akembe, was duly pointed out and gifts were given over. The chief then invited the party to his home, a few hours away. Van Meerhof and his men stayed with the chief for three days before returning, somewhat triumphantly, to Cape Town.

The next mission, with Van Meerhof now in charge, left a few weeks later, in April 1661. Once again, they looked for Akembe's kraal, only to find that the clan had moved north because of a drought. Nevertheless, they made some useful contacts with other Khoikhoi and Bushmen tribes. In November 1661, Van Meerhof was off again, this time under the command of Pieter Everaert. During this journey, one of the men was trampled to death by an elephant, and the group ran out of water—a common problem, since most of these early expeditions set off during the dry summer season.

The indefatigable Van Meerhof (who was by this time married to Eva—Van Riebeeck's ill-fated Khoikhoi ward) made his next trip in October 1662, under the command of Pieter Cruijthoff. This was the first expedition to include a wagon which, as it turned out, wasn't a very practical notion because the wagon had to be unloaded at the foot of the steep mountains, dragged up the pass, reloaded to cross the mountain plateau and then unloaded again to make the trip down the other side. It was a futile effort, however, as the thick vegetation in the Olifants River Valley made the wagon useless. So Cruijthoff eventually packed everything onto the backs of their six oxen and buried the wagon, intending to collect it on the return journey. As it turned out, the party met up with some hostile people near Koekenaap and they didn't bother to reclaim the wagon as they hurried back, leaving it to rot in the sand. Nevertheless, it was during this journey that the Europeans first heard tell of a great river that lay in the north.

Another expedition in 1663, under Sergeant Jonas de la Guerre (and the last for Pieter van Meerhof), also had wagon problems and repeated the burial trick—only this time, when they returned after running out of water, they found that the wagon had been unearthed by the locals and burned down so that the iron components could be collected. Wagons continued to be problematic in the mountainous regions of the Cape until 1682, when it was decreed that henceforth all wagons were to be built in such a way that they could be easily taken apart and re-assembled.

The Copper Mountain

Despite the best efforts of the early explorers, the fabled gold city of Vigiti Magna and/or Monomatapa, and the great river on which it supposedly sat, were elusive. But there was clearly some kind of mineral wealth up in the north because the Namaqua people, first observed by Pieter van Meerhof in 1661, were dripping with copper.

As Van Meerhof wrote in his journal: "Their dress

consists of all kinds of beautifully prepared skin … gorgeously ornamented with copper beads … Their locks they thread with copper beads, covering their heads all over. Around their necks they have chains, slung around them 15 or 16 times. On their arms they have chains of copper and iron beads which go round their bodies 30 or 40 times."

The Namaqua, clearly, were skilled iron workers who were able to extract and manipulate copper. This knowledge was once again demonstrated when a group of Namaqua visited the castle in 1681, bringing with them some specimens of rich copper ore. The Dutch governor, Simon van der Stel, was thus encouraged to send out a number of well-equipped expeditions to try and find the source of the Namaqua's wealth.

The first couple of journeys were under the command of Olof Bergh, who pioneered a route that avoided the Olifants River valley by moving through the Sandveld to the west, thus avoiding the barrier of dry, rocky plains that came to be known as the Knersvlakte (so named because of the sound the wagon wheels made when 'gnashing' over the pebbly quartzite). He also became the first European to visit a cave near Graafwater that soon became a regular stop on the road to the north. This became known as the *Heerenlogement* (Gentlemen's Lodging). On his first trip, Bergh reached the Groen River near Garies and on his second try he got even farther, reaching the vicinity of the Kamiesberg. However, on both occasions, he returned to the Cape empty handed.

Then, in 1684, another party of Namaqua visited Cape Town. This time, Van der Stel sent a party under Sergeant Isaq Schrijver to travel back with the Namaqua. The precise route of Schrijver's group is not known, but he did penetrate far into Namaqualand (probably to Leliefontein) and, when he returned, he presented the governor with some samples of copper ore. These were melted down and the results were sent off to Company headquarters in Holland for investigation.

In the meantime, another expedition had uncovered further information about the existence of a 'Copper Mountain', which was located not too far from the sea. This greatly excited Van der Stel, who promptly put together a massive expedition which he would lead himself. In 1685, with the Company's blessing, the governor set off for the north with all due pomp and circumstance.

By all accounts, it was a very impressive procession. It included 57 whites, two Macassar prisoners (from Indonesia), three slaves, a carriage with six horses for the governor, eight donkeys, 14 riding horses, two artillery pieces, eight carts, seven wagons (one of which contained a boat) and 289 oxen. There were also over 50 Khoikhoi wagon drivers, interpreters and camp followers, as well as six additional wagons each drawn by eight oxen which belonged to freemen who accompanied the expedition as far as the Olifants River. And don't forget about all the provisions, muskets, gunpowder and barter goods that the massive party would need for their five-month journey. The group even had its own artist, Hendrik Claudius, who produced one of the first series of illustrations featuring the plants of Namaqualand, including the kokerboom.

Following the route established by Olof Bergh, Van der Stel pushed his team ever northwards. It was fortunate that the region was enjoying a particularly wet spring that year, so the barren wastes of the Sandveld and the mountainous Hardeveld were unusually fertile. This helped sustain the unwieldy expedition and they made good progress.

After several weeks of travelling, Van der Stel and his gang reached the Kamiesberg. Here, they spent a couple of weeks trying to recruit some local Namaqua who could take them to the Copper Mountain. Eventually, a combination of tobacco, liquor, food and coercion secured the services of two guides who steered the party through the inhospitable hills to the north.

Eventually, on October 21st, 1685, they arrived at the 'Koper Bergen' located near the present-day town of Carolusberg, a short distance away from Springbok. They immediately went to work and sunk several exploratory shafts into the mountainside.

The results looked very promising, with the ore improving the deeper they went. They also sent out prospecting teams who explored the surrounding area, including O'okiep. Van Werlinckhof, the mineralogist, was particularly impressed and, after two weeks at the site, he declared: "I am entirely convinced of the favourable character of these mines; in the event of mining operations being continued, richer and richer, and better minerals will be found, for the hills concerned extend several miles in length and breadth, and hold minerals almost everywhere."

Van der Stel was understandably optimistic as he rode back into Cape Town. The expedition had been a great success. They had found the Copper Mountain and collected numerous ore samples, which were promptly dispatched to Holland for analysis. Moreover, the difficult journey had been completed without a single loss of human life. Even the six-horse carriage had made it back in one piece, apart from a dent inflicted by a charging rhinoceros.

Unfortunately, that's where the good news ended. The assay results from Holland were good, but not outstanding (the ore contained between seven per cent and eleven per cent copper). Furthermore, the country in which the copper was located was dry and remote. There was no suitable grazing land for animals and no practical overland supply route for human provisions. The sea was many miles away, cut off from the mine by a range of jagged mountains, and investigations of the coast between the Groen River and the Buffels River had revealed no suitable anchorages. In short, Van der Stel's copper mine was impossible to exploit—at least for the time being—and no further mining activity would take place in Namaqualand for more than 150 years.

Today, a couple of Van der Stel's open test shafts can still be seen halfway up the side of the 'Copper Mountain'. You can also see the various proprietary inscriptions he had carved on the rocks, identifying them as VOC property. The site is signposted from the N14 highway, just east of Springbok.

The Bastaards and the Trekboers

After Van der Stel's expedition to the Copper Mountain, the route to the far north was set. It wasn't a busy road by any means, but over the next 200 years a number of exotic people drifted into and around Namaqualand. These included hunters, explorers, botanists, European farmers, escaped slaves and a number of so-called Basters or Bastaards (people of mixed blood). With all these new arrivals competing for land and resources, the number of conflicts in the region escalated—especially during times of drought.

First, let's talk about those Bastaards. These mixed-blood 'tribes' were known by a number of individual names, but the colonial powers classified them as either 'Bastaards' (offspring of Europeans and non-whites) or 'Bastaard-Hottentots' (children of slaves and Khoikhoi). As a result of their questionable lineage, most of these people (although technically free subjects) did not qualify for citizenship within the colony. As such, they spearheaded the movement of people into the north, where they sought land for themselves.

Here, they intermingled with the indigenous Nama groups, often dominating them by virtue of their firearms, education or relative material wealth. They also carried a modicum of political clout because of their Christian religion and some even managed to claim farms or grazing rights from the colonial authorities, eventually growing quite prosperous.

The famous Adam Kok, founder of the Griqua nation, was one such individual. Kok moved from the Cape to Piketberg, where he settled on the farm Stinkfontein in 1751. Later, he and his family moved north to the Kamiesberg where his people became active as middlemen in the trade between Europeans, the Namaqua and the southern Tswana people. Around 1780, some members of the family moved again to the Orange River, where they settled in the Kimberley area, before moving on yet again in search of a land of their own. These regular migrations were probably the result of Trekboers moving in and taking over the land.

And who were the Trekboers? Well, initially, all European farmers were obliged to live within a short distance from the Fort at Cape Town, so that the ubiquitous Company could keep an eye on them. By the early 1700s, however, the settlement had outgrown its suppliers and additional lands were required to meet the demand for food and meat. The white farmers were thus allowed to ride out and claim new lands over the mountains.

This was the advent of the Trekboers (literally, travelling farmers) and these hardy Europeans proceeded to usurp territory all over the Cape. Later, this land grab was formalized into a system of loan farms, which allowed farmers to claim huge chunks of territory in exchange for a low annual rent to the Company. Indigenous land rights were, of course, ignored. Even the semi-respectable Bastaards were forced to give up their lands when confronted with a white farmer's claim.

And so, the Trekboers started spreading out, first into the fertile Overberg to the east of Cape Town and then into the land of Waveren in the north-east. Although Namaqualand, with its arid climate, was not initially affected by this white expansion, many Khoikhoi and Bastaard groups were pushed out of their lands by the Trekboers and moved north. This put additional pressure on the territorial and political integrity of the Namaqua.

Soon, the Trekboers and Dutch authorities at the Cape became involved in nominating and appointing Khoikhoi chiefs, even awarding them with a copper-headed 'staff of office' in exchange for their collaboration and support in trading ventures. This further undermined the Khoikhoi's traditional hierarchies. Then, in the 1750s, the first Trekboers started entering Namaqualand itself, where they claimed vast farms for themselves.

In practice, these European farmers were not very different from the indigenous nomadic farmers who had previously worked the land. In the arid Namaqualand region, for example, most of them adopted the traditional *matjieshuise* as their housing unit of choice. They also migrated with their animals, moving with the seasons to seek out the best grazing land. Obviously, this put them in direct competition with the Namaqua herders over the scarce natural resources. However, the European farmers had God and the government on their side and, with their western concept of private land ownership firmly in place, they inexorably took over the countryside. Accordingly, over the next 100 years, the Trekboers effectively marginalized the native Namaqua from their ancient pasturage.

The Namaqua, Bushmen, Khoikhoi refugees and Bastaards were subsequently pushed further and further into the north, where they found themselves competing with one another. The transhumance that had once defined their lives was being constrained and their traditional migration patterns were shattered. Some capitulated and became servants of the Trekboers, or took up work as labourers on their farms.

Others retreated to the relative safety of the mission stations or into remote places of refuge that came to be called 'native reserves', most notably around the Leliefontein Mission in the Kamiesberg and in the Richtersveld (which, until 1847, was beyond the official borders of the Cape Colony). Today, these 'communal' areas comprise 25 per cent of Namaqualand and contain 40 per cent of its population.

Some groups even turned renegade and started raiding the kraals and villages of their neighbours. Indeed, the whole Orange River frontier became something of a 'wild west' during this period, with dozens of robber bands of various racial compositions roaming the area, causing trouble.

One particularly unpleasant incident that lingers in the collective memory of Namaqualand took place in the mid-1800s, when a severe drought gripped the area. As a result, the people at the mission station of Steinkopf moved their families and herds to a small spring about 15km away. Then, one Sunday while the adults were at church, a group of marauding Bushmen invaded the camp, killing 32 Nama children. This site is marked by a small tombstone and is known, simply, as Kinderlê (where the children lay).

Hunters, explorers and scientists

Not all the Europeans who entered Namaqualand were focused on conquest. Many entered the region to explore, collect, trade and hunt. Johannes Rhenius, for example, went on two unsuccessful trading missions to Garies in 1721 and 1724. Co-incidentally, Rhenius was the son-in-law of Olof Bergh, who had pioneered the northern 'highway' in 1682.

The various hunters who prowled around the region are harder to identify. They didn't keep journals and often travelled secretly, without permission. Nevertheless, members of these hunting parties are generally considered to be the first white people to see the Orange River. This may have occurred as early as 1728, when a group of farmers from Piketberg surreptitiously travelled to the north on an extended hunting trip. Here, they came across the wide river known to the locals as the *!Gariep* (Great River). It is also said that they met another white man on the shores of the *!Gariep*, an elephant hunter named Pieter de Bruyn. This account, however, remains somewhat conjectural.

Another expedition, in 1739, did make it into the official records, but for all the wrong reasons. This group of hunters crossed over the Orange into Great Namaqualand (Namibia) where they spent a month at the kraal of Chief Gal. When they left, they persuaded their servants to raid the kraal and steal the cattle, in exchange for a share of the profits. Then, as they rode south through Little Namaqualand, they continued raiding kraals as they went, stealing more than 1,000 cattle and killing several women and children. All of this came to light after representatives from the aggrieved parties travelled to the Cape to protest. Even the servants who had done the raiding complained that they had not been given the cattle they were promised. In the face of popular support for the hunters, the Company decided to confiscate the stolen cattle and keep the booty for themselves!

The first 'official' visit to the *!Gariep* is credited to Jacobus Jansz Coetse who undertook the journey in 1760. He was a farmer from Piketberg who went off to hunt elephants, leaving his wife to look after the family farm. Suitably unencumbered, Coetse travelled with two wagons and 12 Khoikhoi, traversing Namaqualand until he came to the banks of the *!Gariep*. He crossed the river at Ramansdrif near Gu-daos (the sheep path). This was a river crossing that was often used by the Namaqua herders, and it is now known by the corrupted name 'Goodhouse'. In this unassuming manner, Coetse became the first white person to document his journey across the lower Orange River into the country of the Great Namaqua.

Following Coetse's journey, it was decided that a semi-official expedition should go out to explore the region north of the *!Gariep*. This was led by Hendrik Hop, who set out with 15 wagons in 1761. Jacobus Coetse went along as guide and Carel Brink acted as the chronicler. According to Brink, the Namaqua they met along the way were poor, had few cattle and were constantly being raided by 'Bosjesmans'. Hop's party crossed the river at Gu-daos and continued north to the Keetmanshoop area. Here, they were forced to turn back because of the hot and dry summer conditions.

Another member of the Hop expedition, Dr Carel Rykvoet, took the opportunity to do some mineralogical investigations while he was in the area. He examined Van der Stel's Copper Mountain and declared the deposits to be poor. He also ventured into the Richtersveld, west of Gu-daos, where he found deposits that were very rich—up to one-third copper. However, he realized that the rocks were too hard, the land too barren and the distances too great for the minerals to be exploited.

In the 1770s, a new group of explorers entered Namaqualand. They were the scientists, ornithologists and botanists who were attracted by the region's bizarre plants and unusual fauna. This group included Francis Masson, a botanist from Kew Gardens who was sent by the king of England to collect seeds and live plants for the royal greenhouse. Masson spent many years travelling the globe, including two tours of South Africa in 1772–1774 and 1786–1795. He collected Stapeliads from the Kamieskroon district in 1774. Masson was often accompanied by another notable collector, Carl Thunberg, the 'father of Cape Botany'. Together, they visited the southern edge of Knersvlakte, near Vanrhynsdorp, also in 1774.

Two major contributors to the western canon of knowledge on Namaqualand were Robert Jacob Gordon and William Paterson. Gordon, a Hollander, was a prolific traveller who undertook several extensive journeys across South Africa. It was during one of these trips, in 1777, that he came across the 'Great' river near Bethulie and named it the Orange, in honour of the royal House of Orange, rulers of Holland. Gordon suspected that this river ran all the way to the sea, but he could not prove it at this stage.

Then, in 1779, Gordon teamed up with a regular travelling companion named William Paterson to try and find the mouth of the Orange River. Paterson was a young British botanist who had been sent to the Cape by his eccentric patron, Lady Strathmore. He enjoyed some controversy during his stay in South Africa. At one time, he was accused of being a British spy and, later, it was said that he had discovered gold on the banks of the Orange River but kept the secret to himself.

In any case, Paterson had already been to the banks of the Orange in 1778 when he had checked out the old copper mines around present-day Springbok, which he found to be promising. So, he was familiar with the region when he and Gordon set off to the north.

A short distance out of Cape Town, they were fortunate enough to run into Hendrik Wikar, a clerk of the Dutch East India Company, who had fled Cape Town in 1775 because of unpaid gambling debts. Wikar had subsequently spent several years wandering along the Orange River in the company of some friendly locals and wrote an informal report on the region, which he sent to the Dutch Governor, Van Plettenberg. This report was deemed to be so useful that the governor pardoned Wikar, who was on his way back to Cape Town when he met up with Paterson and Gordon. No doubt, Wikar gave the two explorers valuable information about their upcoming journey.

Even so, the trip was arduous. The soft sand of the Sandveld was always tough on travellers, but Gordon and Paterson were determined to keep to the coast instead of heading west to harder ground. So they persevered and continued to push their way from the Buffels River (near present-day Kleinzee) to MacDougall's Bay (near present-day Port Nolloth) and then through the Holgat River Gorge, until they reached the Orange River mouth on 17 August 1779. This short stretch of about 120km took them nine days.

When they arrived, they unpacked a small boat which they had brought with them and, according to Paterson, "launched [the boat] and hoisted Dutch colours. Colonel Gordon proposed first to drink the State's health, and then that of the Prince of Orange; after which he gave the river the name of the Orange River in honour of that prince." This second naming ceremony was probably made because Gordon wasn't sure if this was the same river he had seen at Bethulie.

They then landed the boat on the north bank of the river, where they met some Strandlopers, whom Gordon sketched. The next few days were spent exploring the large bend in the Orange, which curves around the modern Richtersveld National Park. The explorers subsequently returned to the Buffels River, where they parted ways; Paterson headed for Cape Town and Gordon returned to the Orange and followed the river eastwards to the Prieska area, presumably to satisfy himself that this was indeed the same river he had first named in 1777.

There is a sad coda to this story: Upon his return, Gordon became the commander of the Dutch garrison at Cape Town. He continued to travel, draw and categorize the various natural wonders that he saw. The plant *Hoodia gordonii* is named after him. Then, in 1795, Napoleon started making trouble in Europe and overthrew the royal house of Orange. The British took in the exiled Dutch king and sent a fleet of ships to take over the Cape on his behalf. Gordon's loyalties were thus torn between the dethroned royal family and his new Napoleonically controlled masters, the Dutch republic. After the British defeated the Dutch battalions at the battle of Muizenberg, Gordon's indecision was roundly criticized. He was also suffering from ill health and other personal problems. And so, in 1795, shortly after the Dutch surrender, R. J. Gordon killed himself. Gordon's Bay, near Cape Town, is named in his honour.

In the years that followed, several other eminent scientist/explorers from all over the world visited Namaqualand and the Richtersveld. These included the somewhat overblown ornithologist Francois le Vaillant (1783), Carl Ludwig Phillip Zeyher (1830) and Johann Franz Drège (1833/4). The latter is known as the 'father of SA phytogeography' (the distribution of plant species). This may not sound like the most impressive appellation, but more than 100 plants have been named in Drège's honour—which isn't bad going.

In the 20th century, the appeal of Namaqualand, and the Richtersveld in particular, continued to attract collectors intent on identifying new species. These include the brothers Rudolph and Max Schlechter, Dr Louis Leipoldt and Selmar Schönland—a big lover of succulents, as are we all. Interestingly, most of these researchers were from foreign countries and their collections were sent to institutions overseas.

South African botanical studies really got started only after businessman and amateur botanist Harry Bolus established a chair in botany at the South African College (now called the University of Cape Town) in 1902.

The first person to assume the Bolus Chair was Harold Pearson, who had an abiding interest in the plants of Namaqualand. He went on two trips to the region (in 1908–9 and 1909–10) and collected lots of new information and specimens. Pearson went on to become the first director of Kirstenbosch Botanical Gardens in 1913 and helped create the National Botanical Institute (now called the National Biodiversity Institute). The rare *Aloe pearsonii* is named after him.

Then, there was Hans Herre of Stellenbosch University Gardens (who spent 22 years growing a captive specimen of the rare Welwitschia from Namibia), Gilbert Westacott Reynolds (who wrote the essential reference book, *Aloes of South Africa*), Neville Pillans (who gave his name to the Baster Kokerboom, *Aloe pillansii*), R. S. Adamson and Harry Hall, amongst many others. Today, modern botanists are still drawn to the region and new and unique species of plants are regularly identified in the nooks and crannies of Namaqualand.

The missionary's position

As we've seen, the 'Hottentots' and Bushmen were written off by the Europeans as Godless heathens and inveterate sinners. However, the same thing could be said for many of the Europeans who lived at the Cape in the early days of the colony. Van Riebeeck himself warned his colleagues that those who "absent themselves from daily prayer ... attending very little to their religion ... [are] warned henceforth to attend at the place appointed for the purpose ... those remaining absent shall forfeit six days wine rations ..."

In those days, the Company followed the Protestant Dutch Reformed Church of Holland, and the first minister, Johan van Arkel, arrived at the Cape in 1665, more than ten years after the settlement was established. Roman Catholics and German Lutherans were not permitted to practise, and even the ideologically similar French Huguenots were initially restricted in their worship.

Over the next few decades, very few Khoikhoi or Bushmen were converted to the Christian cause. But this is not to say that the locals were without religion. They just weren't particularly interested in what happened to their souls in the hereafter. Instead, spiritual beliefs were organized around practical matters, such as the need for rain, healing of sickness, the fertility of crops, the plenitude of animals and general matters of day-to-day survival.

The Bushmen, for example, believed in a number of 'gods' with the creator /Kaggen being the supreme deity. The Khoikhoi, for their part, worshipped Tsui//Goab, the supreme god, who was offset against /Guanab, the god of evil. For both groups, the ancestors (spirits of deceased relatives) provided a link between the living and the gods (who were often depicted as half-human and half-animal). Shamanistic rituals, trance dances and hallucinogenic plants were a recurring feature of their religious practices.

So, the Khoikhoi and the Bushmen did not provide the church with many souls to save. However, there was another group of 'infidels' at the Cape who were much more receptive: the slaves. At that time, the Dutch East India Company's policy did not allow for the enslavement of the local Khoikhoi, so slaves were brought into the colony from farther afield: East Africa, Madagascar, Java, Bali, Timor, Malaysia, China, India, etc. The first shipment arrived in 1658 and, over the next 160 years, about 63,000 hapless individuals were imported to supply the Cape with labour.

A German Jesuit, Martinus Martiny, administered to the spiritual needs of the slave population at Cape Town, but the conversion of slaves to Christianity was hampered by a number of factors. Firstly, several regulations gave any professed Christians a number of civil rights, and converted slaves were (technically) allowed to buy their freedom. The missionary movement was therefore not supported by the slave owners. Secondly, the religion of Islam had taken root at the Cape with the arrival of a number of Muslim slaves and political prisoners from the East Indies.

For many slaves, the Islamic religion was far more appealing than the rather restrictive faith of their masters, and this alternative ideology grew quickly among the disenfranchised. However, a number of half-caste groups (or Bastaards) tended to adopt Christianity, perhaps because it gave them a greater claim to social and political rights.

In any case, the Khoikhoi themselves were largely ignored until 1706, when two Danish missionaries were sent to work among the reviled Hottentots. As could be expected, the missionaries did not meet with great success and they complained that the Khoikhoi were "truly a wretched and miserable people [who] have no divine worship at all". They abandoned their efforts soon afterwards.

The next attempt took place in 1738, when a missionary from the Moravian Church arrived at the Cape with the blessing of the Company's board (known as the Heeren XVII). His name was George Schmidt and he established a mission station in the Riviersonderend valley, in the Overberg. Schmidt reported that the Khoikhoi in this region were on the edge of extinction and he quickly set about improving their lot. But his activities were heavily criticized by local Dutch Reformed ministers, who complained that he was unordained and therefore not qualified to baptize people into the church. Nevertheless, the authorities in Holland supported Schmidt and he stayed at his post until he was finally forced out in 1744. Much later, in 1775, the explorer Anders Spaarman travelled through the same region and heard the Khoikhoi complain about a preacher who had exploited Khoikhoi cattle and labour—this could only have referred to Schmidt.

Several decades passed before the Moravians sent another group of missionaries to the Cape. They travelled to Schmidt's old mission station in 1792, where they found the ruins of his house, a huge pear tree and an old woman, Magdelena, whom Schmidt had baptized. Ever faithful, Magdelena had remained at the abandoned mission for nearly 50 years, where she taught her daughter to read from an old Bible left to her by Schmidt. Taking this as a sign, the old mission station was resurrected and renamed Genadendal (Valley of Peace). It is considered to be the oldest mission station in South Africa and, at one time, it was the largest settlement in the colony after Cape Town. Genadenal still functions as a mission station to this day (albeit in a greatly diminished capacity). The Moravians went on to establish a number of other mission stations in South Africa.

The first systematic attempt to set up a network of mission stations among the indigenous people of South Africa was undertaken by the London Missionary Society (LMS), starting in 1799. Although these proselytizing activities were initially focused on the Eastern Cape frontier, where they contributed to the general chaos in this region, several stations were set up in Namaqualand, often at the request of the Christian 'Bastaards' who were living there.

Generally speaking, the LMS were concerned with

improving the lot of the 'coloured races' by giving them an education and petitioning the government for more equitable treatment of these 'children of God'. Led by provocative luminaries such as Theodore van der Kemp, John Campbell, John Philip, James Read and David Livingstone (we presume), the LMS was also anti-slavery and therefore less than popular in many quarters for its progressive stance on indigenous rights.

The first exploratory trip through Namaqualand was thus made by Christian Albrecht in 1805. Later that same year, he and his brother Abraham established a mission among the Great Namaqua at Warmbad (in present-day Namibia), assisted by J. Seidenfaden. In 1811, however, Abraham died from tuberculosis, and the mission was sacked by the boisterous chief Jonker Afrikaner. The faithful then fled south into the eastern reaches of Namaqualand, on the western border of what is now known as Bushmanland. Here, they determinedly opened a new mission at Pella (near the modern village of Pofadder).

The LMS and other 'Lutherans' continued to make inroads throughout Namaqualand. In 1813, the Rev. John Campbell called at Pella, and a German missionary, Christopher Sass, opened a mission at Silwerfontein. In 1815 the Rev. J. H. Schmelen established the Bethanien mission in Namibia. In 1816, Rev. Barnabas Shaw was invited to set up a Wesleyan mission at Leliefontein, on a farm which had been given to the indigenous people by Governor Ryk Tulbagh in the mid-1700s. This was done at the behest of Chief Haaimaap, otherwise known as Jantje Wildschut (Johnny Wildshot). In 1818, Rev. Schlemen travelled to Kookfontein (also known as Kokfontein or Besondermied) and established a mission station there, naming it Steinkopf in honour of his mentor and teacher in London. He also founded a mission at Kommagas.

Soon, the Rhenish Mission Society got in on the act and, in 1830, one of their inspectors, Dr E. Richter, visited the far north-west of Namaqualand to inspect this remote region. A mission station was subsequently established at Kuboes in the mid-1800s as a 'sub-station' of the Steinkopf mission. The population at Kuboes was a mixture of Nama and Bastaards, and the entire region came to be known as the Richtersveld in honour of the good doctor's visit. In 1852, the Rhenish Church (meaning from the Rhine River) established the Concordia mission very close to Springbok.

Strangely, the fate of Pella, the first mission station in Namaqualand, is obscure. Some say that it was raided by Bushmen, who killed the minister and his family, causing the inhabitants to flee. Certainly, the traveller George Thompson reported, in 1824, that the place was deserted, but he did find another mission station a few hours away at T'kams—the priest in charge explaining that they moved around during the dry months to find water. Others say that the station endured (perhaps under the aegis of the Rhenish Church) before it was abandoned in 1872 because of an extreme drought that had blighted the region.

In any event, the Catholics established their first mission in Namaqualand at Springbok in 1869. Unfortunately, the copper boom which had been responsible for the creation of the town had gone bust and the place was severely short of Catholics to whom they could preach. Undeterred, the plucky Father Gaudeul, from France, decided to take over the abandoned rectory at Pella. As the Catholic-written history of the Pella mission station hyperbolically recalls: "When the Lutherans got wind of these activities, they wrote to the Cape and made strong objections, but their letters arrived when everything had been settled. There was weeping and gnashing of teeth, but the die was cast."

Alea jacta est, indeed. By 1878, Pella boasted 100

inhabitants, 50 of whom were Catholic. In 1882, Father Jean Marie Simon arrived at the humble mission station in the middle of nowhere. He and his colleagues proceeded to build a small cathedral and a house for the nuns with only an encyclopaedia to guide them in their architectural endeavours. It took seven years. Father Simon would remain at Pella until his death in 1932, 50 years later. He became known as the 'Bishop for the Hottentots' and was an iconic figure in the area. From Pella, the Catholic Church went on to establish a number of missions across Namaqualand, Bushmanland and the Hantam Karoo.

These various mission stations, Protestant and Catholic alike, proved to be a blessing and a curse. On the one hand, they contained clinics, schools and churches, and thus formed a network of social support for the beleaguered Khoikhoi and Bastaards who were reeling under the onslaught of Trekboers and other modern interlopers. On the other hand, however, the permanent villages that grew up around the stations encouraged a more sedentary settlement pattern, which contributed to the decline of the traditional migratory lifestyle. In later years, when schooling became compulsory for all children, the mission stations became essential components of the Khoikhoi's existence and thereby drove the final nail into the coffin of their transhumance.

The indigenous Khoikhoi languages also suffered as a result of the missionaries' education. Few Europeans could master the intricate tongue-clicks of the various local dialects and, although some material was translated into Khoikhoi, most of the communication between shepherd and flock was done in Dutch or English. As a result, only the Nama language (spoken in the remote Richtersveld and in southern Namibia) is still alive today—the sole survivor of a wider linguistic tradition that once covered much of South Africa.

In conclusion, the missionaries can be said to have had a stabilizing yet disruptive influence on Namaqualand. They provided a variety of important social services, and gave the locals a small political voice. In many cases, the mission stations also fought for a 'ticket of occupation' that guaranteed permanent tenure for the indigenous people on the land around the station. This was particularly important in the face of encroachment by white farmers and, later, the mining companies. But all this came at a cost and the government often removed power from the hands of the tribal chiefs and placed it with the heads of the mission stations instead. The mission stations also forced the transient Nama herders to settle in one place, and thus undermined their traditional way of life. As they say, the Lord giveth and the Lord taketh away.

The copper boom

As we've seen, the copper deposits of northern Namaqualand were well known, but impossible to exploit as they were simply too far from market. Sooner or later, however, someone was going to give it another try. After all, money is the root of all invention.

The sequel to Simon van der Stel's expedition of 1685 thus began in 1837 with the arrival of Colonel James Edward Alexander, an avid explorer, prospector and hunter. While travelling through the Richtersveld with a local resident, Willem Joseph, the intrepid Alexander came across some particularly rich copper ore at Kodas (about 7km south of Sendelingsdrif). He collected some samples and forwarded them to Samuel Bennett in Cape Town. The results were very positive—27 per cent pure copper—and Bennett approached the British governor, Napier, for a mining permit. Permission was granted and Bennett travelled to England to form a company that would exploit the deposits. Alexander also returned to England and prepared a report on his findings, but it appears that nothing came of this venture.

Strangely, there are many reports that Alexander did commence mining activities at Kodas and Numees; transporting the unprocessed rocks by ox-wagon to the Orange River and then sailing the ore down to the sea on a flat-bottomed boat. Modern researchers, however, can find no proof of this venture and credit the story to a later prospector, Fred Cornell, who wrote a romantic book about the 'Glamour of Prospecting' in the Richtersveld.

In the 1840s, a missionary named James Backhouse also visited the copper deposits of Namaqualand and sagely observed that, "It might be collected advantageously by Hottentots and transmitted in their skin knapsacks to some place at the coast where they might exchange it for other commodities; but to smelt it in this country would be impractical [because of a lack of wood or coal]."

Undeterred, Bennett pushed ahead with his ambitious prospectus for a 'Cape of Good Hope West Coast Trading and Mining Company' that sought to set up trading posts, mission stations and mines across the region. This prospectus was issued in 1843 but no investors stepped forward to buy shares in the risky proposition. A few years later, in 1845, another attempt was made to form the 'South African Mining Company'. Once again, a glowing picture of untapped mineral wealth was painted, but negative reports from a mining agent put a damper on things.

Several contradictory letters from various stakeholders subsequently appeared in the papers. Thomas Fannin, the Honorary Secretary of the South African Mining Company claimed that the mining agent was misled by members of a rival French faction who wanted to take over the mines for themselves. Opponents to the scheme pointed out that reports from the 1700s found the rock to be too hard to process, that the Orange was not navigable, that there was no fuel or grazing, that there was no suitable harbour on the coast, and so on.

Fannin argued against all the naysayers and, at the first meeting of the SA Mining Company in Cape Town, it was decided that a party be sent out to survey the mine. Fannin was selected to lead the expedition and he headed off in a light ox-wagon, reaching the site of Colonel Alexander's mine on the banks of the seasonal Gannakouriep River at the end of 1845.

Ever the optimist, Fannin found that the mine was "centrally situated" to four mission stations, who would provide labour. He also declared that, "No tribe or individual whatever has any claim, worth a straw, to any part of the district between the Kousie (Buffels) and the Orange River." Furthermore, he said, there was a safe harbour, close to the mouth of the Orange, at Peacock Bay.

This was one of a series of little inlets in this part of the coast that were already being used by small vessels, but were dangerously exposed and unreliable. The others included Homewood Harbour and Alexander Bay—which was not named after Colonel Alexander but for a man named Alexander who ran a trading post at the location with his partner, Mr Peacock, from 1839. Alexander was apparently killed by Peacock in a fight over a girl, but I digress.

The partisan Fannin was obviously overstating the case for mining in Namaqualand. The native Khoikhoi had little interest in becoming wage labourers and the mission stations were far from the mine. The Orange River was riddled with rocks and sand banks, which would make navigation impossible in all but the wettest months (when the river often came down in flood).

Furthermore, Fannin had never seen the harbour at Peacock Bay, so didn't know if it was suitable for larger boats.

Fannin was also wrong about the land rights issue. Technically, the district in question was outside the Cape Colony, which officially ended at the Kousie (now Buffels) River south of Springbok, but there were obviously tribal authorities who had been living in the area for hundreds of years. Furthermore, several white farmers had been granted loan farms in this region, even though the government at the Cape had no legal claim over the land. This last point became moot because Sir Harry Smith, perhaps sensing that something was up in the Richtersveld, annexed this part of Namaqualand in 1847 and moved the northern boundary of the colony up to the Orange River.

In any case, Fannin proceeded to issue a prospectus for the SA Mining Company in 1846. Shares were sold for ten shillings apiece, directors were appointed and a mining team was equipped. They reached the mine later that same year and started digging. Samples were sent to Cape Town and the ore was found to contain 70 per cent copper. But transportation continued to be the major obstacle. There was a rough wagon trail to the coast, but the heavy ore could not be profitably conveyed in this way. Sailing down the Orange, as was originally intended, was no Sunday outing and, in any case, there were few suitable anchorages along the coast. Eventually, Fannin was reduced to transporting the ore overland to Cape Town.

In 1847, shareholders were asked to cough up an additional ten shillings a share to keep the mine going. Fannin, for his part, sold his shares and bought a farm in Natal. By 1848, shares in the South African Mining Company were worthless and the whole enterprise petered out. Nevertheless, this was the first commercial mining site in South Africa.

A few years after the South African Mining Company wound up its affairs, a German named Von Schlicht went to Namaqualand and stopped at a farm called Springbokfontein (also known as Melkboschuil or Koperberg). Here he was amazed to see a rich vein of copper sticking out the mountainside, in plain view. He hurried back to Cape Town to try and raise money for a mining enterprise but, unsurprisingly, he found no takers.

Dejected, Von Schlicht told his sad story to his housemate, a man named Jencken, and then left the colony for several years. Jencken, in the meantime, began working for the company Phillips & King but got himself into financial trouble and wound up owing the company some money. He offered to repay his debts by travelling to Namaqualand to open a trading store on behalf of his employers. To sweeten the deal, he told his bosses about Von Schlicht's copper find and suggested that he check it out.

Jencken's reports from Springbokfontein were euphoric and Phillips & King sent off an agent, John Wild, to investigate further. This was all done under a veil of secrecy because they didn't want to tip the hand of the government, or any other interested parties. Their clandestine approach was just as well because, at that time, the title to the farm Springbokfontein had not yet been granted to the Cloete brothers, who were resident on the land. And, when the deed was granted in 1850, the government didn't retain the mineral rights.

Just then, the story goes, Von Schlicht returned to Cape Town. When he heard that his mate, Jencken, was in Namaqualand, Von Schlicht quickly realized that it had something to do with his copper find. He raced up to Springbokfontein, where he apparently found several sacks of copper ore all trussed up and ready to go. There was no sign of Jack Wild or Jencken, so he rushed to the farmhouse and began negotiating with the Cloetes. The deal was nearly finalized before they all went to bed for the evening.

Late that night, Wild returned to the farmhouse and immediately realized that something was up. He sprang into action, woke up the farmer and got him to sign a deed of sale before the sun rose. And so, on March 15, 1850, Phillips & King purchased the relevant portion of the farm Springbokfontein for the princely sum of £50. This included mineral rights to the entire farm, the right to erect buildings for the purpose of mining, the right to graze such animals as might be needed and the right of access to water. Phillips & King later purchased the remainder of the farm for more than £2,000.

The 'Blue Mine' at Springbokfontein soon began producing considerable quantities of copper ore, which were transported by ox-wagon over the mountains to Hondeklip Bay. The first shipment of eleven tons was sent to Cape Town in 1852.

Von Schlicht was well and truly trumped, but he didn't give up. Instead, he set about prospecting around the area to try and find another windfall. Within a few months, he did indeed identify several additional copper deposits, but these were located on crown lands and not private farms. Reluctantly, he applied to the government for the mining rights to these lands, but the government wasn't about to be duped again. This time, they made a public announcement (in 1853) that the mineral rights to various portions of crown land in Namaqualand would be leased to any interested parties.

Of course, the city of Cape Town went bananas as news of the copper bonanza spread. It was said that the copper mines of Namaqualand "extend, almost without interruption, over a surface of from 8,000 to 9,000 square miles, at all degrees of depth, and that the ore is found almost everywhere at the surface". Several prominent surveyors and geologists (including the redoubtable A. G. Bain) went to visit the area and sent back optimistic reports. Suddenly, everyone wanted to get in on the action. It was a copper rush!

Spurred on by stories of copper lying on the ground, people scrambled to buy leases on 'centres' of land. These were defined as pieces of land no less than ten and no more than 40 morgen to be leased at a rate of £1 per morgen per year, payable in advance. A diagram of the claim had to be lodged within 12 months, during which time the applicant had the opportunity to search within a radius of one mile from the central point described in the lease to identify the best spot for mining. Grazing rights were also included.

Unfortunately, Namaqualand is full of superficial traces of copper that look good on the surface but are not payable. There are also a number of worthless geological formations that look 'green', which were taken to be copper. But the mania for speculation would brook no negativity and dozens of consortiums were quickly formed to take out leases on mining centres. In many cases, these were selected by people who had never set foot in Namaqualand. There was also a hot market for the re-selling of leases, and those who were quick off the mark were able turn a handsome profit by selling their centres to other companies.

As the copper boom increased in intensity, there were some cautionary voices who warned that the bubble was going to burst, as it had done on the Australian and Californian gold fields just a few years before. Rumours of deep-pocketed British investors who were about to step in to buy out the South African leaseholders proved to be without foundation. Transportation remained a problem and several 'mines' had large quantities of ore lying around, with no way to convey it to market. Other companies sent up mine managers with no idea about geology, who often dug up tons of ore that were found to contain not a trace of copper. To add to the confusion, native guides were hired at great cost to lead people to likely copper centres, which usually contained no mineral deposits whatsoever.

But it didn't matter. Copper Fever had gripped the Cape. Even the defunct South African Mining Company was resurrected and proceeded to revive operations at its old mine. This, perhaps, accounts for the story of Patrick Fletcher who is said to have been the first person to transport bags of ore from the old Kodas mine down the Orange in a flat-bottomed boat called the *Enterprise*, in 1854. Apparently, this practice continued until 1857, and some say that the mine remained in sporadic service until the 1920s. Fletcher, by the way, went on to have a long history in Namaqualand and his name crops up several times in the pages that follow.

Although some of these mining ventures showed promise, very few companies were able to present their shareholders with results. After a few months the boom started to lose steam. Then, someone announced that they had discovered gold in Namaqualand and shares soared again, despite the totally bogus nature of the claim (although it is true that Namaqualand copper does contain traces of gold, silver and other valuable minerals).

By now, the sceptics were growing more vociferous. Newspaper editorials poked fun at the gullible public. Parody prospectuses were published for the 'Ladies Mining Company' (its solicitors were listed as 'Mesdames Fleece 'em and Do 'em) and the 'Lunar Mining Company' (which promised to pull the moon down to Earth so that copper could be scraped off the surface). But it was to no avail. More and more people headed north to dig in, heavy mining machinery was lugged over the dry plains and lots of land was taken over by the voracious mining companies. At the height of the madness, applications for over 2,000 centres were made, although only 200 of these were paid for, and it is estimated that between £70,000 and £100,000 was tied up in shares, mostly from small-time investors.

Unlike many of the other mining dilettantes, Von Schlicht knew what he was doing and his consortium, the Namaqua Mining Company, was quick off the mark to purchase a very promising site at Tweefontein (Concordia). Ironically, the Namaqua Mining Company's cautious and realistic prospectus did not find favour with public investors eager for a quick profit and it struggled to get off the ground, eventually relying on a few private individuals for funding. Meanwhile, Phillips & King (which was also a privately held company) made several wise purchases to add to their portfolio. The other companies, however, didn't have a clue and were soon facing bankruptcy.

By early 1855, it was clear that the situation was untenable. After two years, the dozens of mining companies in Namaqualand had only exported 44 tons of ore (with two companies alone accounting for 33 tons). Hundreds of leases were forfeited through lack of payment and proposals were made to amalgamate all the copper mines into a single entity in order to manage the process more effectively. Then, the government abruptly declared that it would grant no more new leases. The boom was over.

By 1857, just three companies remained in operation. These were Von Schlicht's Namaqua Mining Company, the Phillips & King group and the South African Mining Company, which closed soon afterwards. While a few unscrupulous businessmen had made a killing by pocketing the money raised through share offerings, many investors were ruined and limped off into the taverns of Cape Town to lick their financial wounds.

Getting down to business

After the copper boom ended, the two remaining companies got busy consolidating their claims and streamlining operations. The Phillips & King group concentrated on their mine at Springbokfontein—the one that had started the whole thing off.

Before copper, Springbokfontein was a farmstead with one mud house and couple of mat huts. Within a few years, it was a bona fide mining station with houses for officers (mainly Cornish miners) and workmen (from all over SA). There was also a mess room, storerooms, a wagon maker, a blacksmith, stables, a post office and a prison. Everything in town was built and owned by Phillips & King, and uninvited guests were not allowed to stay overnight in the private village. In several cases, thirsty travellers were denied food and water for their horses.

The mine manager (or 'Super') held supreme power over the inhabitants, often behaving like a dictator. Other officials could also throw their weight around and there is one instance of a resident jailer, Genricks, who terrorized the town before he was finally tried (along with his 'tame lunatic') for murder and indecent assault. Even when Springbokfontein got its first resident magistrate, in 1855, he relied entirely on the company for his accommodation and supplies—hardly conducive to an independent judiciary.

The wealth of the Springbokfontein mine was short-lived, however, and the mine was exhausted by 1861. Nevertheless, the village had become established and managed to endure. In 1862, the government declared that it was to become a public village. The town was surveyed by Patrick Fletcher and residential plots were auctioned off. The first clergyman arrived in 1866 and the little town developed a social scene, with race meets and balls. Gradually, the village became something of an urban centre for the region. In 1911, the name was shortened to Springbok.

In addition to the Blue Mine at Springbok, Phillips & King also secured the leases to several other valuable properties, including Spektakel, Nababeep and O'okiep. Collectively, they accounted for the bulk of the copper output from Namaqualand and the company was the most influential player in the region. Their only rival was the Namaqua Mining Company of Von Schlict and his partners, who owned the nearby Concordia mine. Together, these two mining companies made a huge contribution to the colony's balance sheet. In 1860, copper was the second most important export from the Cape after wool (which was, admittedly, a much more substantial industry).

All the productive copper mines mentioned above were located within a radius of about 30 kilometres, and they each had their ups and downs. Drought, fluctuating copper prices, transport woes, shortage of labour, variable ore qualities and other vagaries caused the mines to increase production, prosper, slow down, wither and grow again in a constant cycle.

The Blue Mine at Springbokfontein was the first to fail, as we've seen, but the settlement was maintained as a municipal centre. A smelter was set up at the old mine in 1866 to process ore from the other Philips & King mines, although this was later superseded by the reduction works at O'okiep. The company then dealt the town another blow by relocating its headquarters to the more important mine at O'okiep and, by 1877, Springbok was nearly deserted. Then, in 1881, shipping costs decreased and Springbok mine re-opened for another ten or 15 years. W. C. Scully, the new magistrate, got to work improving the town, often using the prisoners held in the jail as a labour force.

By 1904, there are reports that the town was once

again on the skids. In 1906, about 100 people lived there. A school was established in 1911 but, by 1913, the village still had only one hotel. Clothing and lodging were very expensive in Springbok, and some civil servants asked for a transfer because they would've gone broke on their current salaries. Still, there were obviously some folks with money because, in 1914 when the first registration of cars in South Africa took place, there were ten licensed drivers in Springbok (out of a total of 13 for the whole of Namaqualand).

The mine at Spektakel was another precarious proposition. The lease was granted in 1853 and pits were sunk. By 1856, only one pit had proved worthy of exploitation, but it was really rich. In 1861, it produced more ore than the mighty O'okiep mine and, by 1863, Spektakel had grown into the largest village in Namaqualand. A school was established a few years later, but the mine was already petering out. Workers were transferred to other mines and the school closed down less than a year after it opened. In 1867, production slowed to a meagre 49 tons of ore. The following year, production resumed but on a small scale, and smelting works were constructed to reduce the ore to more profitable grades (known as regulus).

Things seemed to be looking up. In 1869 a mission school was established and, in 1871, the grandly-named *Spektakel Examiner and Times and Namaqualand Advertiser* began its circulation to a reported 600 inhabitants. Two topics that were regularly discussed in the hand-written circular were the lack of a law officer and the ongoing problem with stray dogs. Then, in 1872, the mine failed again, but work continued sporadically. The town dwindled, only to recover a few years later when the mine improved.

The year 1886 was a bad one for the mines, with a slump in the price of copper causing many mines to close down. Prices rebounded two years later, thanks to the efforts of a London-based syndicate funded by the copper companies, and Spektakel was opened yet again. But, by 1890, there were reports that the people at the nearby village of Kommagas were suffering because work had been suspended at Spektakel once more. The mine was now valued at £100 (£2,000 if you included the value of buildings and equipment). Nevertheless, the mine stumbled on until 1901 when it was finally put to rest as a result of the Anglo–Boer war. The last entry in the mine manager's journal reads "Mine abandoned due to marauding Boers". Today, Spektakel is a small village, and a popular site on the spring flower route.

Nababeep was a more substantial proposition. It began as a farm, Lelykepad (bad road), which was granted to Pieter van Zyl in 1850. In 1852 it was purchased by Phillips & King for £1,000. For the next few decades it was considered to be a very promising trial mine, slowly growing into a complex with several shafts, a smelting works, winding engines, stone breakers etc. By 1902, it was the secondmost important producing mine in the group. By 1908, it had a population of more than 2,000 people. Nababeep closed during the copper slump of 1919, but reopened in 1937 and continued to operate, albeit under constant threat of closure, until the early 1980s. Today, there is a sleepy village at Nababeep and an interesting mining museum. Amazingly, a private consortium is currently trying to re-start the mine after all these years.

The big one, however, was O'okiep. It began life in 1856 with one small shaft and by 1860 it was the most important mine in the region. Ten years later, it was described as the richest copper mine in the world. Accordingly, it was a large settlement with stores, stables, workshops, machinery, steam engine, school, store, infirmary, residences and cottages. By 1870, the mine was 75–90 metres deep with a population that was approaching 1,500. A few years later, the mine was nearly 150 metres deep and it took 20 minutes to climb up the ladders from the lowest levels to the surface.

Labour at O'okiep was divided into 'tut-work' (sinking shafts) and 'tribute work' (getting ore to surface). Most of this was done by black labourers under the supervision of white miners. Salaries were relatively high, with qualified miners from Britain earning between £8–£12 per month. In stark contrast, the black workers were paid 1s/6d per day. Women and children, who were employed to sort the ore by hand and do other 'menial' jobs were paid four pennies a day. At the time, this wage gap was considered to be entirely appropriate given the difference between "the skilled labour of civilisation and the unskilled labour of barbarism".

Despite the professed generosity of the company, O'okiep (and the other mines in the area) often experienced a shortage of labourers, especially when the rains were good and locals returned to their farms. As a result, workers were brought in from all over the world. By 1875 the population totalled 1,752 people, living in 73 houses and 367 huts and tents. A contemporary traveller described the 'copper wonder' as follows: "There is a perpetual clatter which, to a stranger, is very fidgeting, but which is not noticed by those resident, unless there is a stoppage, when everyone looks up to see what is the matter. The people are called to work by a huge steam whistle, which can be heard for many a mile. Almost every nation finds its representatives there, English, French, German, Italian, Portuguese, the colonial Dutch and 'Africanders', and as for the numerous native races, I would scarcely like to say what African race is not there. Here you see men from the far interior, west and east coast of Africa, Lascars, Indians, Kafirs, Fingoes, Hottentots, Bushmen and the various Damara nations, and all the wonderful crosses produced by marriage amongst such a mixed population."

And still the mine continued to grow. In 1882, it had a population of around 2,000, eight stores, two churches, two schools, a hospital, a post office, a telephone service and a telegraph line. By this time, the mine was so successful it had started to pollute the environment and many people died from the bad air and contaminated water.

But the mine was too good a proposition to slow down. In 1884, production was reported at 15,000 tons of 30 per cent copper ore, the mine had over 900 employees and the resident magistrate said that, "I have never been in touch with a community where there is such a constant undercurrent of scandalous innuendo as there was at O'okiep." Apparently, moral decline is a sure sign of prosperity.

Four years later, the mine had 2,000 employees, with huts of the Damara labourers (from Namibia) on one side of the valley and Khoikhoi huts on the other. Popular prejudice against the Khoikhoi had not diminished over the years and it was declared that, "The Damara is a steady, hardworking, reticent, thrifty native. The Hottentot on the other hand is thriftless, careless and happy-go-lucky. He is altogether a most disreputable character with one god—'dop' [booze]."

Despite these misgivings, O'okiep continued to produce ore through most of the 20th century before it was closed for good. Today, Okiep (as it is now spelled) is a quaint place. The smoke stack of the old reduction works is still standing, as is the steam-driven Cornish pump—the only complete example of its kind in South Africa. The massive mine dumps are also visible on the edge of town, with their dark-green ore glistening in the hot sun. The town currently contains about 7,500 inhabitants, and the unemployment rate is sitting at 75 per cent.

The Namaqua Mining Company's property at

Concordia was said to be more of a quarry than a mine. It began in 1853 and a neat compound was quickly laid out. It was never a particularly rich mine, but it was regular. In 1873, it had between 150 and 500 employees, depending on the season, and a reported output worth £15,000. A few years later, the population numbered 961, who were living in ten houses and 219 huts and tents. In 1875, mine activities were greatly reduced and things remained very quiet until 1881 when reduced shipping costs made it feasible to resume operations. In 1886, the mine improved but a few years later, things had gone belly-up and the mine's land was valued at a mere £150 (with equipment and buildings, £10,000).

But you can't keep a good mine down. A smelting works was constructed in 1905 and, by 1908, the mine employed around 650 people. The mine finally closed for good in 1931. It was the plucky underdog of the Namaqualand copper mines, paying out a 400 per cent dividend between 1888 and 1928. Today, it is a dusty village with little in the way of economic opportunities.

The fates of the companies that owned these mines are similarly full of vicissitudes. The Namaqua Mining Company, in particular, went through several changes of fortune. In the 1860s, the original consortium was bought out by Von Schlict and Henry Home Ley. Then, in 1869, Von Schlict was bought out by Ley, but the mine soon went into liquidation (partly as a result of their rival's monopoly over the railway line to Port Nolloth—see below).

In 1872, a group of Glasgow capitalists bought the company for £15,000. It then changed hands a couple of times before it was re-incorporated as Concordia Copper Company in 1877. The name was changed again a few years later to the Namaqua Copper Company, which then became the Namaqua United Company in 1886. This concern also went bang, only to be resurrected in

1888 as, once again, the Namaqua Copper Company.

In 1902, the Anglo–Boer War came to Namaqualand, and all the mines were affected. Concordia surrendered to the Boers without a shot being fired. This was greatly resented by the other mines as the Boers used Concordia as a base from which to launch a month-long siege on O'okiep. The siege was unsuccessful, but the Boers did manage to take Springbok and they also blew up the railway line, as they were wont to do. As it turns out, all this was of little consequence as the war ended a few months later.

At the outbreak of World War I, all copper mining in Namaqualand was suspended. This was because the government stopped the shipping of copper ore to Britain, preferring to keep the cargo space for products that were more important to the war effort. The Namaqua Copper Company never fully recovered. Major operations were stopped in 1918 and smelting stopped in 1930. By 1931, the company was defunct, retaining only the mineral rights to its lands.

The Phillips & King group, on the other hand, had all the good mines and enjoyed a more sustained corporate history. After commencing operations in 1853, the company did well until two partners in the firm died in 1862. This necessitated the dissolution of the concern and the whole enterprise was taken over by the newly formed Cape of Good Hope Copper Mining Company Ltd. This soon became known, simply, as the Cape Copper Company. In the new company prospectus, it was announced that the company-owned mines had already exported 19,000 tons of high grade ore, worth £500,000 (with a profit of £115,000).

For the next couple of decades, the Cape Copper Company continued to deliver solid results. But the outbreak of World War I put a serious dent in its finances. To make matters worse, 1918 was a bad year all

Above: The charming white-washed Catholic church in Port Nolloth
Below: Sunset at MacDougall's Bay, Port Nolloth

Above: Diamond and fishing boats at anchor, Port Nolloth
Below: Flocks of flamingos perch precariously in the Orange River Mouth wetlands, Alexander Bay

Above: Diners enjoy the warm and friendly clutter of Anita's Tavern, Port Nolloth
Left: Two young go-cart enthusiasts, Sizamile township, Port Nolloth

Top: A purple haze covers the fields near the Rooiberg Guest House, Richtersveld Community Conservancy
Above: The gravel road to the Rooiberg Guest House curves around a lonely windmill, Richtersveld Community Conservancy

Left: Thin branches are tied together to create the framework of a traditional *matjieshuis*, Kuboes.

Below: A *matjieshuis* that needs a facelift, Rooiberg Guest House, RCC

Top left: A botterboom *(Tylecodon paniculatus)* blooms in the wild open spaces of the Richtersveld Community Conservancy
Above: The stoep of the Rooiberg Guest House is the perfect place to enjoy a hot cup of tea as the sun sets behind the mountains
Below left: The peaceful, dreamy village of Eksteenfontein, in the middle of the RCC
Below: The fully equipped self-catering cottages of the Mountain Valley Guest House, Kuboes

The Rooiberg lives up to its name as the setting sun turns the rocky slopes red

Auntie Kniekie, one of the hosts at the Rooiberg Guest House

A friendly passer-by, strolling down the main road of Eksteenfontein

Gert Swartbooi, 86 years old and still going strong, Kuboes

A cowboy in Kuboes, yee-hah!

Students at the Eksteenfontein Primary School

The stern face belies a friendly welcome, Kuboes

Left-hand page: A quiver tree at sunset, Kokerboomkloof, Richtersveld National Park
Above: The tentative gravel track that leads through the lunar landscape of the Richtersveld National Park
Left: Going in style—the attractive ablution blocks at the Kokerboomkloof campsite, RNP
Below: Camping on the banks of the Orange River, De Hoop, RNP

Above: The surreal Hand of God stamped into the stone of the Richtersveld National Park
Left: The eerily accurate profile of Queen Victoria etched into the rocks by wind erosion, Kokerboomkloof, RNP

Left: A dramatic kokerboom casually grows outside a cottage in Concordia, near Springbok

Below: Spring flowers grace the gardens of Bergsig township, Springbok

Above: The Springbok Café has an extensive gemstone display and a good selection of books on Namaqualand

Left: The gracious sandstone church at Springbok

round; falling ore grades, shortage of supplies and lack of access to markets all exacerbated the situation. Then, in 1919, the Cape Copper Company suddenly suspended its operations with "a callousness and want of consideration and forethought [for their employees] which [was] nothing short of culpable". In fact, on a single day, the company dismissed all the staff in one fell swoop, most with just a week's severance pay. The shareholders, however, had done very well, making £217 for every initial share of £8.

In 1920, the company started up again, mining on a small scale and selling off its accumulated stocks of ore. It was eventually bought by an American consortium, which paid $750,000 for the company's property. This new concern was named the South African Copper Company Limited, and it was involved mainly with exploratory work. In 1937, the O'okiep Copper Company was incorporated to buy out the South African Copper Company. Shares in the new enterprise were taken up by a variety of international mining companies, with the Newmont Mining Corporation, based in America, as the largest shareholder. The O'okiep Copper Company's assets included 105,000 acres of land, mineral rights to another 50,000 acres, equipment, the railway to Port Nolloth and the jetty at Port Nolloth.

In 1939, the company bought the mineral leases held by the defunct Namaqua Copper Company for £2,125. It now owned all the mines in Namaqualand. In 1940, it began milling and smelting operations and, in the following year, it posted sales of £467,010, £109,125 of which were profit. These returns improved during World War II, when the company secured contracts with the British and American defence departments. After the war, East Okiep mine was opened and a pipeline to the Buffels River was constructed to supply the mines with water, which was always in short supply. In 1951, another mine called Wheal Julia opened. Several others followed: Hoit's mine, Homeep, Jan Coetzee (famous for its quartz crystal formations), Carolusberg (the location of Van der Stel's original excavations in 1685) and Nigramoep.

By 1975, the O'okiep Copper Company employed 1,036 whites, 1,996 coloureds and 2,080 Africans. But the life of their mines was limited and, by the 1990s, only Carolusberg and Nigramoep remained in operation. In 1997, the company gave all the houses in Okiep, Carolusberg and Nababeep to the current occupants, irrespective of their status. At that time, the company was managed by Goldfields of South Africa, but it was bought by Metrorex in 1999. Nigramoep, the last active mine, closed in 2004 and surface explorations were abandoned in the same year.

Processing of stockpiles continued until 2005, when it was announced that the equipment of the O'okiep Copper Company was to be transported 'meccano-like' to a new copper mine in the Democratic Republic of Congo. Today, there are no active copper mines in Namaqualand (apart from the small, speculative operation at Nababeep). One of the region's most important industries had come to an end.

Transport problems

As we've seen, the biggest problem facing the copper mines of Namaqualand was the lack of effective transport routes. The region had few roads, and those that did exist were in a terrible state. The heavy ore couldn't be profitably transported overland to Cape Town and the Orange River wasn't an option. This meant that the rocks had to be taken to the sea (about 120km away) and then shipped down to Cape Town, from whence they could be sent to England. But this required the establishment of a port on the hostile coastline.

Accordingly, in 1854, Captain H. J. Nolloth surveyed

the entire Namaqualand coast up to the Orange River mouth. He declared that there were two potential anchorages, although neither was particularly good. Both had an outer anchorage about a mile from the shore and an inner anchorage (for smaller boats) with a pronounced sandbar. They were called Hondeklip Bay and Robbe Bay (Bay of Seals), and the good captain's preference was for the latter, which was soon re-named Port Nolloth in his honour.

For the mines clustered around Springbok, 120km away from the coast, neither port was ideal as the overland routes to reach these harbours each had their own problems. The Hondeklip Bay road was very mountainous, while the Port Nolloth route had a poor supply of water for the draught animals. Furthermore, while both routes had to traverse the western Hardeveld mountains and then cross a strip of soft, deep sand (which was a nightmare for the heavy wagons), the Port Nolloth route had a wider expanse of Sandveld to negotiate.

Previously, in 1852, the first shipment of eleven tons of ore had been sent by wagon over the rough path to Hondeklip Bay. This tortuous route thus became the preferred route to the sea and a new profession was created to take on the challenge—the era of the copper rider had begun.

Despite the best efforts of the copper riders, who were local farmers of various ethnic groups, the problems with the primitive road were manifest. Sacks of ore burst open. Wagons fells to pieces. Water for the animals was scarce. Wheels got stuck in the sand. And it was slow going. Each journey to the coast took roughly six days, and another four days to get back.

Nevertheless, a procession of heavily laden wagons, each weighing up to one and a half tons, soon began bumping along the rough gravel path (although many wagons arrived at the coast about 500 kilograms lighter as a result of ore falling off en route). By 1866, there were about 300 wagons and 6,000 draught animals plying the route.

Most of these wagons were hauled by sorry asses, arranged together in teams of up to ten mules. In times of good rain, oxen were used. The copper riders also tried using Scotch carts, but these light-weight vehicles couldn't withstand the battering. The geologist-surveyor, Wyley, even suggested importing camels to use as draught-animals during the dry summer months. While this is a somewhat ridiculous idea, it's not as bad as an earlier idea, expressed in 1802, that proposed using giraffes!

Transporting the copper was not only difficult; it was expensive. By 1855, the cost of getting ore to the coast equalled the total cost of mining the stuff in the first place. The figures broke down like this: copper riders were paid £7/10s to travel to the coast, and £3 to return back to the mines; shipping to Table Bay cost £1/10s; shipping to London cost between £2 and £3; transport from London to the smelting works at Swansea cost a mere 10s or 15s; amounting to a total cost of £16 per ton (£10 of which was for the short overland route of 120km).

These high prices meant that only the highest grade ore could be profitably exported, while hundreds of tons of lower grade ore were stockpiled at the mines. Furthermore, the riding season was limited to the wet winter months, when there was enough water for the draught animals, so transportation of ore was sporadic.

The mines made repeated calls for improved roads or, even better, a railway that would make transport more efficient. However, the government didn't want to pay for the construction of proper roads, as they believed the mines were making a decent profit as things stood. The mine owners, for their part, felt that their leases were too short to justify spending large amounts of money on infrastructure and, in any case, they were generally low on capital and high on speculation. It was a stalemate.

In an attempt to settle the issue, two Select Committees were set up (in 1854 and 1855). Both committees considered the development of the mines in Namaqualand to be of national importance, and both recommended the construction of railway line from Hondeklip Bay across the Sandveld, as this would facilitate a cost-effective bulk transportation system that would unlock the value of the lower-grade ores.

The government refused to budge, despite the sage advice of respected surveyors A. G. Bain and Charles Bell. There were some suggestions of floating a railway consortium, which would construct the railway as a profit-making exercise, but this didn't materialize because, just at that moment, the copper boom went bust and no-one was prepared to invest.

The two remaining copper companies (Phillips & King and the Namaqua Mining Company) were left to their own devices. Phillips & King, the larger of the two, took it upon themselves to repair the road to Hondeklip Bay at their own expense after each riding season, but the road continued to deteriorate year on year. Various government agents protested that this wasn't fair, as the mines brought a lot of money into the colony, but nothing was done.

To compensate themselves, Phillips & King quietly bought up almost all farms along the route from Springbok to Hondeklip Bay. This left their rivals in a tenuous position, but the Namaqua Company did manage to secure their own outspan on one of the farms along the way. They also sent their wagons to Port Nolloth, when the erratic water supply would allow.

Things proceeded in this manner until 1862, when another Select Committee was appointed to investigate the construction of a road, which it soon recommended. The committee also considered an application from Phillips & King (now called the Cape Copper Company) who wanted to construct a railway line from Hondeklip Bay to Riethuis farm, 16 miles away. This section of track would eliminate the difficult stretch across the Sandveld, and the committee agreed to the proposal on condition that public goods would be transported and that the line be sold back to the government at cost after ten years. But the funds were still not forthcoming and the status quo was maintained.

By this time, Hondeklip Bay had developed from a single trading store (owned by a Mr Grace) into a ramshackle village with four trading stores, dozens of wooden shacks and a jetty. It was, by all accounts, a horrible place. There was no inn, tavern or canteen in the settlement, and drinking water had to be shipped in from Cape Town. The only other liquid available was brandy, which was sold in 16-gallon casks. This led to widespread drunkenness and regular outbursts of violence among the copper riders. There was also no jail and the lone peace officer certainly had his hands full dispensing rough justice.

The anchorage at Hondeklip Bay was similarly problematic. It was exposed to the strong winds and rough seas, and there was a shortage of moorings in the inner harbour. Nevertheless, this was now the main transport hub in the region and the Cape Copper Company set about constructing houses, storerooms and other utilitarian buildings. In 1862, Hondeklip was made a magisterial district and a customs officer was appointed. Within ten years, exports from the port amounted to 800,000 pounds, with imports of 450,000 pounds (which consisted mainly of supplies destined for the mines at Springbok).

But the town was still a dump. A contemporary visitor

described it thus: "The wood [of the houses] is covered with tar, which prevents decay, but does not improve its appearance. The ground on which it stands, and for miles around, is loose sand, which is blown about by the wind. The frequent sea fogs are very damp and unpleasant … It would be difficult to find a more disagreeable place."

By 1865, nothing had been done about either of the roads to the coast, and the situation was getting worse. The Divisional Council of Namaqualand (which was established in 1861) complained that it spent most of its revenue keeping the Hondeklip Bay road in repair (even though it was still terrible). The farmers living in the Hardeveld and at Kamiesberg were also unhappy that their rates were going into the road, even though it was of little use to them. So, yet another Select Committee was established 'on Namaqualand Roads and Tramway'. This time, the government brought a roads inspector, our friend Patrick Fletcher, to decide on whether the road should be constructed to Hondeklip Bay or Port Nolloth. Meanwhile, the Cape Copper Company got in their own engineer, Thomas Hall.

Surprisingly, Hall advised that a Springbok–to–Port Nolloth road was preferable and proposed building a tramline from Port Nolloth across the Sandveld to the farm Muishondfontein. Fletcher, however, suggested improvements to the Hondeklip Bay road, even though it would be expensive to build and maintain. This latter recommendation was apparently based on the needs of the copper riders who were already based in the Hondeklip area. It was subsequently decided that a new road to Hondeklip Bay should be built and permission was granted for the Cape Copper Company to build a tramway from Hondeklip Bay across the Sandveld to the farm Riethuis (although this tramway never materialized).

And so, in 1867, construction on the long-awaited road

to Hondeklip Bay was commenced, under the supervision of Patrick Fletcher. It was called the Messelpad (Mason's Road) because of all the high dry-stone retaining walls that had to be constructed to push the road over the mountains. Convicts were used to supply the labour, and accommodation and transport for these road gangs was supplied by the Cape Copper Company. Even so, by the time the road was complete in 1871, it had cost a total of £10,000. This road still exists today and offers the modern motorist a wonderful scenic drive. The ruins of the old convicts' compound can also be seen.

Unfortunately, the Messelpad came too late for Hondeklip Bay. In the late 1860s, the Cape Copper Company revamped its transport operations by putting the riders under contract. From then on, only 30 or 40 men were allowed to transport the company's ore, and they were paid at O'okiep and supplied from company stores, thus depriving the Hondeklip traders of their most important customers.

Then, in 1869, the decision was made to develop Port Nolloth as the major sea port in the region and the Cape Copper Company was granted permission to build a railway line across the Sandveld from the port to Muishondfontein. Thomas Hall was recalled to begin construction and the first 46 miles of line was opened in 1870. The new wagon route from O'okiep over the Anenous Pass to the railhead at Muishond proved very popular. Ore exports almost doubled within the year and copper riding over the nearly completed Messelpad decreased dramatically.

Within a few years, Hondeklip Bay was a shadow of its former, boisterous self. The copper riders had departed and all but one of the shopkeepers left town. By 1877, Hondeklip Bay had ceased to be a separate magisterial district and was no longer regarded as a port. The town barely survived and only became viable again with the growth of the fishing industry. A cannery was built in 1925, but this closed in the latter part of the 20th century. It still smells though.

Port Nolloth, meanwhile, boomed. In 1856, the town had only a couple of inhabitants, four or five wooden houses and a single trading station, run by F. W. Dreyer. By 1870, a few months after the tramway opened, it contained around 200 residents. Captain Nolloth himself, now retired, was appointed as the first harbour master. Unfortunately, it remained an unattractive place. Makeshift houses sprawled across the soft sand, along with a number of canteens and bars. There was no jail or magistrate, and living conditions were very rough.

But it was, in many ways, a far superior port to Hondeklip, with a safe inner anchorage protected from the elements. In the early days, sacks of ore were carried down to the beach and into the sea by 'coolies', who then heaved the bags into the bobbing boats. By 1874, a jetty had been constructed with a miniature railway that ran along its length, allowing the ore to be dumped directly into the waiting vessels. Moorings and navigational beacons were erected, and a fortnightly ship from Cape Town brought in the much-needed supplies. In the same year, Port Nolloth became a magisterial district and a customs officer was appointed. Drinking water for the settlement was sourced from a spring about five miles away and transported into town on a *rol-vaatjie* (basically a barrel fitted to an axle).

By 1882, the town had 2,000 inhabitants and the *Namaqua*, a Union Castle steamer, regularly plied the Cape Town–Port Nolloth route. Unfortunately, there was no proper landing area for passengers and, to get from a boat to the jetty, you either had to climb up a rocking ladder or get hoisted ashore in a basket that dangled from a wire pulley.

The town continued to grow apace. The year 1886

saw the establishment of a newspaper and a cricket club. In 1896 a sanitation system was installed. A lighthouse was erected in 1909. But the fortunes of Port Nolloth took a tumble when the Cape Copper Company stopped production in 1919. Poverty overwhelmed what was, essentially, a mining town. Visitors in the 1930s reported seeing young children begging for a cup of fresh water. Fishing turned out to be the saving grace of Port Nolloth and today it is an attractive town with a well-developed tourism infrastructure.

Meanwhile, back in the 19th century, the Cape Copper Company applied for an extension of the narrow-gauge railway from Muishond to O'okiep. This was granted in 1871 and work began on the Anenous Pass section (which climbs 400 metres in only 12 kilometres). The railway finally reached O'okiep in 1876. The total cost of the railway and its complementary jetty at Port Nolloth was £170,000. This is a bargain when you consider that an estimated £500,000 of lower grade ore was stockpiled at the mines, just waiting for a more cost-effective transportation method.

At first, teams of mules were used to pull the railroad trucks along the track, as was stipulated in the various government acts that authorized the construction of the line. However, Hall wanted to try a steam engine. Two of these locomotives arrived in 1871 and were put to use over a section of the line, but they required a lot of water (which was always in short supply) and often broke down. So, the trusty mules were put back into service and continued to pull coaches along the track, as follows: freight trucks were grouped into threes and pulled by six mules in single file, while passenger 'specials' were pulled by three mules. This was doubled for the uphill section of the Anenous Pass. The mule teams were changed every 28 miles.

The only notable exception to this system was on the

down run, when the cars were tied together at the top of the pass and allowed to coast all the way down to Port Nolloth, with a brakeman checking the speed. If that sounds hairy, consider that when going up the pass, a man sat at the front of the locomotive scooping sand onto the tracks to prevent the wheels from slipping. Contemporary passenger accounts of trips up the pass are full of wonder and terror, in equal measure.

From 1878, the light rails were replaced by heavier rails, in anticipation of the re-introduction of steam locomotives. This took place in 1886, when special condenser-type engines were brought in. These didn't work too well in the high temperatures, however, and were soon replaced with Kitson 'mountain type' locomotives. This shortened the travelling time from two days (during which people would overnight at the Klipfontein Hotel, at the top of the Anenous Pass) to an eight-hour trip that could be completed in a single day. By 1896, steam traction was used along the entire line, although the mule teams were still maintained for times of drought.

All in all, the railway line was a huge success and the Namaqualand copper fields were finally placed on a firm footing. However, it wasn't all sunshine and light. The line, as you'll remember, was owned by the Cape Copper Company and, although they were legally obligated to act in the interests of developing the country, they often made things very difficult for members of the public and their rival, Concordia Mine. Discriminatory tariffs were charged and numerous complaints were made. However, the government was reluctant to act against the mighty Cape Copper Company and, after ten years of operation, they declined to exercise their option to purchase the line at the cost price of construction, thus forfeiting the right entirely. The Cape Copper Company was then pretty much free to do as they pleased with their line.

But progress is inevitable, even in the wilds of Namaqualand. In 1927, the South African Railways line from Cape Town reached Bitterfontein (a couple of hundred kilometres to the south). Now, the mines found it more effective to transport the ore by road to the new railhead, thus effectively ending the life of the Port Nolloth railway. It remained in the possession of the O'okiep Copper Company (successors of the Cape Copper Company) and continued to operate until 1942. The line was then scrapped and sold in 1944. Its cannibalized remnants can still be seen in the pylons that carry the power lines over the mountains.

Diamonds in the sand

The Namaqualand copper fields were already on the decline when a new form of mineral wealth was discovered in the desolate north—diamonds! We've already seen how, millions of years ago, diamond pipes intruded from the Earth's mantle to the surface, only to be washed into the sea by the Orange River. The northern Namaqualand coast, and the southern Namibian shore, was thus coated with several diamond-bearing terraces, located both above and below the current waterline.

Strangely, none of the early explorers and prospectors who roamed the region found any trace of these gems, and the secret wealth of Namaqualand lay hidden for hundreds of years. Then, in 1886, a German named Franz Lüderitz set off from Angra Pequena (Lüderitz Bay) on a prospecting mission.

Lüderitz was an interesting bloke. He was a merchant from Bremen who had grown bored of working in the family business. One day, he looked at a map of Africa and saw a big, empty space that no other colonial power had claimed. He decided that he would take it since "nothing better (was) left". In 1882, he approached the

German government and got their permission for his venture. Then, through an agent named Vogelsang, Lüderitz persuaded the local chief, Joseph Fredericks, to sell him a large chunk of land around Angra Pequena for 10,000 reichmarks and 260 rifles.

Within a few months, Vogelsang had made several additional purchases and Lüderitz became the proud owner of a country that stretched from the north bank of the Orange River to the Kunene River. Fearing that the British would annex his territory, Lüderitz asked the imperial German government to take over the land as a protectorate. This was completed by 1885 and German South West Africa was born, with Lüderitz retaining several key concessions.

Unfortunately, by 1886, Lüderitz was broke. He sold his concessions to a chartered company, the Deutsche Kolonialgesellschaft für Südwest Africa, and embarked on a fateful journey to discover new mineral deposits. His trek took him through the sandy wastes of Namibia to the Orange River, where he unpacked a small boat from his wagon. He then sailed down to the sea at Alexander Bay before turning the vessel to the north, intending to sail back to his eponymous bay. Unfortunately, he disappeared and is presumed to have drowned in the cold Atlantic waters off the aptly named Skeleton Coast. The rumours were that he had discovered diamonds on this journey but died before he could tell anyone.

The first official diamond find was made 22 years later, in 1908, when a railway worker named Zacharias Lewala picked up some shiny pebbles on a beach near Lüderitz Bay. Lewala showed these gems to his supervisor, August Stauch, who immediately applied for a mining permit. News of the find soon spread and a major diamond rush was sparked. At that time, it was claimed that the diamonds were so abundant that all you had to do was crawl along the beach and pick them up.

They were even said to be visible in the moonlight!

But the German colonial government simply couldn't handle such a disorganized set-up and, realizing that the extensive diamond fields were no flash in the pan, stepped in to institute control. A central market was established in 1909 and, in 1911, a Sperrgebiet or 'forbidden zone' was declared. This vast single-concession area extended 360km northward from the Orange River and 100km inland from the coast, and was enclosed by two tall, barbed-wire fences.

The first mining town to be established was at Kolmanskop, where five million carats were recovered in just six years of mining. The town grew so rich that, apparently, water was shipped in from Cape Town to irrigate the rose gardens. Kolmanskop also got electricity at a time when most towns in Germany still had gas streetlights. The first X-ray machine in southern Africa was installed at the Kolmanskop hospital.

After the First World War, however, Germany lost control of South West Africa and South Africa took over. The diamonds of SWA were thus up for grabs and Sir Ernest Oppenheimer was quick off the mark. He hurriedly formed Consolidated Diamond Mines of South West Africa (CDM) in 1920 and, in 1923, CDM signed the Halbscheid Agreement with the South West African Administration. This granted CDM the mining rights for the Sperrgebiet.

In 1928, vast diamond reserves were found in the south, around the Orange River mouth, and operations moved away from Kolmanskop. The company-built town of Oranjemund was established by CDM in 1936, and Kolmanskop was abandoned in the 1950s. It is now a well-known ghost town in the desert. CDM continued to operate out of Oranjemund and, after Namibian independence in 1990, CDM became Namdeb, a joint partnership with De Beers and the Namibian government that retained all of CDM's old concessions.

Oranjemund is still the centre of Namdeb's operations and is reached by crossing the highly restricted Oppenheimer Bridge over the Orange River, just outside Alexander Bay. The 26,000-square-km Sperregebiet is also intact and special permission has to be arranged for visitors. However, now that the onshore diamonds in the northern part of the forbidden territory are finally running out, there are plans to create a Sperregebiet National Park, which will allow people to experience this pristine section of the Skeleton Coast.

Today it is thought that Namibia has the richest diamond reserves in the world. More than 100 million carats have been recovered since 1908, and there is still an estimated 1.5 billion carats waiting in reserve. Fifty-five per cent of the diamonds recovered are on-shore (along the coast and the northern banks of the Orange) and 45 per cent are off-shore (under the water). All in all, diamonds contribute about 45 per cent of Namibia's GDP.

But back to the south side of the Orange River, and the diamonds of Namaqualand ...

In the early part of the 20th century, several prospectors picked their way along the north-west coastline, looking for anything that glittered. Fred Cornell was the best known of this generation of fortune-seekers. He spent 20 years in South Africa and his wanderings took him through most of Namaqualand, the Richtersveld and Namibia. As he went, he kept his eyes open for gold, copper and diamonds, but he didn't report any significant finds. Instead, he wrote a book, called *The Glamour of Prospecting*, which was very popular.

Some say that Cornell did indeed find diamonds but kept it a secret. And it does seems hard to believe that he could spend so much time in the area and not stumble across at least one. However, many others had come before Cornell and similarly failed to discover anything. In any event, Cornell served with honour in World War I and returned to England to receive an award from the Royal Geographical Society for his work. Sadly, in 1921, while in London, he died in a motorcycle accident.

Then there was Ernest Martin, from Aus in Namibia, who apparently found diamonds at Alexander Bay some time in the early 1920s. He supposedly put up beacons to mark his claim, but didn't get round to working them—which seems rather daft—and nothing came of the discovery.

It was only with Jack Carstens' discovery of a diamond in 1925 that the ball really got rolling. Carstens was from Port Nolloth, the son of a storekeeper who was also the local Reuters correspondent. One day, Jack was exploring the Oubeep farm, south of the port, when he picked up a shiny lump of rock. News of this, the first diamond found on the Namaqualand coast, spread fast thanks to his father's newspaper connections, and the hunt was on. Soon, dozens of treasure hunters headed up to Port Nolloth to see what they could uncover.

The next find was made soon afterwards by Robert Kennedy, an experienced prospector, who was taking a swim in the cold water off 'The Cliffs', north of Port Nolloth. By chance, Kennedy looked up at the rocks above him and spotted a chunk of diamond-bearing rock. He soon recovered 14 diamonds from the site.

Then, amazingly, a teacher spotted a diamond embedded in the wall of a newly built school building on the farm Kleinzee, near the mouth of the Buffels River. Jack Carstens was called in and a syndicate was formed to buy the farm. Within a week, 500 carats had been found.

Meanwhile, another prospector named Solomon Rabinowitz was scratching around the gravel beds near the mouth of the Orange. Hidden among the oyster shells, he found 334 diamonds. Clearly, there were rich pickings to be had and, by 1926, the mining rights to most of Alexander Bay had been snapped up. The lower elevations were claimed by the Luderitzbucht Syndicate, and the upper elevations by Caplan's Syndicate (headed by a storekeeper from Port Nolloth).

That same year, the famous German geologist Hans Merensky hurried up to Namaqualand. He had a theory that the diamonds were linked to fossilized oyster beds on old marine terraces. He quickly formed a syndicate with Dr Ernst Reuning, Dr I. B. Celliers and J. J. Buschau to search for this 'oyster line'.

Now, things were really hotting up and deals were being brokered at a feverish pace. Accordingly, a police sergeant, Van Wyk, sold his claim to Caplan for £15. Caplan then gave Merensky permission to inspect the upper levels of this claim, unaware of his 'oyster line' theory.

While this was going on, Reuning offered to buy the claim from Caplan and a price of £17,500 was agreed on. Almost immediately, a 16.5 carat octahedron was found. With Caplan kicking himself, Merensky scrambled to find the money to pay for the claim before the offer expired. A deal was subsequently made with H. O. Althauer and Julius Jeppe to form HM Associates, with Merensky getting 50 per cent of the company and the other two backers getting 25 per cent each. Merensky's previous partners were thus pushed out of the deal and Reuning only got a token £150 per month plus a bonus of £5,000 if the claim was successful.

With the stakes rising, Merensky optimistically applied to the Minister of Mines for a mineral lease over all public lands in the area, but this was refused. Instead, the government stopped the prospecting on crown lands and transferred all mineral rights to the crown. The only exception to this was the private farm Kleinzee, which was offered to the government for £200. Inexplicably, this sale was turned down and Kleinzee was sold to the Cape Coast Exploration Company (CCEC). This company was soon bought up by De Beers—which still operates the Kleinzee mine to this day. Visits to the mine can be arranged, but must be booked at least five days in advance.

In the face of this government clamp-down, Merensky's HM Associates fought to have their original claim recognized. This was eventually accomplished and Merensky also managed to get another five claims honoured by the Department of Mines. The first shipment of diamonds from the HM Associates claims totalled 12,253.5 carats. Ernest Oppenheimer immediately bought a 74 per cent interest in HM Associates.

Then, in 1927, the Precious Stone Bill was passed, which empowered the state to establish a State Alluvial Diggings around Alexander Bay. This developed into the company known today as Alexcor. The Bill also allowed for the government to monitor and control the output of all diamond producers. This was bad news for HM Associates who, by now, had recovered 461,393 carats. Fearing an oversupply of diamonds, the government froze the sale of these gems.

In 1929, Merensky sold his company to Oppenheimer for £3 million and went into voluntary liquidation. In 1932, the Merensky diamonds were ceded to the Diamond Corporation, a newly established central selling organization which sought to control the sale of all diamonds to prevent over-supply. Finally, in 1937, the Merensky diamonds were released for sale in London and at the New York World Fair of 1939. A final sale took place in 1942 in Bermuda.

Over the decades that followed, Alexcor built a town at Alexander Bay which was, until recently, highly restricted. De Beers expanded their operations at Kleinzee to include the Koingnaas Complex, near Hondeklip Bay. In the 1960s, a new company was formed and it secured leases along the southern banks of the Orange River. This became the TransHex Corporation, which now mines at Baaken and Reuning (at the entrance to the Richtersveld National Park).

Most of these mines did exceedingly well. The De Beers mines alone recovered 31 million carats in 75 years. At Reuning, a 43-metre-deep splash pool formed by the Orange River collected a glut of diamondiferous deposits with as many as 41 carats per 100 tons of gravel. This so-called 'Glory Hole' yielded diamonds worth a modern equivalent of R4 billion.

But those 'glory' days are in the past. Today, the on-shore diamond fields are almost worked out and attention has shifted to the marine deposits. The exploitation of underwater diamonds began with a Texan, Sam Collins, who had a company that specialized in sub-marine pipelines. In the early 1960s, Collins heard a story about a farmer who was pumping up diamondiferous gravel off the Namibian coastline. He leapt into action, bought the farmer's concession and started working out new ways to profitably suck up the sand from the sea bed.

Obviously, De Beers kept a close eye on Collins' operation and, as soon as they saw that the scheme was payable, they bought him out in 1965. A slump in diamond prices caused De Beers to abandon the sea-diamond enterprise in 1971, but prospecting continued. Then, in the early 1990s, sea-diamond mining started up again because the supply of on-shore diamonds was drying up.

Today, sea diamonds are big business. In 2003, for example, a team near Alexander Bay found the Cirrus Diamond, a fabulous 111-carat gemstone, which must have got people very excited! Nevertheless, Alexkor and De Beers no longer operate their own sea-diamond boats. Instead, they have divided up their respective ocean areas and assigned them to independent contractors on a concession basis.

These 'blocks' are now worked by small diamond boats, which suck up gravel from the sea bed through a big tube operated by a diver. Once on the boat, the gravel is packed into sacks and sent to on-shore sorting facilities. The diamond boats have become a valuable source of employment in an impoverished region, although rough seas and adverse weather conditions limit the number of days that boats can go out.

Despite the success of the sea-diamond operations, the output of the on-shore mines continues to dwindle and most have a life expectancy of five to ten years. With the imminent closure of these mines, there is a question of what to do next. Alexander Bay has already opened its gates to visitors, and the private towns of Kleinzee and Koningaas may soon be turned into public villages. When this is done, it is hoped that tourism will step in and fill the economic gap left by the departing diamond mines. After all, the extensive land holdings of the various mining operations has ensured that the coast is in a pristine condition and, once land rehabilitation is complete, the area should offer some unique leisure activities.

Land affairs

The indigenous people of Namaqualand always came second with regards to land rights. This subjugation began with the arrival of white farmers and was continued by the mines.

As early as 1842, a memorandum was presented to the government by the Steinkopf missionaries on behalf of the local people. This was occasioned by rumours that the colony was going to extend its border to the Orange, thereby including this formerly 'unclaimed' part of the country. The government confidently replied that there were no plans to move the boundary "or of interfering with the rights of those inhabiting the country beyond the boundary, by granting those lands to colonial farmers". Despite these calming words, land beyond the frontier had already been granted to farmers, starting from around 1776, and no formal 'ticket of occupation' was issued to the native inhabitants.

In 1846, new rumours about the annexation of northern Namaqualand started bubbling up from the Cape. This time, there was some consultation with the local chiefs about the plans, one of whom commented, "What the great chief or governor does, I cannot object to; but this only I say, that I will keep my ground, for me and my people, in order to lead a quiet and honest life."

In 1847, the border was indeed moved north to the Orange but no official government officers were installed, leaving the missionaries and the chiefs to go about their business in the usual way. Nevertheless, it was an uncertain time.

In 1851, Rev. Brecher of the Steinkopf mission wrote to the government requesting clarity regarding the land rights of the indigenous people in the area. He noted that, "The chiefs and natives residing here wish to be placed under the protection of the British Government, and that the ground occupied by them may be reserved for their occupancy against the encroachments of farmers, traders, or any others wishing to settle on the same, as much unpleasantness has already arisen on this point."

In reply to this entreaty, the Colonial Secretary wrote back, saying the government would not "countenance any encroachments on the land occupied by the people of the institutions … nor has His Excellency any desire to disturb them in his occupancy". However, the desired ticket of occupation was still not granted to the indigenous people of Steinkopf, and tenure on their ancestral land was not guaranteed beyond these vague promises.

The matter came to a head in 1853, at the start of the copper boom, when the Namaqua Mining Company applied to the government for a lease on a promising mining centre at Tweefontein (later Concordia). This lease was happily granted but, when the first miners arrived, they were greeted with a letter from Rev. Brecher which pointed out that their new mine was actually located within the mission's grounds. Speaking on behalf of the local people, Brecher went on to say that the land was protected by the government's previous letter which had promised not to countenance any encroachment etc.

Unwilling to start a ruckus, the Namaqua Mining Company signed a deal with the Steinkopf office bearers which granted them exclusive mineral rights over the ground in exchange for £100. The company then wrote to the government asking them about the legality of the whole situation, as they didn't want to pay twice. The reply was, predictably, self-serving. As far as the government was concerned, they had only guaranteed that the people of Steinkopf would not be ejected from the land, which was now said to be the property of the crown by virtue of the same letter of 'protection' mentioned by Brecher.

As such, the government retained all mineral rights to the area and said that any deal entered into between the company and the Steinkopf mission had nothing to do with them. The people of Steinkopf, however, didn't realize that their appeal for protection had been opportunistically interpreted as a sign of ceding the land to the government. No prizes for guessing whose version of events won out in the end …

Nevertheless, the government did graciously agree that the indigenous people should be compensated for the "use of land in respect of water and pasturage". The Namaqua Mining Company subsequently concluded an agreement with Steinkopf for water and grazing rights, on condition that no alcohol was to be sold within mission lands. This uncomfortable division between the occupational rights of indigenous people and the mineral rights to the land on which they lived was only finalized when the Mission Stations and Communal Reserves Act of 1909 was passed. This piece of legislation explicitly "prohibited the 'natives' of the territory from any legal claims to mineral rights on the land which was reserved for them".

As a result of this policy, the local people did not derive any direct benefit from the mining industry that came to dominate the region. The only way they could make money from all the activity was by taking up employment on the mines, or by selling supplies to the mines. Charles Bell, surveyor-general of the colony, believed that this was only fair and fitting. As he wrote in the 1850s: "I asked [the indigenous people] if they were fit to open all the mines … or whether they could smelt and work up and use the copper themselves. The reply usually was 'no, no; take the copper, we can't raise it, and don't want it.'… You say you apprehend oppression; rest quiet … Are the present prices you receive for labour, for the carriage of ore, and for your crops, symptomatic of oppression? I think not, but your waste of these prices … in folly and vice, to the destruction of yourselves and your oxen, is an oppression from which no government can effectually shield you. And if, hereafter, your sons have difficulty in finding healthy and respectable wives of their own race, you will recollect, with bitterness, the drink, food, clothing, or indifference that induced you to shut your eyes while your daughters tempted the crowds of single men now landing on your coast."

Meanwhile, up in the far Richtersveld, the Kuboes mission station was being presided over by the good Reverend Hein, of the Rhenish Church. The population was made up of Nama Khoikhoi, some Bushmen and a couple of Baster families (formerly known as Bastaards). The settlement was controlled by a 'Groot Raad' (great council), which was made up of community-elected representatives and chaired by the head missionary.

A contemporary report states that, "The inhabitants of Richtersveld count only 47 families, comprising say 380 souls, nearly all of whom are Hottentots, with Paul Links, son of the late Captain Paul Links, as their headman; their live-stock consisting of about 50 horses, 560 horned cattle, and 3,200 sheep and goats. Most of them are very poor, and I fear they are in a retrogressive state."

The 'Groot Raad' presided over the day-to-day affairs of the community. These included the "maintenance of order, settlement of disputes and granting of residence and grazing rights". However, this system was not without its critics and the above-mentioned Mission Stations and Communal Reserves Act forced the separation of civic and religious authorities, replacing the missionaries with a secular Advisory or Management Board (made up of white outsiders).

The precise boundaries of this mission station (and, indeed, most mission stations in South Africa) were ill-defined. By the 1890s, however, the people of the Richtersveld requested clarity on the issue as their land was being usurped by various colonial forces. They subsequently specified an area of nearly 700,000 morgen (600,000 hectares) as their traditional grazing land and requested an official ticket of occupation to guarantee their rights. But Mr S. Melvill, Second Assistant Surveyor-General, had other ideas.

In his report to parliament "in regard to lands occupied by natives on certain Missionary Institutions and other places in Namaqualand", Mevill stated that the land claim was much too large. He suggested reducing the land to 450,000 morgen (385,600 hectares) by excising most of the fertile land along the banks of the Orange as well as the coastal belt, which might be used for farming or fishing. In the event, nothing was done about these recommendations, and no ticket of occupation was issued as the people were considered too primitive to look after themselves.

Despite the legal limbo, five farms on the coast were leased to white farmers in 1904. In 1919, a farmer named Cloete even tried to claim the whole of the Richtersveld as his own, which provoked a bemused response from the Rev. Hein who said that, "the Richtersveld belongs to the community, no individual can claim it". Then, when diamond fever struck in the 1920s, land around the Orange River mouth was leased to prospectors, even though this too was part of the original Richtersveld land claim.

Perhaps galvanized into action by the flurry of diamond mining, the South African government finally got around to settling the Richtersveld land issue. Thus, between 1925 and 1926, a commission was set up to formulate recommendations, and they decided that Melvill's proposed allocation was still too large. Another 143,000 morgen (122,500 hectares) was lopped off and the final size of the Richtersvelders' land amounted to a little more than 300,000 morgen, less than half their original claim. On the up side, this truncated piece of land was approved for the use of 'Hottentots and Bastards', under the authority of the Minister of Native Affairs. Eventually, in 1930, a formal ticket of occupation (or reservation) was issued by the Minister of Lands—although the land was still technically held in trust by the state.

The same process played out at several other former mission stations around the country. The resulting entities came to be known as 'coloured reserves' or 'coloured rural areas'. In Namaqualand, five of these were established: Richtersveld, Steinkopf, Leliefontein, Komaggas and Concordia. They were among the largest in the country, totalling over 1.5 million hectares.

The old management boards and councils were maintained as the political authorities in these coloured reserves. They decided who qualified for 'citizenship' in the reserves and therefore who was entitled to housing, grazing land, voting rights for the council etc. Special concessions were also granted to *bywoners* (literally sub-farmers or squatters—who worked as herdsmen, sharecroppers or servants) and *vreemdelinge* (outsiders or strangers—who included missionaries, traders, teachers and even some white farmers). These two groups had to get permission from the council for temporary housing and/or grazing land in exchange for a gift, tribute or service to the community.

By now, the various racial groups who lived in Namaqualand had intermingled and assimilated to a considerable extent. Although this meant that there was a peaceful co-existence between these former rivals, the concept of a distinct Nama or Khoikhoi identity was severely undermined. This sense of 'nationhood' was further squelched by the apartheid-era population registration mania which *sommer* classified the whole *bleddy* bunch of them as 'coloured'.

Accordingly, the Basters came to assume a more prominent role in the political life of Namaqualand's coloured reserves. They were, by and large, slightly better off and numerically superior to the remnant Khoikhoi population, and they also had the benefits of a more sustained education at the hands of the missionaries. In the Richtersveld, this presence was significantly bolstered by the arrival of the Bosluis Basters in 1949.

This new group of 'Bastaards' had been forced to move from their home in the Pofadder district of Bushmanland by the Group Areas Act, which was officially passed in 1950. It was an insidious piece of legislation which stipulated that all racial groups had to be geographically segregated from one another. This act (an extension of the old Land Act of 1913) was the cause of a string of forced removals that traumatized the country during the 1950s (including Sophiatown, District 6, South End etc.).

And so, when the apartheid government of D. F. Malan cracked the whip, the Bosluis Basters (comprising about 68 families) had no choice but to pack their belongings into ox wagons and trek more than 300km through the thirstlands in search of a new home. Their destination was the remote stretches of the Richtersveld, which was considered to be a dumping ground for unwanted and/or disreputable people.

It must have been an arduous journey, but they were assisted by the benevolent leadership of their pastor, the Reverend Eksteen, who had been with the community since 1945. Finally, a site was selected on the banks of a small spring, in the middle of nowhere. A church was soon built and the new settlement was named Eksteenfontein, in honour of their spiritual leader.

Incidentally, the Bosluis Basters get their name from their original home, the farm Bo-Sluis (above the sluice), and not from the Afrikaans word *bosluis*, which refers to a parasitic bush tick or louse. It's also worth nothing that the equally unfortunate term 'Baster', which is derived from the earlier form 'Bastaard', is maintained with some degree of pride by several Baster groups (including the Rehoboth Basters in Namibia). Several commentators have written that the reason for this dates back to the 1800s, when their status as 'half-castes' distinguished them as being slightly better off than the inferior 'Hottentots' and other natives.

In any event, the arrival of the Bosluis Basters proved to be somewhat disconcerting to the local Khoikhoi. I was told that, at first, the two groups were rather wary of one another and, as recently as the 1980s, a marriage between a Nama and a Baster would raise eyebrows in Eksteenfontein. Today, however, the various groups in the Richtersveld have become unified as a community and work together for the good of all.

In closing, allow me to point out that the Group Areas Act did cut both ways. In the 1950s, about nine families of white farmers (who were now technically squatting on a coloured reserve) were removed from the Richtersveld. These included: the Avenant family who farmed at De Hoop in the present-day Richtersveld National Park (the graves of several Avenant children can still be seen if you know where to look); the Van Rensburgs who had a homestead at Grasdrif; the Graaff family at Gelykwerf; the De Vries brothers who farmed on the summit of the Vandersterrberg and at Koeskop; and the Bosman family who resided at Stinkfontein (now Eksteenfontein).

Rebirth of a community

In 1957, the 'coloured reserve' of the Richtersveld was given a tangible boundary with the erection of a fence that ran between the communal lands and the 'corridor' farms along the river and the coast. This physically curtailed the movements of the nomadic herders and drove another nail into the coffin of the old transhumance patterns.

As a result of this, the remaining land became overgrazed and the subsistence lifestyle of the stock farmers became unsustainable. Many people decamped from their villages and stock-posts, and moved to the mines, farms, fishing boats, towns and faraway cities to seek wage labour. The community of the Richtersveld was in what appeared to be terminal decline.

Even today, less than ten per cent of Nama consider themselves farmers, and most of these are elderly. The old stock-posts are still inhabited but, again, it's the old folk who remain and they are only visited by their children on weekends and holidays. After all, it's a tough life out in the wilds. Herders in the field have to survive on very little water, which is often brackish with high levels of fluoride and other unpalatable minerals. This causes white flecking and dark brown staining of the teeth, which is sometimes called the trademark of Namaqualand.

Meanwhile, the diamond mining industry on the coast was flourishing. In 1989, the Alexander Bay Development Corporation was established by the government to take over all "assets, liabilities, rights and obligations of the … State Alluvial Diggings". This generous deal included ownership of the land around the Orange River mouth and all the lovely diamonds therein. Three years later, this entity was converted by an act of parliament into a company that was named Alexkor Limited, with the government as the only shareholder. Title deeds to the land and all associated mineral rights were transferred to Alexkor by 1995.

But change was in the air. The democratic elections of 1994 ushered in a new age of land restitution and many dispossessed communities approached the new government for compensation or reclamation. Accordingly, a new act was passed, called the Restitution of Land Rights Act of 1994. This landmark act (pardon the pun) made it possible for communities or individuals who believed they had been unjustly removed from their land to lodge a land claim "to provide for the restitution of rights in land to persons or communities dispossessed of such rights after 19 June 1913 as a result of past racially discriminatory laws or practices". Sixty-nine thousand land claims were subsequently lodged across the country.

In the Richtersveld, the Sida !hub Communal Property Association (CPA) was formed to make a land claim on the Alexkor property, which extended for 85,000 hectares along the coast between Port Nolloth and Alexander Bay. This was duly lodged before the specified date of 31 December 1998 and heard by the Land Claims Court in 2000.

The plaintiffs in the case comprised various local communities and stakeholders, namely the Richtersveld community, the Kuboes community, the Sanddrif community, the Lekkersing community, the Eksteenfontein community and the adult members of the Richtersveld community. Due to the valuable nature of the claim, it was fiercely contested by Alexkor Limited and the government of the Republic of South Africa.

The defendants (Alexkor and the government) threw everything they had at the Richtersvelders. It was said that they weren't a real community; that they didn't 'beneficially' inhabit the land because they were nomadic; that they had been deprived of the land by virtue of the 1847 annexation of Namaqualand which fell outside the mandated 1913 cut-off date. Although most of these tactics failed to win support with the judges, the 2001 judgement did rule that the claim was invalid. This was primarily because the court found that the community had not been removed from the land as a result of any 'racially discriminatory laws', since white farmers and prospectors had also been removed by the same process.

This finding was appealed and the Supreme Court of Appeal overturned the Land Court's decision, finding that: "their dispossession resulted from a racially discriminatory practice in that it was based upon and proceeded from the premise that due to their lack of civilisation, to which their race was inextricably linked, the Richtersveld people had no rights in the subject land". Round two to the Richtersvelders.

But Alexkor and the government appealed the appeal and took the case to the Constitutional Court. This court also found in favour of the community and the land was finally and unequivocally granted to the people of the Richtersveld in 2003. Several years of negotiation followed until, in April 2007, an agreement was reached between Alexkor and the Richtersveld community.

Then, just weeks before the whole deal went before the Land Claims Court for final ratification, a dissident group of Richtersvelders lodged a complaint against the already-signed contract. Apparently, there were some problematic clauses and it was claimed that the wider community had not been consulted about the details of the deal.

For a few nerve-wracking weeks, it looked like it could all go pear-shaped. But last minute negotiations successfully resolved the crisis and on the 9th of October 2007, Land Claims Court Judge Antonie Geldenhuys confirmed the revised settlement. The legal battle had taken almost ten years and cost the government more than R50 million, but the people of the Richtersveld had triumphed.

On the 1st of December 2007, Public Enterprises Minister Alec Erwin (who was the man responsible for contesting the claim) and Land Affairs Minister Lulu Xingwana formally handed over the title deeds to the land to the Richtersveld leaders. Willem Diergaardt was quoted in the press as saying, "I am overwhelmed with joy. I can't hold back my tears." He went on to say that there was going to be a celebration in the Richtersveld, "and I can promise you it will not be a little celebration. It will be a celebration like South Africa has never seen before." Erwin wryly commented that it was a "great occasion after an amazing legal battle".

The final settlement, which is worth well over R440 million, is intended to provide the community with some sort of reparations for all the diamonds previously extracted from their land. It also looks to the future by establishing a secure financial foundation for future development. More importantly, perhaps, it properly acknowledges the land rights of the Richtersveld people for the first time in modern history. In this sense, the legal battle was about more than money. It was about giving the Richtersvelders a new sense of pride in their cultural identity, and this has already led to the rejuvenation of once-neglected traditions.

Briefly, the main terms of the Alexkor deal are as follows. The state will hand over 194,600ha of land, including the crucial 84,000ha of diamond territory along the coast and a strip of fertile land along the Orange River, which currently supports citrus, oyster and ostrich farms. It will also give the community an 'extraordinary reparation payment' of R190 million plus a development grant of R50 million. Furthermore, the Richtersvelders and Alexkor will enter into a joint mining venture, in which the community will hold a 49 per cent interest. This part of the deal isn't as great as it sounds because Alexkor has been losing money for quite a few years. However, the stability of the settlement will now allow the state to invest up to R200 billion in a much needed re-capitalization programme.

And there's more! The Alexkor-owned town of Alexander Bay will be transferred to the community, and Alexkor will pay R45-million to allow its staff to remain there for the next ten years. Plus, thanks to the efforts of those 'dissident' community members, all Alexkor's obligations are now underwritten by the state, particularly with regard to the rehabilitation of the landscape after decades of mining (which could cost many additional millions). Several 'good governance' clauses have also been included to control the behaviour of the various community trusts and companies that will be established to administer this historic settlement.

So, it's good news all round. But what is the nature of this 'community' who will reap all the rewards? Well, the ownership of the land first had to be determined in terms of the Transformation of Certain Rural Areas Act of 1998. Under this act, communities could decide whether the ownership of the former 'coloured reserve' land should be lodged with a Communal Property Association (CPA), given over to a local municipality, or split up and granted to individual owners.

In 2002, the various communities within the Richtersveld voted to transfer ownership of the land to a CPA which would own and administer the land on behalf of the people. This entity had already been established the previous year as the Sida !Hub CPA. It includes every adult member of the four Richtersveld towns of Eksteenfontein, Kuboes, Lekkersing and Sanddrif, where adult members are those over the age of 18 who have lived in any of the towns for five years or more. The aims of the CPA include "improvement of the infrastructure, development of agriculture, tourism, and economic opportunities to support job creation, and capacity building of committee members so that they can make the right decisions on behalf of the community".

To accomplish all this, the CPA has set up four commercial companies to run their considerable interests. There's an agricultural company that's going to develop the farms along the Orange River. An environmental rehabilitation company is going to reverse the damage done by years of mining. A property holding company is going to be responsible for renting out the houses in Alexander Bay. And there's a mining company that will administer the community's 49 per cent holding in Alexkor.

The proceeds from these four companies go into a development company and a community trust. Each division of the CPA has community directors, one from each town, as well as independent directors who are appointed either by the CPA or its trustees. The Richtersveld Community Conservancy has also been set up to oversee the tourism and environmental activities of the CPA.

So, the future is looking bright for the Richtersvelders. They have their land. They have a considerable amount of money for development. And they have a large share in a major diamond mining company. Not bad for a bunch of Hottentots, Bushmen and Bastaards.

And speaking of developments, there are several in the pipeline. The ailing Alexkor is about to be revitalized and discussions have been held with both De Beers and Transhex to amalgamate and/or establish a joint diamond cutting and processing plant, which will create employment. The Sida !Hub CPA is also embarking on a number of new development projects. These include the improvement of infrastructure and public services, entrepreneurial loans for small businesses and an agricultural school.

Of course, tourism initiatives rank high on the agenda and the conservancy is busy developing visitor centres, museums and a range of exciting tourism activities. So, get out there and visit the Richtersveld. It's not just an amazing travel experience; it's an active contribution to the rebirth of a much-maligned community.

Conserving the landscape

The landscape of the Richtersveld is unique and unforgettable. Its barren beauty may not be as eager to please as the more obsequious vistas of the Western Cape or the Garden Route, but its unmistakable majesty is imprinted in the mind of every visitor. Thankfully, this precious and precarious ecosystem is now being preserved in a number of conservation areas.

The first attempts to formally protect the dramatic mountain desert and its unusual plants began in 1975, when the National Parks Board agreed to investigate the establishment of a national park in the northern part of the Richtersveld. However, this was communal land that couldn't be bought, transferred or otherwise appropriated. It took nearly 20 years of negotiations with the local council to reach a deal.

By 1989, a contract had been drawn up. Then, just as the park was about to be proclaimed, a group from a 'Community Committee' lodged an injunction against the whole process. According to them, the council was "unrepresentative and autocratic" and the community had not been given an opportunity to provide their input.

In truth, the terms of the original contract were extremely prejudicial against the local people. The 99-year lease stipulated that all livestock had to be removed from the park, no resources (plants or water) could be utilized and there were no employment guarantees for community members. In other words, the establishment of the park would have entirely excluded the local people from land they had lived on for over 2,000 years. It almost seemed as if the Parks Board wanted to save the land *from* the locals instead of *for* the locals.

The signing ceremony was postponed and a series of meetings was held between all parties concerned. During the course of these consultations, the Parks Board came to a new realization that local populations are an important component of any conservation initiative, in terms of environmental management, ownership and even as visitors. Furthermore, in the case of the Richtersveld, the indigenous people were actually an integral part of the eco-system and their traditional lifestyle was just as endangered as the rare succulents.

A new contract was subsequently drawn up with much more equitable terms. The lease was reduced to 30 years, the grazing rights of local people were acknowledged (subject to a limitation of 6,600 small stock units), access to natural resources within the park was similarly allowed, and a certain number of jobs were reserved for local people.

With this agreement in place, a joint management committee was established to run the park and the contract was signed in July 1991. This was the first contractual national park in South Africa (independently owned land, jointly managed by the Parks Board and the local community). Later, this model would be used to help solve the thorny issue of land claims in other national parks, such as the Makuleke concession area within the Kruger National Park.

Initially, the newly established 162,000ha Richtersveld National Park (RNP) was very rugged indeed. The roads were virtually non-existent, the campsites were very basic and the wilderness reigned supreme. For the adventurer who really wanted to get away from it all, it was heaven. Unfortunately, for a place so disconnected from the modern world, there were some very contemporary complaints from the local community. This mainly revolved around the stipulated registration of herders (only 28 families were allowed into the park at its inception) and the selective appointment of staff members.

Today, however, things are much more settled. The community has come to accept the park on its doorstep. Campsites have attractive ablution facilities. The roads are much improved (although a 4x4 is still recommended). And there are even several chalets and hutted camps available. This is a cause of distress for old-timers who miss the untamed wildness of the park, but most visitors will be thrilled by the current combination of untrammelled nature and moderate creature comforts.

Meanwhile, up in Namibia, the Ai-|Ais Hot Springs Game Park had been declared between 1968 and 1988, which included the mighty Fish River Canyon. In 2002, the formidable Huns and Chum mountains were also incorporated to form a vast 440,600 hectare reserve that stretched all the way down to the Orange River, adjacent to the RNP.

This paved the way for the formation of a Trans-Frontier Conservation Area (TFCA), defined as "the area or component of a large ecological region that straddles the boundaries of two or more countries, encompassing one or more protected areas as well as multiple resource use areas". This very important conservation initiative is spearheaded by the Peace Parks Foundation, and there are already six TFCAs in various stages of development around southern Africa.

In terms of the Ai-|Ais-Richtersveld TFCA, discussions began between Namibia and South Africa in 2000. A memorandum of understanding was signed between the two state parties in 2001. Consultations were held with local stakeholders and management plans were drawn up and signed in 2002. And, finally, the treaty was signed by presidents Thabo Mbeki and Sam Nujoma in 2003.

The Ai-|Ais-Richtersveld TFCA currently measures around 36,000 square km, but this is just the beginning. There are already plans in place to enlarge the protected area into an enormous Greater *!Gariep* TFCA. This ambitious project would incorporate a number of additional land units to create a truly mammoth transfrontier park that stretches from the Richtersveld to the sea and far into the north. These areas include: the Namib-Naukluft Park, the //Gamaseb and Brukkaros

Community Conservancies, the Orange River and Orange River mouth, and the vast Sperrgebiet (already declared a national park, but not yet developed). There is even a possibility that World Heritage status may be expanded to cover this entire area, but only once mining has ceased and the land has been rehabilitated.

And even that's not the full picture. Some environmental visionaries have formulated plans to create the Three Nations Namib Desert TFCA. This mega-park would stretch from the Richtersveld all the way to the Iona National Park in Angola. Although still in its early stages, this initiative seeks to "involve rural communities productively in conservation through sustainable use of natural resources and in local economic development". The possibilities are endless.

At the moment, however, all eyes are on the Ai-|Ais-Richtersveld TFCA, to see how it performs. And things are looking good. Visitor numbers are up and the TFCA process has already stimulated investment in the area. On the South African side, poverty alleviation funds have been used to upgrade roads, interpretation centres, entrance gates and rest camps in the RNP. A new border post has also been opened at the Sendelingsdrif gate and the entire region is hoping that tourism will provide some much needed economic stimulation.

The other major conservation area in the Richtersveld is the Richtersveld Community Conservancy (RCC). This entity began life as a concept paper in 1998 and evolved hand in hand with the World Heritage application process. It was supported by various international and local heritage agencies (such as the NORAD—the Norwegian Agency for Development Co-operation, the Northern Cape Department of Arts and Culture and Eco-Africa environmental consultants).

Through extensive workshops and consultations, the conservancy concept firmed up as part of a wider

Integrated Development Planning process for the region. The community thus got behind the idea of creating a heritage area where natural and cultural resources would be protected under a policy of sustainable development. Various management plans were drawn up and, in 2004, a management committee was elected with a full-time conservancy manager and administrative officer. The headquarters of the RCC are in Eksteenfontein.

In 2005, the Department of Environmental Affairs and Tourism (DEAT) coughed up R6 million to help the conservancy develop infrastructure and accommodation. The Northern Cape provincial administration also started negotiations to hand over the adjacent (and wholly undeveloped) Helskloof reserve to the conservancy.

Today, the Richtersveld Community Conservancy (RCC) is a remarkable place. It is a biological reserve dedicated to biodiversity conservation and plans are in place to establish a scientific research station. But it is also a cultural reserve where ancient human traditions are protected and encouraged to resume their previous vitality.

Unfortunately, tourism is a double-edged sword. The ecosystem in the RCC (and the RNP) is fragile. It is already under threat from overgrazing and other environmental factors, and uncontrolled tourism could make matters worse. The thing is, tourists are (by their very nature) destructive beasts. Their feet trample delicate plants, their cars (if driven irresponsibly) can scar the landscape, and their mere presence in a village can corrupt the cultural traditions that attracted them in the first place.

So, all new tourism initiatives in the Richtersveld are being carefully planned and monitored so that the tourist cash cow doesn't kill the ecological golden goose. In other words, all the stakeholders in the region are working together to make sure that tourism and development strategies are being implemented in a responsible and sustainable manner. And, after speaking to some of the people involved in this initiative, I am confident that they will succeed in their very important endeavours.

Exploring the Richtersveld

Okay. So now we know all about the Richtersveld. But how do you get there, where can you stay and what's to do? The answers to all these questions and more can be found in the pages that follow …

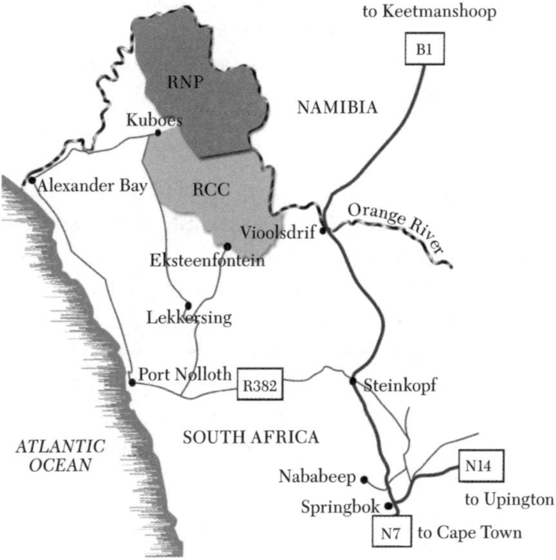

Getting there

From Joburg or Pretoria: Get on the N14 and drive to Springbok. This is a long haul, about 1,200km, so I would suggest breaking the journey in two by spending a night at either Kuruman (550km), Upington (820km) or the wonderful Augrabies Falls National Park (a substantial 910km).

The drive takes you through a succession of non-descript towns. You know the type; bottle store, butchery, grain silos and an N. G. Kerk. Nevertheless, here are some potential highlights, with distances from Joburg in brackets:

- At the town of Sannieshof (280km) there's a restaurant called The Turning Point, which seems appropriate.
- Birdwatchers might want to stop off at the Barberspan Bird Sanctuary (300km).
- Delareyville (320km) and Vryburg (400km) are good places to get petrol, supplies and takeaways.
- Kuruman is a rather nice little town with parks and trees, and the perennial spring called Die Oog forms a pretty pond in the middle of town.
- There's the Kalahari Raptor centre at 570km (www.raptor.co.za).
- Kathu (600km) is the location of the Sishen iron ore mine and you'll see the colossal mine dumps looming up on your right. This is the start of an industrial railway line that runs all the way down to Saldanha Bay on the lower West Coast.
- Upington is quite a big town with the Desert Palace casino glittering avariciously in the savannah. This is the heart of the so-called Green Kalahari.
- The long road up north to the Kgalagadi National Park can be accessed from Upington.
- The road between Upington and Keimoes is incongruously marketed as the Orange River Wine Route, which might appeal to adventurous winos.

- The landscape really starts drying up after Keimoes and by the time you reach the punchline dorp of Pofadder (1,040km) it's positively desiccated. You'll finally reach Springbok about 160km later.

From Cape Town: Take the N7 and drive for a relatively moderate 560km to Springbok. This route is discussed in greater detail in the 'Exploring Namaqualand' section on page 178.

Flying in: There are no commercial flights into Springbok—the nearest airport's in Upington.

There is no rail link either, as the tracks end at the town of Bitterfontein about 200km to the south. Besides, you need a car to get around the Richtersveld so load up your iPod with everything you've got and hit the road.

Then, from Springbok: drive about 50km north on the N7 to reach Steinkopf—the gateway to the Richtersveld. From here, take the tarred R382 down the Anenous Pass until you reach the turn-off to Eksteenfontein. This is where your adventure really begins …

You can now turn onto the gravel road to Eksteenfontein and enter the Richtersveld Community Conservancy (*see* page 142), or continue on tar to Port Nolloth and Alexander Bay if you want to go directly to the Richtersveld National Park (*see* page 163).

Websites:

- www.upington.co.za
- www.upington.com
- www.kakamas.co.za
- www.greenkalahari.co.za
- www.northerncape.org.za

Suggested itineraries

The question here is, always, how much time do you have? In the case of the Richtersveld, however, you definitely need more than a night or two. After all, you wouldn't schlep out all this way for a quick weekend getaway, unless you already live in Springbok. Furthermore, it seems a waste to visit the Richtersveld National Park (RNP) without visiting the Richtersveld Community Conservancy (RCC), and vice versa.

So, here are a couple of suggested itineraries, starting from Springbok. You can get more detailed information about each of the destinations in the sections that follow. Please note that the roads in the RCC are all untarred but in good condition, so they are accessible for most vehicles. The roads in the RNP are much rougher and some soft-sand driving is necessary, so a 4x4 or a 4x2 with good ground clearance is essential. And take spare tyres, a toolkit and emergency petrol cans!

If you have fewer than four days, or a non-4x4: Concentrate on the RCC. Spend a night at Rooiberg Guest House, Eksteenfontein, Lekkersing and/or Kuboes, then return to Springbok. Alternatively, if you do have a suitable vehicle, forgo the RCC and spend your time at one or more of the RNP's fantastic campsites.

If you have four days: Drive to Eksteenfontein and spend a night in the town or at the nearby Rooiberg Guest House in the RCC. Then drive through the conservancy to the RNP and spend the night at either the comfortable rest camp at Sendelingsdrif or the nearby campsite at Potjiespram. Next day, drive to another campsite, preferably at De Hoop or the spectacular Kokerboomkloof. Leave the RNP via Helskloof Pass and drive to Port Nolloth for the night. Then, return to Springbok. Please note that this will be a very rushed trip and most of your time will be spent in the car. There is also very little margin for error if you have any mechanical problems.

If you have four to six days: Spend one night at Rooiberg and one night at Eksteenfontein. Then drive to Kuboes and spend a night there. Drive into the RNP and spend a night at De Hoop and another night at Kokerboomkloof (although all the campsites have something special about them). Then head out to Port Nolloth for a night in a guest house before returning to Springbok. This is a more leisurely trip that will give you some time to explore each of the sites in the RCC and RNP.

If you have more than six days: Follow the itinerary above, but spend a couple of nights at each place. You should also take more time in the RNP, where you could easily pass a day or two relaxing at any one of the various campsites. Then, if you can, cross the border at Sendelingsdrif and drive up into the Namibian part of the TFCA to visit the Ai-|Ais hot springs and the Fish River Canyon. When you're done, return to Springbok via the Vioolsdrif border post on the N7 highway. It's a trip you won't forget in a hurry.

When to go

The Richtersveld is, essentially, a desert so the usual rules apply. The summer months (mid-October to mid-February) are very hot and dry, and temperatures peak at nearly 50°C. The winter months (May–July) can be cold and soggy, especially in the evenings and early mornings. So, the shoulder seasons are your best bet.

Ideally, try to visit the Richtersveld during flower season in early spring (end July to mid-September). The temperatures are comfortable and the weather is usually good. Furthermore, this is the time of the year when many of the plants burst into flower, splotching the landscape with colour like a Jackson Pollock painting.

Do note, however, that there are no guarantees. When

I was at Eksteenfontein, for example, the rain set in for a solid 24 hours and a freezing wind blew in from the coast. We even had to make space at the guest house for an impromptu party of five very wet bikers who were forced to seek shelter from the miserable weather.

In case you're interested, these bikers were all mates from Pretoria. Every year, they go on long motorbike expeditions across the country. This time, they had railed their bikes to Cape Town and were slowly scrambling up the west coast to Alexander Bay, sticking mainly to sand roads. They carried all their camping gear on their bikes and Eksteenfontein was one of the few places where they spent the night under a roof. Sounds a bit nuts to me, but then they are from Pretoria. In any case, it was good to have the extra company and, that night, we all sat around the TV and watched 'Survivor'.

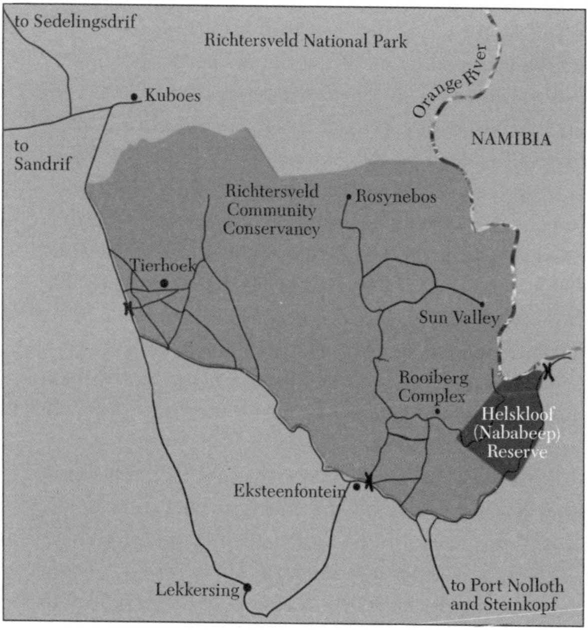

Getting there

From Springbok, follow the N7 north to Steinkopf (about 50km), then take the R355 towards Port Nolloth. After about 10km, you'll start to descend the Anenous Pass, which will give you great views out over the Grasvlakte. This is the route of the old Port Nolloth–Okiep railway, so imagine doing the trip in a narrow carriage pulled by mules!

After about 36km, you'll come to a turn-off for Grasvlakte/Eksteenfontein. Take this untarred road to the right and drive for about 50km. You are now in the RCC. The turn-off for the Rooiberg Guest House is on your right (10km off the main road) and Eksteenfontein is about 6km straight ahead.

If you are feeling adventurous, you can also enter (or leave) the RCC via the Helskloof Nature Reserve. This can be accessed by following the N7 north of Steinkopf to Vioolsdrif (70km). Then, before you cross the border into Namibia, turn left and follow the gravel road along the south bank of the Orange River, past the Peace of Paradise campsite, until you enter the Helskloof/ Nababeep reserve. The condition of this road is variable, especially after wet weather, so it might take you a while and it is only suited for 4x4 vehicles. But, apparently, the views are amazing. I've also heard that the road is being rehabilitated, so it may not be as rough as I've been told. The Helskloof road will bring you out on the main road to Eksteenfontein, just below the turn-off to the Rooiberg Guest House.

From Eksteenfontein, it is suggested that you follow what has been dubbed the Richtersveld Circle Route. This tour takes in the other Richtersveld towns of Lekkersing, Kuboes and Sanddrif. Then, you can choose to enter the Richtersveld National Park or return to

Steinkopf via Alexander Bay and Port Nolloth. Please note that all the roads in the RCC are untarred, except for the Alexander Bay–Port Nolloth–Steinkopf leg. The gravel roads are in pretty good condition and can be negotiated by most ordinary cars (unless there has been heavy rainfall—check before you go). The roads in the Richtersveld National Park, however, are for 4x4s only.

Rooiberg Guest House

This is a very special spot and the best place to experience the wild open spaces of the RCC. Originally built as a mining office, the Rooiberg compound consists of a couple of cosy houses nestled in a small valley, with a huge, eponymous red mountain acting as a backdrop.

Apparently, they used to mine ore from the top of this mountain, flying the rocks down to the house by helicopter. From here, the ore was transported by car for analysis and processing. They found traces of copper, gold and lead on the mountain, but the amounts were too small to be payable and the operation was abandoned. The community has since taken over and improved the buildings, and it's been running as a guest house for a couple of years.

The main house has a fully equipped kitchen, a large lounge and an expansive stoep for enjoying the long, lingering sunsets. There are several bedrooms with a number of single and double beds (sleeps 12 in total) and two functional bathrooms. There's also a small Honeymoon Suite which is separate from the main house. In summer, you can even choose to sleep in a genuine *matjieshuis* built at the back of the property. It's all very basic, but very comfortable.

There's no electricity at Rooiberg, but there are gas geysers, a freezer and a stove. There's also a newly built braai area. A gas fridge is on the cards, as are solar panels for lights. I'm not sure if this latter development is such a good idea. At night, the soft lighting provided by the supplied paraffin lamps and candles is perfect. And, with no other human activities for miles around, the darkness is immaculate and the stargazing, simply overwhelming.

Unfortunately, the compound is fenced off (which is rather unattractive) but I'm assured that this is necessary to keep the animals away from the water tanks and the delectable reeds of the *matjieshuis*. When the wind blows, it whistles through the holes in the steel poles of the fence, making a high-pitched noise that sounds like an off-key choir. This strange song combines with the low roar of the wind to create an eerie polyphony that is disquieting and beautiful at the same time.

The guest house used to be run communally, but this system has changed. It is now run as a private concern by people from the community who pay a commission to the RCC trust for each guest. The staff who look after the place stay here for about a month before they are rotated with other members of the team. They will book you in at the gate when you arrive and graciously show you around the house. They live in a separate building a short distance away, should you need anything, and are very friendly.

My hosts were the marvellously photogenic Hendrina (known as Auntie Kniekie), her son and an *oom* whose name I sadly didn't catch. They only spoke Afrikaans, but we managed to communicate well enough when they came to chat with me on the stoep. They also had a very friendly dog, Fooitjies, who kept us all company.

Rooiberg is self-catering, so bring all your own food and drinks. The nearest shop is in Eksteenfontein, and this has limited supplies, so I would suggest that you do your shopping at Springbok. There is no petrol available, so make sure you arrive with a full tank (the last petrol station is at Steinkopf). If you want, meals can be provided by the guest house staff, but this must be booked and paid for in advance as supplies have to be brought in.

If you are feeling active, you can hike up the Rooiberg or simply wander through the jagged foothills. There are also several 4x4 routes that lead through the mountains. One track leads to the Kannikaip campsite on the banks of the Orange River. Another takes you to the forbidding Black Face mountain and on to Eksteenfontein via the back road.

Rates are around R100 per person per night. Entrance to the conservancy is R30 per person per day.

Contacts:

- Rooiberg Guest House bookings: 027-851 7108

Eksteenfontein

This friendly village is the 'capital' of the RCC. The administration offices are here and there is a tourist info centre and a museum (which is a work in progress). So, it's a good place to get all the latest info on the RCC.

The town is built along the banks of a small stream called the Stinkfontein. This rather unappetizing name dates back to a time when the Khoikhoi and the Bushmen were engaged in a bitter rivalry. The story goes that after one particularly fierce battle, a number of bodies were left in the river and it started to smell. Ugh!

Despite its grisly etymology, Eksteenfontein is an attractive place surrounded by wonderful mountains. Goats roam through the village, their bells tinkling as they trot between the colourful houses. There's a humble church, built by Reverend Eksteen and his congregation of Bosluis Basters. The primary school is full of romping children. The name of the town is even spelled out in white stones on a prominent ridge above the settlement. All in all, it seems to be a place with a growing sense of pride.

Indeed, the people of Eksteenfontein are actively

working towards the cultural and economic rejuvenation of the community. The school has recently appointed a teacher from Riemsvasmaak to teach students the Nama language, and the museum staff are busy collecting oral histories from people in the village. The large community centre on the banks of the river houses the conservancy offices, a library, a community hall, a crèche, a postal agency and a textile and needlework workshop which makes T-shirts and other interesting things.

The famously nomadic farmers who live in their traditional *matjieshuise* are usually found in the vicinity of the town, and visits can sometimes be arranged. However, these herders are real people and not tourist attractions so visits are at their discretion. Make arrangements ahead of time if you really want to meet these living recipients of World Heritage status.

Visitors may also be disappointed to know that you won't see many women wearing the traditional *kappies* (bonnets) that are featured so prominently in the photographic portraits taken by people such as the estimable Obie Oberholzer. In days gone by, these brightly coloured items of clothing were worn all the time for protection against the sun. Now, they are only worn on ceremonial occasions and at cultural events.

The town has a population of around 800. However, most of the men work on the mines, either at Transhex, Alexander Bay or Kleinzee. The mine shifts are considerately arranged so that workers work seven days on and seven days off. This allows them to return to the village every second week, so they are able to maintain contact with their families. A regular shuttle service from the mines keeps this system functioning smoothly. Unfortunately, there is no high school in the village, so students have to go to Alexander Bay, Steinkopf, Springbok or Concordia to complete their schooling. Nevertheless, there is a sense of continuity in

Eksteenfontein and the town looks like it is doing well.

Currently, the only tourist accommodation in Eksteenfontein is at the Kom Rus 'n Bietjie (Come and rest a while) Guest House. The main house has several bedrooms and bathrooms, a large kitchen with all the necessary equipment and a TV room with couches. There are also several stand-alone chalets that sleep two, with an en-suite bathroom. These units are newly built and very comfortable. Rates are about R100 per person per night. Conservancy fees will set you back an additional R30 per person per day. There are also several campsites tucked away in the surrounding mountains.

There is no petrol in Eksteenfontein, so fill up at Steinkopf. There is a small general store that sells meat and a few other basic supplies, but it's a good idea to stock up before you get here. There is no restaurant in town, but meals can be arranged if you book them in advance. These home-cooked repasts are prepared by members of the community and brought to you on their very own plates, covered with lace doilies. It's a homely arrangement that seeks to spread the economic benefits of tourism across the village. There are no banks or ATM facilities in town, so make sure you bring enough cash with you.

There are a number of activities available in Eksteenfontein. Guided town tours and donkey-cart rides can be booked, and are very worthwhile. If you have a 4x4, take a trip to the campsites at Fluorspar Valley, Sun Valley (both old mining sites) and Rosynebos. Hikers can choose between three beautiful trails:

- Eksteenfontein to Rooiberg: an easy hike of about 12km (three to four hours) past old stockposts and tall kokerbooms.
- Rooiberg Guest House to the top of Rooiberg: a steep walk of about three hours each way, with panoramic views from the summit.
- Rooiberg Guest House to the Kannikaip campsite on

the Orange River: a moderate but long walk of 17km (five to six hours), with beautiful scenery and a swim in the river as a reward at journey's end.

A range of other activities are in the planning stages, so phone ahead and find out what's on the menu.

Contacts:

- Tourism office: 027-851 8619
- Kom Rus 'n Bietjie Guest House bookings: 027-851 7108
- Richtersveld Community Conservancy offices: 027-851 7026/7082/7420, 083-618 4480; contact person: Volenti van der Westhuizen (tourism officer), Joani Cloete (RCC administration) or Gert Links (RCC manager)

Just as you leave Eksteenfontein, the road splits. The right-hand fork will take you in a north-westerly direction towards Kuboes—this is the shortest route to that town (65km). The left fork will take you south to the town of Lekkersing. If you take the left fork, after about 37km you'll see a turn-off to the left towards the Koerdap campsite. Keep to the right and drive for another 5km to reach Lekkersing.

Lekkersing

In spite of its charming name, Lekkersing (Nice singing) is a small and rather unlovely little settlement. It was established in 1926 by the farmer Ryk Jasper Cloete (who once tried to claim the entire Richtersveld as his own) and it is named after the beautiful 'song' made by water bubbling out of a nearby spring.

Although the landscape is not as mountainous as the eastern part of the conservancy, Lekkersing is surrounded by stark black hills covered in white quartzite pebbles. It's an alien scene, made even more uncompromising by the dumps from the Diamond Quartzite Stone Mine. Established in 1964, this quarrying operation produces many beautiful stone slabs in shades of red and gold, which have been exported around the world.

In terms of things to do, Lekkersing is not as developed as Eksteenfontein. A hike to the Skurwehoogte caves can be arranged, and the Rusoord Club for the Elderly sells arts and crafts from its small shop. There is no petrol station, restaurant or convenience store in town, but you can get traditional Nama food from the local Nama Cultural Group. The Protea Elderly Club Food Garden (which has twice won best garden in the Northern Cape) can also be visited. Horse riding and donkey-cart trips can be arranged if you book them in advance.

But there's a somnolence about Lekkersing that saddened me. The people wave as you drive past, but they don't do so with any real enthusiasm. Perhaps the new developments that are on the cards will turn the town around.

There's no official guest house in Lekkersing, although they are planning to build one. You can arrange for overnight rooms through the municipal office. The town has no petrol and no ATM facilities.

The campsite at Koerdap is about 15km south of the village. It has four chalets, which sleep two people each, and several hiking trails. A nearby farm, Kalkfontein, also offers hiking and horse riding, with dormitory-style accommodation. It is self-catering, but meals can be arranged. Please bring your own sleeping gear.

Contacts:

- Municipal office: 027-851 8580; contact person: Marie Sampson or Mina Adams
- Koerdap Campsite: 027-851 8136 (Sintie Cloete); 027-851 7192 (Sarah Cloete)
- Kalkfontein Farm: 073-507 4301 (Pastor P. Groenewald)

From Lekkersing, continue driving north for 67km. Along the way, you will see rows of stark mountains rolling away to your right. The turn-off for the Tierhoek campsite and cave can be found on this part of the road. When you reach a junction with the Alexander Bay–Kuboes road, turn right and drive for another 5km to arrive at Kuboes.

Kuboes (also spelled Khubus or |*obes*)

Originally founded as a Rhenish mission station, the delightful village of Kuboes takes its name from a Khoikhoi term meaning 'round fountain or spring'. It is a beautiful town built around the elegantly simple, whitewashed church complex, established in 1893. The lofty mountains of Kuboesberg, Vandersterrberg and the granite pluton of Ploegberg surround the town.

Kuboes is considered the stronghold of the Nama people and their culture. Local choirs still sing songs in the soft, clicking Nama tongue and dance groups perform the traditional 'Nama-stap' (Nama-step dance) at ceremonial events. If you ask ahead, a cultural programme can be performed for guests. You may even get to hear an ancient folktale narrated by one of the local storytellers.

The CPA that now owns and administers the RCC land on behalf of the local communities has its headquarters in the centre of town and, in the afternoons, groups of people gather around the steps of municipal offices to chat. All in all, it's a very friendly place and I thoroughly enjoyed driving around and meeting the people. Photographs of the locals may be taken, but do ask permission first.

Even if you don't speak Afrikaans (the lingua franca of the town) some basic sign language will suffice in this regard. Here is my personal procedure: I hold my camera in a non-threatening position, with the lens pointing away from my prospective subject. I then point at my camera and point at the person whom I am stalking, I mean propositioning. If they shake their head, I smile and walk away. If they nod, I'm in! And I usually do get a nod. In fact, in Kuboes I was positively swamped by kids and young adults who all wanted their picture taken—thank goodness for digital photography …

There is no petrol in Kuboes (the nearest place to get fuel is at the Baken mine at Sanddrif, about 25km away). At this stage, this is the only town in the Richtersveld with cell-phone reception. There are no banks or ATM facilities.

Accommodation for guests is available at the Mountain Valley Guest House, which consists of four stand-alone, whitewashed cottages, built in a lovely river valley on the outskirts of the town. Each cosy cottage has three bedrooms and is fully equipped. If you want a real Nama experience, you can also stay in one of three traditional *matjiehuise*. Costs are about R100 per person per night, and conservancy fees of R30 per person per day apply. The guest house is self-catering, but meals can be arranged if booked in advance. A traditional Nama meal is also available at around R100 per head. The guest house has electricity and hot water geysers.

Contacts:

- Tourism office: 027-831 2375
- Sida !Hub CPA: 027-831 1648
- Contact person: Carmen Cloete (CPA) or Jacoba de Wet (municipal office)
- Field guide: Seth Domroch 027-831 1589
- Mountain Valley Guest House Bookings: Johanna Obies 027-831 2363; 076-643 1575 or Katriena de Wet: 027-831 1940

From Kuboes, head back towards Alexander Bay. After about 10km, you'll see a turn-off to the right that leads towards the Richtersveld National Park (40km to Sendelingsdrif—see *page 165). Alternatively, keep going straight for another 8km until you see the turn-off for Sanddrif/Baken. Turn right and, about 10km down this road, you'll see the turn-off for the Baken mine. A short distance further on you'll find the town of Sanddrif.*

Sanddrif

This rather dusty collection of houses is closely associated with the mining industry. The first settlers arrived at Sanddrif in the early 1900s, when the Nama people along the coast were moved out and relocated to these sandy dunefields. Then, in the 1970s, the Transhex Corporation opened up a new diamond mine at nearby Baken and many Xhosa and Sotho workers were brought into the area to work on these deposits.

Sanddrif therefore contains a strong Nguni influence, which mixes with the Nama cultural tradition. As a result, Sanddrif is sometimes called the District Six or Rainbow Town of the Richtersveld, referring to its multi-cultural heritage. For example, the Sanddrif Youth Forum Basotho Stars and groups doing the Nama-stap dance are both regular features at local functions.

As such, Sanddrif is a very welcoming place. I spent quite some time driving around, taking pictures and chatting to the people. One of the guys I spoke to, by the name of Kosie Fredericks, told me a bit about his life in the town. At school, he said, he was forced to learn Afrikaans and then, as soon as he could read and write a little bit, he was kicked out. He described these days as *swaar jare* (heavy years), but he went on to say that things were better under apartheid because there wasn't so much murder and crime. This isn't the first time I've heard this kind of sentiment, but it was surprising coming from a remote and economically dispossessed town like Sanddrif.

The Baken mine, close to Sanddrif, is the only place in the area where you can get petrol (unleaded, LRP and diesel). There is also a well-stocked convenience store and this is a good place to get supplies like bread, tinned food, meat, firewood and the like. They even had copies of the *Sowetan* newspaper. The mine complex includes an extensive residential settlement with neat little houses, a school, an ATM and a sunburnt miniature golf course. The mine is a restricted area, but they'll let you through the gate if you tell them that you want petrol. Tours of the mine can be arranged.

At present, there are no official guest houses at Sanddrif. There is a camping site, Stofbakkies, but this is not always operational. South African National Parks has recently built an interpretation centre in the town that does valuable community outreach work and encourages local people to get involved in the national park up the road. Other activities include walks to the Hangklip (which offers great views out over the Orange) or the Island Trail (which lets you hop across the small, reed-covered islands that pepper the channel of the Orange River).

Contacts:

- Municipal office: 027-831 1457; contact person: Catherine Slaander
- Emily Smith: 082-538 9585
- Hein van Wyk: 083-949 9389
- Transhex head office: 021-937 2000

*From Sanddrif, head back to the Kuboes–Alexander Bay road. You can now either turn left to head up to the Richtersveld National Park (about 47km—*see *page 163), or right to Alexander Bay (55km).* As *you drive* *towards Alexander Bay, the road rises over several ridges that give you views out over the Orange River with its green strips of farmland and other agricultural structures. Most of these farms were established by Alexkor, and now belong to the Sida !Hub CPA. A short distance outside of Alexander Bay, you'll see the turn-off to Oranjemund in Namibia. The road to this Namdeb-owned settlement crosses the Orange River over the Ernest Oppenheimer Bridge—but don't even think about taking this route unless you have the necessary permits.*

Alexander Bay

Located at the mouth of the Orange River, Alexander Bay is a very typical company town. Built entirely by and for the state-owned Alexkor diamond mining operation, the town was once heavily restricted and you needed a permit to gain entry. Now, with the on-shore diamond mines almost exhausted, the town is a shadow of its former self and much more open to tourism. So, all you need to do is stop at the boom gate, sign in, show your ID and they'll let you right through.

Once inside the settlement, it all looks very institutional. Rows of low brick houses vary in size, according to the status of the employees who live inside. There are several churches and schools, and a couple of walls are painted with murals that are supposed to lighten the mood. But it's a rather sombre place. The tall wire fences that separate the town from the mining area along the beach are omnipresent, and ugly industrial structures seem to tower over everything. There's no doubt that this was a utilitarian town with a one-track mind; nothing has been put here for beauty's sake. It's all very functional.

The one attraction of Alexander Bay is the Orange River mouth. This vitally important RAMSAR wetland can be reached by following a series of hand-painted signs (marked 'Riviermonding') through the town and down a long sand road to a small parking area on the beach. On your left, the fence is covered with severe signs that say 'Warning. Mine Area. No Entry'. Behind the wire, you can see an enormous old mine building that is now abandoned and crumbling into the sand that is creeping up around its base. The lifeguard's hut on the public part of the beach is similarly neglected and even the muddy ocean seems forlorn and angry.

You now have to leave your car and walk along the beach to your right. It's a wild scene, with long strands of seaweed and huge pieces of driftwood littering the blackened sand. The actual river mouth is quite a distance away, but you can clamber up one of the sand dunes and get a good view out over the beautiful wetlands, which stretch back from the narrow mouth.

Birders, in particular, will do their nut. Thousands of flamingos perch in the waters of the estuary and many other water birds wheel across the sky. In the distance, you can see the Boegoeberg twin mountains and, if you look carefully, you can just make out the town of Oranjemund in Namibia.

Unfortunately, there is no established visitor infrastructure that allows you to access the wetlands directly. You either have to organize a local guide who can unlock one of the gates in the fence or find yourself a good vantage point from the beach. The mouth has also been degraded by years of mining, but efforts are currently underway to rehabilitate this natural wonder. One hopes that improved tourist facilities are part of these plans.

Alexander Bay has a population of 1,600 people, but only about 450 of these are permanent residents. Everyone else is here either on contract to the mine or stationed at the nearby naval base. It will be interesting to see what happens to the town now that it has been given over to the Sida !Hub CPA.

Surprisingly, Alexander Bay has several guest houses: Af-en-Toe, Frikkie Snyman, Uitsig, New Horizon and Lieflot. Other tourist facilities include a small shopping centre with a convenience store, post office, a place selling shoes and clothes, and the Koffiekan coffee shop. There's also the Dunvlei sports club with the Zonneblom restaurant and ladies bar. A 24-hour petrol station with an ATM machine and a workshop can be found just outside the boom gates. The town has a hospital and emergency services, just in case you run into trouble.

There is also a museum but, unfortunately, the woman who used to run it has left town and I can't determine if a replacement has been found. The museum also used to organize tours into the restricted area to visit an operational diamond mine, but I'm not sure whether this service is still available. Try phoning ahead to check on the status quo.

There are two camping sites in the vicinity of Alexander Bay. Patchvlei is located on the banks of the Orange River, about 8km out of town along the Kuboes road. It has a picnic spot and a braai area, but facilities are limited. Farther along the same road, you'll find Brandkaros (27km from Alexander Bay). This is a more established campsite, with chalets, ablution facilities, a restaurant and a swimming pool.

Finally, if you're a lover of lichen, don't miss Lichen Hill. This little rise is covered with dozens of species of lichen and is the only one of its kind in South Africa. It's located a short distance to the south of Alexander Bay, along the Port Nolloth road.

Contacts:

- Museum and mine tours: 027-831 1330
- Guest house bookings: 027-831 1855
- Brandkaros campsite: 027-831 1856

From Alexander Bay, turn right onto the tarred R382 towards Port Nolloth (85km). This part of the road is very dry and sandy, with an endless series of rolling koppies leading down to the dark green waters of the Atlantic Ocean. The coast, which is still restricted, is dotted with mine dumps and other relics of the decaying mining industry. Rehabilitating the landscape once the mines are finally shut down (in about ten years) is going to be a major project. Oh, and keep an eye on the telephone poles along the road side. Hawks, owls and other birds of prey can be seen on every second pole, just waiting to scoop up a bug or some road-kill from the tarmac. In spring, this is quite a pretty drive, with dustings of bright purple and yellow flowers brightening up the dusty palette of brown sand and khaki bushes.

Port Nolloth and MacDougall's Bay

I really like Port Nolloth. I arrived at the town during the golden hour before sunset and the warm light made everything look quite beautiful. The town also has a well-developed tourism infrastructure, so it's a good place to start or end off your Richtersveld adventure. There are dozens of guest houses, inns, hotels and motels, and several restaurants specialize in fresh seafood straight off the fishermen's boats.

The harbour, which was once the busy terminal of the copper-era Okiep–Port Nolloth railway, is now filled with picturesque fishing and diamond boats. There is an excellent museum on the beachfront, located close to the old lighthouse and the delightful, baby-blue Catholic church. The museum is a good place to get tourist information about the town and the surrounding region. It also has extensive displays on the natural and cultural history of the region and an internet café. It is housed in the old Cape Copper Company's Officials Club, dating from the 1880s.

A few kilometres down the coast, you'll find the holiday resort of MacDougall's Bay, with more guest houses and a well-known caravan park that is literally on the beach. This beautiful, unspoilt spot was once a diamond area and thus out of bounds. It was opened to the public around 1986 and, since then, it has blossomed. The presence of several real estate agencies and numerous residential developments indicate that this is a resort town on the up. Long-time residents told me that they can't believe how much the town has grown in the past few years, and property prices are already quite considerable.

The most well-known place to eat is definitely Anita's Tavern. This charming bistro is decorated with a cosy clutter of nautical paraphernalia. It's a great place to spend an evening. The hosts are warm and welcoming and the food is excellent. It's even been featured on several TV shows, so it's got to be good. I tried the house speciality, the Calamari Carpetbagger—two calamari steaks (breaded and deep fried) stuffed with mussels and cheese sauce. It was all a bit rich for my palate, but they serve a wide range of food so you should find something that appeals. Advance booking is recommended in season.

In terms of nightlife, there ain't much to speak of. But curiosity got the better of me and I did check out the little disco at the back of the Scotia Inn. It turned out to be a rather enticing pool bar, with lots of face brick and loud 'sokkie' music. The crowd was nicely multi-racial and I quite enjoyed myself.

In MacDougall's Bay, try eating at the Pondok, next door to the Port Indigo Guest House. This is one of the original, low-roofed tin shanties that was built when the area first opened to the public in the 1980s. There's sea sand on the floor, the breakfasts are excellent and the service is very friendly. The main beach is right across the road and this sandy shingle is perfect for a late-afternoon stroll. Just don't try to swim in the visually inviting water because it's bloody freezing!

Between Port Nolloth and MacDougall's Bay, there's Sizamile township (meaning 'we have tried'). While driving through this location, I took some pictures of two kids riding their homemade go-carts down the sand dunes. When I was done, they came over to me. I was expecting them to ask for some money but, instead, they wanted to know if I had a screwdriver or a hammer to fix their vehicles. I respected their priorities.

On the outskirts of town, you'll find several motor workshops, panel beaters, auto-electricians, hardware stores and tyre places. So, this is the place to go for mechanical repairs either before or after your Richtersveld odyssey. There's also something here called the Richtersveld Experience, which offers information on the area, a restaurant, a pub, a guest house, river rafting excursions, hiking trips, 4x4 hire, tours, you name it. There are also several other tour operators who run trips to the Richtersveld from Springbok (*see* page 177).

Port Nolloth is renowned for having four seasons in one day. It also has the most number of fog days for any town in South Africa. Apparently, the easterly wind is the one that brings the sunshine, and the westerly wind is the one that brings the fog and the mist. Either way, it's an enchanting place that is sure to delight its visitors.

Contacts:

- Municipal offices and tourist info: 027-851 1111
- Port Nolloth Museum: 027-851 8350/8865 (closed Saturday afternoons and Sundays); for more information contact Bedrock Lodge
- Anita's Tavern: 084-726 7090
- Dine & Wine Restaurant: 027-851 8245/8353
- Elza's Kitchen: 072-183 7664

- Mamma's Restaurant: 027-581 8027
- Mar E Sol Espresso Bar: 082-821 2083
- Port Fisheries Take Aways: 074-363 9045
- Port Nolloth Fish Shop: 027-851 8701
- The Royal Pub and Restaurant: 083-416 2523
- Vasco Da Gama: 027-851 8515

Accommodation:

- Bedrock Lodge***: 027-851 8865; www.bedrocklodge.co.za
- De Duine: 027-851 7707
- Higgo's Accommodation: 027-851 7532
- Kusweg: 027-851 7410
- La Rochelle: 083-411 1024
- MacDougall's Bay Caravan Park and chalets*/**: 027-851 1110
- MacDougall's Beach House***: 027-851 8856
- Muisvlak Motel: 027-851 8046
- Nollothville Guest House B&B: 027-851 7180
- Port Indigo***/****: 027-851 8012; www.portindigo.co.za
- Port Nolloth Country Club: 027-851 7433
- Richtersveld Experience Tours & Lodge: 027-851 8041
- Scotia Inn Hotel**: 027-851 8353
- Self-Catering House: 027-851 8811; www.richtersveld.co.za
- Sizamile Guest House: 027-851 7628
- Woonstel Accommodation: 027-851 8041

From Port Nolloth, continue on the tarred R382 towards Steinkopf (92km). This returns us to our starting point and completes the circular route through the Richtersveld Community Conservancy.

Steinkopf

Another former mission station, Steinkopf is a small town developed around the old Rhenish church (built in 1840). There isn't much of a tourism industry here, but the petrol station on the outskirts of town is a good place to fill up before entering the fuel-less expanse of the RCC. The adjoining convenience store and café also makes a surprisingly good chicken burger.

For those who do wish to spend some time in town, there are several things to see. The Immanuel Succulent Nursery and tea garden, run by the local home for the disabled, displays numerous succulents as well as arts and crafts. The Steinkopf Art Gallery is located inside the old Rhenish Mission Church, featuring paintings donated by the Brecher family.

For 4x4 enthusiasts, you can take a trip up into the mountains to see the old Anenous station and Nonahams watering point (both part of the old Okiep–Port Nolloth railway line). Historically minded visitors may also want to pop in at the Kinderlê memorial or visit the ruins of the old Klipfontein Hotel, which has several gravesites dating back to the Anglo–Boer War.

The only official overnight accommodation at Steinkopf is at the nearby community-run Kookfontein Rondavels and Info Centre. Traditional Nama food, such as roosterbrood, chicken noodle potjie, lamb's-neck potjie and 'curry tripe', is served at the Kookskerm foodstall.

Contacts:

- Kookfontein Rondawels: 027-721 8841
- Kookskerm Foodstall: 078-126 0808; 076-550 3555
- Tour Guide, Calitz: 073-635 7021

Activities in the RCC

Although the conservancy is only in its infancy, there are already a number of enticing tourist products on offer and many more are on the way. The infrastructure of the RCC is also being improved, with a number of museums, interpretation centres, guest houses and entrance gates in various stages of development. The lack of good road signage is being addressed.

In terms of people skills, several funders have helped more than 40 community members train up as accredited tour guides and field guides. These local experts are available to accompany you on village tours, hikes and 4x4 trails. This is highly recommended as the well-informed guides will greatly enhance your appreciation and understanding of the RCC.

A number of hiking trails, 4x4 routes and campsites are already open and waiting to captivate visitors to the RCC. Workshops and brainstorming sessions have also been held to identify new tourism opportunities, and these are currently being investigated. So, phone ahead to find out about the latest offerings.

Just to whet your appetite, these upcoming attractions could include:

- Multi-day hikes with overnight stops at various campsites
- Angling and fly-fishing in the Orange River
- Mountain-bike trails
- Horse-riding trails
- Canoeing and white-water rafting trips on the Orange River
- The establishment of an indigenous nursery, medicinal garden and botanical garden
- Rock climbing
- Airplane flights over the conservancy
- Stargazing and astronomy tours
- Hot air balloon trips
- Cultural home-stays
- Bird-watching tours

Websites:

- www.richtersveld-conservancy.org
- www.richtersveldguesthouses.co.za
- www.richtersveld.net
- www.richtersveld.gov.za
- www.south-north.co.za
- www.northerncape.org.za
- www.diamondcoast.co.za

The Richtersveld National Park

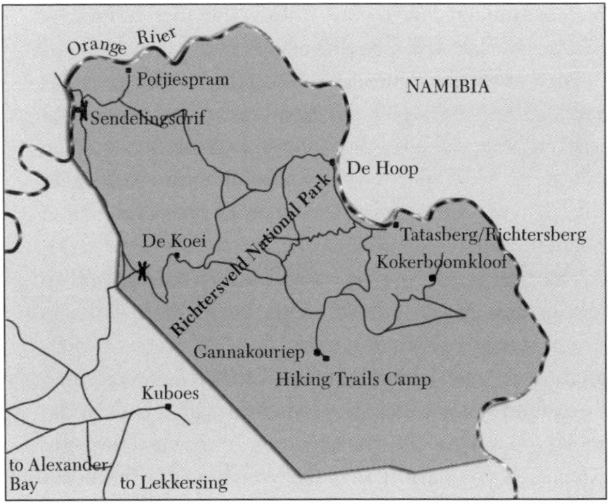

RNP

Administered by South African National Parks (SANParks) on behalf of the Richtersveld community, the Richtersveld National Park (RNP) is, quite simply, breathtaking. It is a place out of time, out of the ordinary and out of this world.

Here, in the most mountainous part of the Richtersveld, the rocks are laid bare. The mountain slopes are starved of soil and the dry desert plains are barren and beautiful in equal measure. You need a 4x4 to drive in this rugged park, and it's really only geared for camping, but recent improvements to the park's infrastructure make it relatively easy to explore.

Getting there

From Steinkopf, take the tarred R382 towards Port Nolloth. From this road, you can either drive through the gravel roads of the RCC, via Eksteenfontein and Kuboes, to reach the entrance gate at Sendelingsdrif (about 200km), or you can keep on the tar to Port Nolloth and Alexander Bay before hitting the dirt (a total of 262km, the last 83km on gravel).

Both of these routes are described in the previous section. So, we'll pick up from the point where you turn off the Kuboes–Alexander Bay road (about 50km outside of Alexander Bay) and head up to the park itself. The distance from this intersection to the main gate at Sendelingsdrif is about 45km.

The first intriguing sign you'll see is the turn-off to Wondergat (Mystery hole). This deep, dark sinkhole drops straight down for more than 20 metres before angling off and descending even further. It was formed by ground water which percolated through a fault in the rocks, dissolving the limestone as it trickled through. Nama legends have it that the Wondergat is the home of Heitsi Eibib, the great spirit. Other stories say that it is the home of the 'Great Snake', which swims through underground channels into the nearby Orange River where it transforms itself into a young maiden in order to lure men to their death.

In any case, the sinkhole is indeed dangerous and should only be approached with extreme caution. If you want to walk up to the Wondegat, drive around to the south side of the hill, where you'll find a parking area. Then follow the neat little path, marked out in white stones, up the side of the koppie. I must say that, when I got to the top, I couldn't actually find the mouth of the sinkhole, but the view was astounding nonetheless.

Shortly after the Wondergat, you'll see a turn-off to Bloeddrif (Blood drift). I'm not sure what happened at this river crossing, but it must have been pretty sanguineous. Bloeddrif is part of the Transhex mining company's holdings, but there are a number of petroglyphs here which can be visited with permission (contact Transhex head office or the RNP reception).

From the Bloeddrif turn-off, keep driving north through the mountains. Eventually, you'll come to a neat-looking visitors' centre. This is the entrance to the Helskloof gate. However, if you haven't been to the park before, I would suggest that you start your visit at the main reception office at Sendelingsdrif and then exit the park via the Helskloof Pass, if you wish.

So, keep driving for another 20km until you get to Reuning mine. This small village, cluttered with heavy machinery, conveyor belts and 'no entry' signs, is actually the unlikely location of the RNP reception. But rest assured that you'll see no sign of mining once you enter the park itself.

Sendelingsdrif

The main gate to the RNP is at Sendelingsdrif (Missionaries' crossing) and it is important that you check in at reception before driving into the park. After all, it is a wild place and the staff want to know where you'll be staying and how long you intend to be inside. That way, they'll know when to send in the rescue team.

You will get all the necessary maps and brochures at reception, and these are essential for successful navigation through the park. There is also a new interpretation centre that was still under construction when I was there. Unfortunately, the staff tend to only speak Afrikaans and I had some trouble communicating with them because my Afrikaans is *vreeslik*.

The reception office has a store that sells basic supplies (open weekdays) and petrol pumps—diesel and LRP only. There is a coin-operated public phone at reception but please note that there is no cell phone reception. The new border post and pontoon across the Orange River are also located at Sendelingsdrif.

If you are planning to arrive late, it's a good idea to book in at the rest camp at Sendelingsdrif. There are 12 campsites with a good ablution block and a number of very attractive chalets, which have been recently refurbished. These excellent units (four four-bed and six two-bed units) are fully equipped with an air-conditioner, basic kitchen (fridge and hot plate), bathroom and braai area, with great views out over the Orange River and Cornell's Kop. There's also a swimming pool in the camp.

Alternatively, if you want to forsake your last chance for a hot shower and soft bed, book your first night at the Potjiespram campsite (10km from Sendelingsdrif).

Potjiespram

The road down to Potjiespram runs along a dry riverbed. It is quite rocky and, since I was there at the end of the wet season, there were many water-filled depressions that had to be negotiated with care. Still, it's not nearly as fearsome as I was led to believe.

When you arrive at the campsite, you have to choose from one of three sections, each with its own ablution block (cold water only). All the sites are arranged along the Orange River, and you can walk down through the tree-lined verge along the rocky riverbanks for a stroll. This is an amazing experience, with the wide, flat waters of the river curving through an otherwise blistering assortment of boulders and mountains.

Unfortunately, on the far bank, you can see the huge pit of a mining operation, which is a bummer. Having said that, the mountains sides are so shattered and decomposed that it's quite hard to tell what has been mined and what is just collapsed scree. My initial thoughts were that the mountains look like crumbled Flake chocolate, with the dark rocks jutting out of light-brown ice-cream—but maybe I was just hungry.

The three main camps contain a total of 18 campsites. There is also an environmental education centre, where students can sleep over in traditional *matjieshuise*.

De Hoop

After leaving Potjiespram, it's time to venture deeper into the RNP. The first intersection you come to is marked for the Oena mine and the Hand of God. Take this road for 200m to see this amazing imprint in the rock face, which does indeed look like an almighty handprint. Then, turn around and go back to the main road to continue on your journey.

Now it's time to tackle the Akkedis (Lizard) Pass. This is a rather rough, twisty track with lots of rocks; a bit of scrambling may be required to get your car over the steeper sections. Take it slowly, so that you don't degrade the road any further by spinning your wheels. And keep an eye out for some halfmens trees that grow along the roadside (although I must confess that I missed them completely). It should take you between 45 minutes and an hour to complete the ascent.

At the top of the pass, you come out onto a wide plain. I was there during spring, so the ground was absolutely covered in bright yellow and purple flowers, creating a transiently fertile bowl, ringed by fierce, naked mountains. I found the contrast to be profoundly beautiful.

In the middle of this plain is a small homestead with

quite a few goats. This is currently being used as a research station for the many different scientific missions that conduct research in the park each year.

The road to De Hoop campsite now leads along a wide, flat, sandy riverbed. Drive carefully so that you don't get stuck in the soft sand. It's worth the effort, however, because De Hoop is a heart-stopper.

Set out along the banks of the Orange, De Hoop is a popular campsite with open access to the cool river. The peace is overwhelming, broken only by the sound of birds and the splashing of water as it rushes over some small rapids. As with the other campsites, the newly built ablution blocks are both beautiful and functional. Although do remember that there is no hot water and no flush toilets.

There are 12 campsites at De Hoop but these are not demarcated, so you just pick a spot on the sandy banks and pitch your tent. You can swim in the river, go fishing, or just relax. The choice is yours. And don't worry about crocodiles or hippos. The water's too cold to support crocs and the last hippo in the Orange River, Humphrey, died near Alexander Bay in 1921.

Richtersberg and Tatasberg

From De Hoop, you used to be able to follow the riverbanks to the Richtersberg campsite. However, the sand on this road is very deep and too many cars were getting stuck, so this route is now closed. Instead, you must head back to the hard road and drive through the mountains, which is fine by me.

Once you drive out of the riverbed, the road leads up a low rise, which crests the hill to reveal a spectacular panorama across the plains, with row upon row of red mountains heading off into the distance. About 10km further on, you'll see a road marked for Richtersberg/ Tatasberg. This is also closed due to the sand traps that it contains, and your passage is barred by rocks and a big 'no entry' sign.

Just keep going as the road dips down into another riverbed, with some deep sand patches. Keeping to the left, you'll eventually turn down into a narrow canyon that twists between two parallel walls of russet rock. It seems impossible that there's anything at the end of this road, apart from some hungry vultures waiting for their next meal. But the rocky path turns the corner and leads you to yet another pristine waterfront campsite.

Richtersberg is similar to De Hoop, with 12 campsites and ample space to pitch your tent along the riverbanks. The eternal mountains form a serrated backdrop against the blue sky, reflecting imperfectly back at you from the rippled water.

The Tatasberg reed cabins can be found a short distance away from Richtersberg, along a soft sand road. These are comfortable self-catering units (four two-bed units) with hot showers, a 12-volt lighting system and a gas fridge and stove. Paraffin lanterns are supplied in case the lights fizzle out and a resident caretaker is on site if there are any other problems. Although the units are kept clean by the park's staff, guests must do their own washing up and make their own beds.

Kokerboomkloof

After De Hoop, my favourite campsite has to be Kokerboomkloof, located on the top of the Tatasberg pluton. This is a large granitic dome with enormous boulders that are slowly weathering away to form a variety of weird and wonderful rock formations. Many of these natural features have been given fanciful names like The Toe, The Witches and the uncannily lifelike Queen Victoria.

Then, there are the hundreds of kokerbooms, growing in haphazard profusion across the plateau. Walking through these bizarre aloe trees is an otherworldly delight that somehow defies any attempts to put it down in writing. Needless to say, I spent hours watching the setting sun blanket the colony of kokerbooms in a golden light. That night, I sat among the quiver trees and stared at the bright stars in a clear, moonless sky until my eyes got sore, because I could hardly bring myself to blink. The next morning, I spent another couple of hours watching the sun rise, as I absent-mindedly fed my breakfast to the fearless birds who hopped around my feet. It was all quite marvellous.

There are eight campsites at Kokerboomkloof and several ablution blocks. Unfortunately, the water supply is erratic and, at the time of writing, the campsite was temporarily closed because the toilets kept backing up.

Gannakouriep and Hakkiesdoring

Driving back from Kokerboomkloof, the rocks seem exposed and raw. Here, the geological processes that formed the landscape of the Richtersveld are laid bare, and distinct streaks of colour on the mountain slopes clearly indicate the transition from one rock suite to another.

After a while you'll see a sign for the panoramic Gannakouriep valley, in the heart of the RNP. Overlooking Mount Terror and the Rosyntjieberg, the Gannakouriep Wilderness Camp offers accommodation in four two-sleeper canvas cabins. Like the Tatasberg Reed Cabins, there are hot showers, a battery-powered lighting system and a gas fridge and stove. A resident caretaker is on hand to sweep up the unit, but guests must do their own cooking and cleaning.

The Gannakouriep valley is also the location of the Hakkiesdoring hiking trails base camp. This facility sleeps nine people, and contains gas stoves, fridges and hot showers. The three hiking trails that have been laid out in the RNP start from here: the Vensterval Trail (four days, three nights), the Lelieshoek-Oemsberg Trail (three days, two nights) and the Kodaspiek Trail (two days, one night).

Unfortunately, at time of writing, none of these guided trails is open due to a shortage of qualified guides. However, the camp may be booked by motorists who wish to explore this part of the park. You can even walk the trails by yourself, but groups must get permission from reception and be under the guidance of a suitable leader. The base camp costs R600 for the first four people and R100 for each additional person.

Helskloof

The time has come to, reluctantly, leave the RNP. If you do not want to backtrack to Sendelingsdrif, I can recommend the alternative route out via De Koei and Helskloof Pass.

De Koei was one of the original campsites in the park, but it is now closed and overnighting is not allowed. The road, however, is magnificent. It leads along a pretty, well-watered valley before climbing up the mountains and rambling across a high ridge. The road is quite rough, but enchanting nonetheless. In flower season, this part of the park is bursting with colour. Several windmills and stock pens also indicate that the valley is favoured by the registered herders who graze inside the park's boundaries.

Then, the road rounds a spur and the cleft in the mountains known as Helskloof appears, in all its precipitous glory. This is the home of the rare *Aloe pearsonii,* which blanket the slopes on either side of the road as it descends the pass. In the distance, jagged ridges recede into the desert sands. For me, it was a highlight of my journey through the park and an appropriate ending to my adventure.

At the base of the pass, the road leads along the banks of a dry river. A large herd of goats swarmed around the car as I trundled along—although I couldn't see the herder responsible. Finally, I reached the Helskloof Gate on the main access road to Sendelingsdrif. I signed out and, sadly, turned my back on the RNP, until next time.

The Ai-|Ais Hot Springs and the Fish River Canyon

If you can afford the time, take the opportunity to cross over into the Namibian side of the Ai-|Ais-Richtersveld TFCA. This can be done at Sendelingsdrif, thanks to a new border post and pontoon that ferries vehicles across the Orange River. Last in operation in 1988, the pontoon service is a boon for TFCA visitors.

Previously, if you wanted to go from the RNP to Ai-|Ais, you had to backtrack all the way to Steinkopf, continue on the N7 to cross the border at Vioolsdrif (a detour of over 400km), and drive another 185km to reach the entrance to the hot springs. Now, the whole trip is just 160km, door to door.

The highlights of the Namibian part of the TFCA are undoubtedly the Ai-|Ais Hot Springs and the Fish River Canyon. These are conveniently located within easy driving distance from one another and, collectively, they make one helluva destination.

Located in a barren valley surrounded by black mountains, the hot springs at Ai-|Ais bubble out of the ground at a toasty 60° Celsius. The mineral-rich water is then channelled into a large outdoor pool and a rather ritzy indoor complex with fountains and thermal baths. The resort offers a range of accommodation and spa treatments, and has recently re-opened after extensive renovations.

Ai-|Ais (meaning 'burning hot') is open throughout the year, although it does get very warm in the summer months. I was there a few years ago in mid-December and the temperature was hovering around 40°C. But for some reason, swimming in the hot water with the hot sun beating down on my head was fantastic. I felt like a lobster.

A short drive north of the springs is the Fish River Canyon. This is the second largest canyon on Earth (after the Grand one in the USA). It is 161km long, up to 27km wide and the inner canyon reaches a depth of almost 550m. It's a genuine spectacle of nature that has to be seen to be appreciated.

There are several viewpoints along the main section of the canyon, which allow you to peer over the edge into the abyss below, where the incongruously small Fish River is still cutting its way through the rocks. I spent the whole day there, just looking out over the scene and chatting to the various people who came and went. Perversely, my camera battery chose that particular day to go flat and I had to buy some spare batteries off a passing German tourist. The same day I also met Moogie, another German, who was driving an old Mercedes bus from Berlin to Cape Town—a trip that would take him two years to complete. The Fish River Canyon is that kind of place.

In terms of accommodation at the canyon, there's the Hobas campsite at the main entrance gate (N$100 per person, per day) and several luxury lodges run by the Gondwana group. The nearby Cañon roadhouse is an excellent place for a meal and a cold drink.

Planning your trip

In the old days, the RNP was really wild and you had to bring everything with you. Now, the campsites have ablution facilities (albeit with cold water) and there are even a couple of wilderness camps with proper beds and other luxuries.

Nevertheless, you still need to be prepared and pretty

much self-sufficient. Make sure your vehicle is in good repair. Take spare tyres, tools and recovery equipment. If you do break down you're going to have to wait for a passing vehicle to raise the alarm as there is no cell-phone reception in the park. During the winter months, the park is relatively busy so this shouldn't be too much of a problem. In the hot summer months, however, the visitors are few and far between so you might be stranded for a while.

The good news is that the roads are generally not as bad as people make out. Don't get me wrong, you still need a 4x4 or a sturdy 4x2 with good ground clearance and, preferably, a diff lock. A low-range gearbox is nice to have, just in case, but not essential. If you can, take along a portable air-compressor (available at most outdoor suppliers) so that you can deflate your tyres to help you across the soft sand and then inflate them again to tackle the rocky sections. Also, plan your day's driving carefully so that you can make it to your next overnight destination before the sun sets. Driving at night is dangerous and not permitted. Besides, pitching a tent in the dark sucks big time!

In terms of food, take along all the supplies you will need for the duration of your trip. There are no shops inside the park and, if you run out, you're going to have to beg from other campers (not good form) or go hungry. Also, the water within the park is suitable for washing utensils but not really drinkable, so bring plenty of fresh water for you and your party.

Fuel is another concern. The store at Sendelingsdrif sells diesel and Lead Replacement Petrol, but no unleaded fuel. The closest filling stations with unleaded are at Alexander Bay (90km away) or at the Baken mine near Sanddrif (55km). So make sure you top up your tanks at one of these places and carry some spare fuel in a jerry can or two.

However, the distances within the park are not that great (a complete circuit is only about 200km) and you'll be driving slowly so you can probably make it on a single tank. Personally speaking, I only used three-quarters of a tank on my journey, and it was a pretty comprehensive trip. But then I was driving a 4x4 with a 2.4 litre engine and I didn't turn on my air-conditioning very often because the outside temperature was quite comfortable. So, use your discretion but err on the side of caution.

Finally, don't be afraid to try out a couple of different campsites. Each site has its own look, character and appeal. This will also give you the opportunity to explore different parts of the park without having to drive back and forth from one location. But remember, you have to specify which campsites you will be staying at when you make your booking.

Other things to bear in mind:

- Be careful where you walk. The flora of the RNP is fragile and your big feet can destroy the plants.
- Always stay on the marked roads and only camp at official campsites, so that you do not cause any environmental damage.
- All rubbish must be taken out of the park with you, so bring along plenty of plastic refuse bags.
- Make sure your camera is working! Having extra batteries, film and/or memory cards is a good idea because you'll be taking pictures constantly and you won't want to run out of resources.
- Take clothes that are suitable for extreme temperatures, both hot and cold. Scarves can protect you from dust and wet towels are useful in extreme heat.
- Heavy dew-falls can occur at night.
- Gas cookers are recommended due to evening winds.
- Firewood and kindling may not be collected in the park, so bring your own.

- o The picking of plants, or removal of seeds, rocks, crystals or driftwood, is an offence.
- o Take a good insect repellent and bug spray.
- o This is scorpion country, so do not sleep on the bare ground and keep your shoes inside your tent.
- o No pets or generators are allowed, obviously.

Contacts and details:

- SANParks central reservations: 012-428 9111
- RNP reception: 027-831 1506
- Sendelingsdrif office hours: 08:00–16:00
- Gate hours: 1 October to 30 April 07:00–19:00; 1 May to 30 September 07:00–18:00
- The pontoon and border post operates from 08:00–16:15 (weather permitting). Pontoon crossings cost R150 per vehicle, one way and R200 with a trailer. Namibian cross-border charges are N$160 for an SUV. N$1 = R1.
- Fuel (diesel and LRP only) available Monday to Friday: 07:30–18:00, Saturday: 08:00–16:00, Sunday: 08:30–13:00
- Accommodation rates (valid from Nov '08 to Oct '09, incl. VAT):
  - o Campsites—R130 for the first two people, R42 for each additional adult and R21 for extra children (subject to a maximum of six people per site)
  - o Chalets and huts—about R480 for the first two people, R124 for each additional adult and R62 for extra children (where applicable)
- Daily conservation fee (valid from Nov '08 to Oct '09, incl. VAT):
  - o SA citizens (with ID): R35 per person per day
  - o SADC nationals (with passport): R48 per adult; R35 per child under 12, per day
  - o Standard conservation fee: R96 per adult; R48 per child under 12, per day

Left (above): All dressed up—to attract pollinators, some flowers develop markings that mimic the appearance of specific insects
Left (below): *Gazania rigens* on the road between Matjieskloof farm and Nieuwoudtville

Top: Say 'Cheese'—Snapping pics of the breathtaking wild flower display at Matjieskloof Farm, Nieuwoudtville
Left: A mystery blue flower, Groot Toren farm, outside Calvinia—see if you can identify it because at time of going to press we couldn't!

Every spring, the village of Nieuwoudtville is transformed into a floral wonderland

The Quiver tree forest (or colony) that grows on a mountainside outside Nieuwoudtville

Top left: The awesome Nieuwoudtville Falls
Top right: A thick carpet of flowers can contain hundreds of different species, Matjieskloof farm
Far left: A dazzling spray of colour pushes the dull shrubs aside, Groot Toren farm, outside Calvinia
Left: Playful *Bulbinella floribunda*, also known as *katsterte* (Cat's Tails) growing on the Bokkeveld plateau, Nieuwoudtville

Top left: The Clanwilliam Wild Flower Show, held every year in the 'Flower Church'
Far left: *Conicosia pugioniformis* shows off its inflorescence, Namaqua National Park
Left: The beautiful *Gazania krebsiana* blooms in the veld outside Hondeklip Bay
Top right: The artist known as 'The Villain' stands tall outside his humble home, Hondeklip Bay
Above: The Villain's artwork on display in the sand, Hondeklip Bay

Above: The Namaqua National Park, outside Kamieskroon, is one of the most reliable places to see a good display of flowers

Top right: You have been warned!—the farmstall adjacent to the Namaqua National Park has some fun with the visitors

Right: Enjoy a leisurely stroll through the amazing floral displays of the Skilpad Wild Flower Garden, Namaqua National Park

Fishing boats line the beach at Hondeklip Bay

A flock of birds slice through the late-afternoon sky at the Cape Columbine Nature Reserve, Paternoster

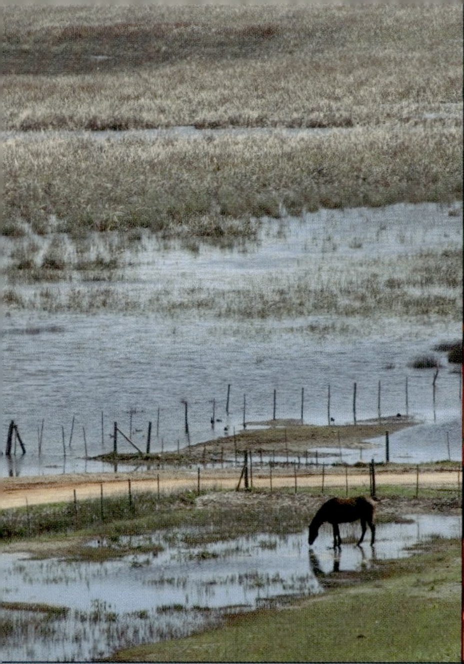

Top left: A horse takes a graceful drink from the wetlands of the Verlorenvlei River, outside Elands Bay
Far left: A splash of Pietsnot (*Grielum humifusum*) brightens up the wonderful coastal road from Elands Bay to Baboon Point
Centre: *Gazania krebsiana* is a blatant show-off, Elands Bay
Above: The sun sets over the rocky coastline of the Cape Columbine Nature Reserve, Paternoster

The tranquil waters of the Langebaan lagoon, West Coast National Park

Top: Small and delicate, *Lapeirousia jacquinii* grows low to the ground, Elands Bay
Above: The superlative Beach Camp in the Cape Columbine Nature Reserve, Paternoster

- o Holders of a valid Wild Card do not pay conservation fees

Websites:

- www.SANParks.org/parks/richtersveld
- www.peaceparks.org
- www.nwr.com.na—Namibia Wildlife Resorts
- www.namibiatourism.com.na
- www.gondwana-canyon-park.com
- www.nacobta.com.na—Namibian Community Based Tourism Assistance

Richtersveld tour operators:

- Aukwatowa Tours: 027-851 8026; 073-651 8833; Conrad Mouton; Port Nolloth
- Diamond Tours Unlimited: 053-861 4983; 083-265 4795; Dirk Potgieter; Kimberley; www.diamondtours.co.za
- J.C. Botha Tours: 027-712 2685; Pieta; Springbok; www.jcbotha.co.za
- Koperberg Tours and Safaris: 027-713 8755; 083-873 3390; Springbok; www.namaqualand.net
- Namakwa 4x4 Route: 027-712 8035/6
- Richtersveld 4x4 Hire: 027-831 2511; 082-805 4253; Springbok
- Richtersveld Challenge 4x4 Tour: 027-712 1905; Rey van Rensburg; Springbok
- Richtersveld Tours: 082-335 1399; 083-928 3571; Johan and Magda; Port Nolloth; www.richtersveldtours.co.za
- Southern Cross Adventures: 027-712 2624; Springbok; www.scadventures.co.za
- Virosa Tours: 027-712 3650; 073-229 5014; Piet van Heerde; Springbok; www.virosatours.com

Exploring Namaqualand

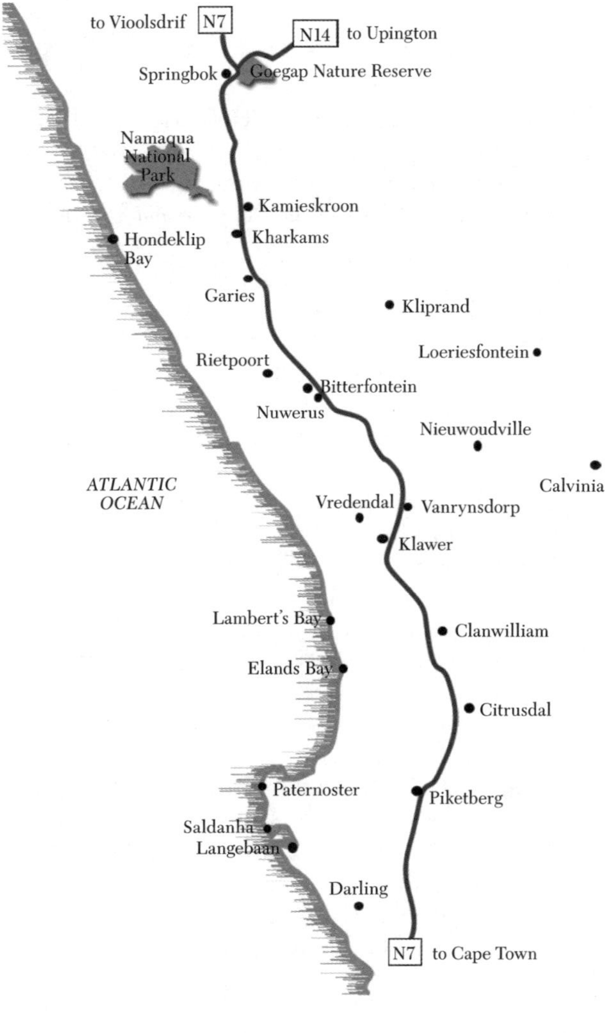

In this section, we'll have a look at the remainder of Namaqualand, south of the Richtersveld. Since this region is famous for its spring flowers, special attention is given to flower-spotting routes and destinations. Then, just to be complete, we'll also travel south of Namaqualand to discuss some of the popular wild flower havens in the Cederberg and along the West Coast.

Getting there

For the purposes of this section on the wider Namaqualand area, we are going to look at the various towns along the N7 highway from Cape Town to Springbok. This is the major transport corridor through the region and the main access road for the annual spring flower spectacle.

So, since we're already in the area, we're going to start with Springbok and work our way down south. Most people, however, will be starting in Cape Town and driving up to the north, so they are going to have to read this section backwards!

General info websites:

- www.namaqualand.com
- www.namaqualand.net
- www.namaqualand.co.za
- www.namakwa-dm.gov.za
- www.namaquainfo.com
- www.namakwa.com

Suggested itineraries

Once again, it all depends on how much time you have available. The total distance from Cape Town to Springbok is about 560km, but this can be broken up in a number of ways.

Briefly, the two main centres for flower watching are Springbok and Nieuwoudtville (315km from Springbok and 350km from Cape Town). The Namaqua National Park (near Springbok), the west coast around Elands Bay and the Cederberg (near Clanwilliam) are also good places to catch the flower show. So …

Starting from Springbok

If you have one to two days: There is plenty of flower action in the various hills and towns around Springbok, so pick a place to stay and drive around a bit. The Namaqua National Park near Kamieskroon is a definite must. You'll find more information in the Springbok and Kamieskroon sections later.

If you have two to four days: After a couple of nights in Springbok, drive the 300-odd km to Nieuwoudtville and spend the rest of your time there.

If you have four to six days: After a few nights in both Springbok and Nieuwoudtville, spend a night or two somewhere on the West Coast (I would suggest Elands Bay). When you're done, you can return to Springbok, but you'll probably be closer to Cape Town.

If you have more than six days: Once you've had enough of Springbok and Niewoudtville, head south to the Cederberg and/or the West Coast. Apart from Elands Bay, I would recommend staying over at the Cape Columbine Nature Reserve near Paternoster and/or the West Coast National Park at Langebaan. Then head back to Cape Town via Darling.

Starting from Cape Town

If you have one day: Plan a conservative route from the Mother City to the West Coast National Park at Langebaan (about 90km) and then return via Yserfontein and/or the pretty town of Darling, with its wild flower reserves—a round trip of roughly 200km.

If you have two to four days: Spend your time along the West Coast and the Cederberg, exploring the West

Coast National Park at Langebaan, the Cape Columbine Nature Reserve at Paternoster, Elands Bay and/or the area around Clanwilliam. Alternatively, drive straight to Nieuwoudtville and spend a couple of nights there before returning directly to Cape Town (a round trip of roughly 700km).

If you have four to six days: Plan a route that combines elements of the West Coast strandveld, the Cederberg mountain fynbos and the flowers of the Bokkeveld plateau around Nieuwoudtville.

If you have more than six days: Head north from Niewoudtville and spend some time at the Namaqua National Park at Kamieskroon and Springbok. If you can, spend a few days in the Richtersveld as well, while you're in the area.

Starting from Joburg

Due to the distances involved, I would suggest doing a large circular route: from Joburg to Springbok on the N14, then Springbok to Cape Town on the N7 and returning to Joburg via the N1 (or the other way around). This round trip is about 3,150km. Alternatively, you can just drive from Joburg to Springbok and back (about 2,200km in total). A side-trip from Springbok to Nieuwoudtville, returning to Springbok, will add about 640km onto the journey.

Personally, I hate driving back the way I came, so if you are planning to visit Nieuwoudtville, I would say that the extra 300-odd kilometres it takes to complete the Joburg–Springbok–Cape Town circuit is worth it. If these distances are too much for you, your only other viable option is to fly to either Cape Town or Upington and rent a car. Chartered flights to Springbok may be available, but this would be beyond the means of most wage-bound mortals.

Flower power

Much has been written about the annual wild flower spectacular that turns the dry plains of Namaqualand into a 'carpet' of colour every spring. In fact, it tends to send most writers into paroxysms of poetic platitudes that border on the hysterical. I, however, am made of sterner stuff and will do my best to remain calm.

Nevertheless, flower season in Namaqualand is hugely and profoundly impressive. In other words, it's blooming marvellous. But what causes this natural phenomenon and why is it over so quickly?

Well, basically, every plant species in Namaqualand has developed a strategy to cope with the low rainfall. Succulents store water in their leaves or stems, geophytes (or bulbs) store water in underground organs. Others (such as trees and shrubs) grow deep roots or confine themselves to water courses. But the annuals (which include the daisy family) have a different method.

After the winter rains, these cunning plants grow quickly; germinating, flowering, dispersing their seeds and then dying all in a matter of weeks. The seeds then wait in the soil for the next good rainfall, whereupon the whole cycle begins again. Some seeds can survive for years underground, until there is enough rain to coax them into life once more.

So, if the winter rains have been good, a few weeks later the stage is set for a collective eruption of yellow, white, orange and purple blooms that will pop the eyes and delight the soul. And the sheer volume of flowers on display is jaw-dropping.

However, Hendrik van Zijl, one of the botanical gurus who lives in the Nieuwoudtville area, says that it's not just about the numbers. He believes that it is the diversity of different species that makes the flower displays so amazing. All in all, there are about 3,000 species of flowering plants in Namaqualand, some of which are very rare or narrowly endemic. Therefore, if you really want to be a good flower spotter, do your homework and get the necessary wild flower guide before you start driving around. After all, it pays to know your *Iridaceae* from your *Asteraceae*.

Unfortunately, I am no botanist and, in the pages that follow, I will refrain from listing all the different species you will find in the different regions of Namaqualand. There are other books available that can do this with a much greater degree of accuracy, and I don't want to clutter up this text with lists of Latin nomenclature. So, see the back of the book for some suggested further reading, and don't make me go binomial on you!

With all this simultaneous germination, the millions of flowers blowing in the breeze are desperate to get pollinated by the limited supply of suitable insects. This leads to fierce competition and every plant species has developed its own ingenious ways to attract the right kind of pollinators. Many rely on showy displays of big, bright petals in seductive hues of yellow, white, red and orange. The petals of many vygie flowers are positively iridescent, luring bugs with their shimmering purple power.

Additionally, the petals of some plants have developed markings that look like specific insects, which attract either mates or feeders to the pollen. Monkey beetles, for example, like to use the flower heads of daisies as a mating platform. The subsequent roll in the pollen covers the insects with, what is in effect, the plant's sperm, which they then carry with them as they visit other flowers. So, to encourage the attention of young beetle lovers, several species of *Gazania* have developed markings that mimic female monkey beetles. Similarly, the Bee fly is attracted to the shiny dots around the flower head of the mis-named Beetle Daisy, which reflect light as if from the body of a fellow Bee fly.

Other plant species have evolved in harmony with their pollinators, developing flower structures that are uniquely suited to the anatomy of their symbiotic partners. For example, some species of *Pelargoniums* and irises have developed flowers with slender tubes that fit only the mouthparts of one or two suitable species of tangle-winged flies. Talk about hard to get.

Now, with all this talk of frenzied procreation, don't go getting the idea that the entire Namaqualand region is blanketed with wall-to-wall daisies. Instead, the flowers tend to occur in clumps and patches. So, throughout the region, you will often see isolated stands of colourful flowers growing in an otherwise brown landscape. Even in the floral heartlands, one field may be covered with colour, while another may not appear to contain even a single petal.

The erratic distribution of the flowers is caused by several factors, including soil composition, the wind-blown dispersal of seeds, ambient temperatures, rainfall patterns, topography and other geographical inscrutables. So, during flower season, you have to drive around to bit to find the best sites, either in terms of volume, diversity or rarity. This quest can become all-consuming and every tourist seems to have only one question on their lips, "Where's a good place to see the flowers?" It's kind of like looking for lions in the Kruger Park.

The one thing you should be aware of is that the flowers tend to grow on disturbed ground where the established vegetation has been removed or reduced. This usually occurs on farmlands used for grazing animals or on disused fields that have been previously ploughed but not sown, sometimes called 'oldfields'.

This is because the flowers are part of what is known as primary ground cover, i.e. the first plant species to start growing on freshly turned land. If the land is left alone too long, it will be colonized by bushes and shrubs (secondary ground cover) and flowers will not have the space to grow once secondary plants have become established. So, the best places for flower spotting are on fallow farmland, grazing ground and untended roadside verges.

As an example, consider the miraculously rich flower site at Matjieskloof farm, near Nieuwoudtville, which follows a very simple method to encourage this process. The secret, they say, is as follows: the sheep are let into the fields at the end of September to *mis* (do their business) and graze on the dried-up flowers. The animals are taken out in March to give the plants a chance to rest and then, in August/September, the flowers come out again, and the cycle is repeated. The Skilpad wild flower garden at the Namaqua National Park uses a similar method, but a good ploughing will also work.

When to go

This, my friends, is the million-dollar question. And it's not an easy one to answer.

Firstly, there are actually flowers blooming throughout the year. Summer-flowering succulents (such as crassulas) add a dash of colour during the hot months from November to February. Many geophytes and bulbs (such as the Amaryllis family) bloom as the temperatures start getting cold, in late autumn to early winter. The Scented Candelabra Lily, *Brunsvigia bosmaniae,* puts on a particularly spirited display, flowering three weeks after heavy rains in March–April (although this doesn't happen every year). Then, in winter, many aloe species start to bloom.

The main event, however, kicks off when the weather starts getting warmer in late winter to early spring. So, broadly speaking, the famous spring flowers come out between early August and mid-September, give or take a couple of weeks on either side. Mid to late August is usually considered the peak season, but there are several variables to consider.

Firstly, there are several different kinds of wild flowers, including annuals (such as daisies), vygies (mesembs), perennials, geophytes and shrubs, that all come into bloom during the spring season. These various species have different life cycles and will bloom and die at different times during the season.

Secondly, you have to find out when the winter rains fell. The flowers will start to spring up a month or two after the main rains, and this may occur at different times in different parts of the region. The intensity of the rain is directly related to the intensity of the bloom—the more rain, the better the display.

Then, you must ask yourself, where are you? The flowers tend to bloom as temperatures start to rise. This increase usually occurs first along the coastal areas and in the north, before moving in an easterly direction across the interior of Namaqualand. Altitude also plays a role as the higher up you are, the colder it's going to be and the later the flowering will begin. The heights of the Kamieskroon mountains may even have flower displays well into October.

You also have to consider the vagaries of the spring climate. If there is a sudden transition from a cold winter to a hot spring, the flowers will die faster. If, however, the spring temperatures are low, with cold nights, the flowers will stick around a lot longer. Local conditions are another factor as a strong, hot Berg wind blowing down the mountains can shrivel an entire colony of flowers overnight, so you have to be on your toes.

Therefore, depending on where you are and what kind of flowers you want to see, the season can start as early as mid-July and go on until the end of September. Nevertheless, August is the safest bet, especially in

Nieuwoudtville and Springbok. However, there is a problem. You cannot wait until the flowers start to bloom and then jump in your car and race off to Namaqualand.

This is because, during flower season, the entire region gets booked up months in advance. I found this out first-hand when I arrived in Vanrhynsdorp without pre-booked accommodation, only to find that every single hotel, guest house and campsite was totally full, and I mean full to bursting. The nearby towns of Vredendal and Nieuwoudtville were also chock-a-block.

It's a horrible feeling to be stuck in a strange town, at night, making desperate phone calls from the petrol station, only to find that there is literally no room at any of the inns, at any price. I eventually drove to Klawer (20km away) and booked into the last room at a guest house that was, until recently, a farm school. As I sat in the converted gym, eating my breakfast, I realized that it was foolish to think that I could just rock up at the height of the season and waltz into a hotel room. But I took solace in the fact that I had made my mistake on your behalf.

One of the reasons for the shortage of accommodation is the tour groups. You see them everywhere; huge buses hauling thousands of rather elderly people across Namaqualand on flower expeditions.

Now don't get me wrong. For many people, organized tours are the best way to access Namaqualand, and who am I to denigrate their fun? Tours offer you security, supervision and convenience. They can also be very cost-effective. So, if this is your kind of thing, see page 188 for a partial list of operators who specialize in flower tours. Personally speaking, however, I don't respond well to this kind of tourist experience and prefer to travel under my own steam.

Namaqualand flower tour operators:

- Afrika Safaris: 027-216 1071
- Happy Holiday Tours: 021-855 2108; www.happyholiday.co.za
- Impala Namaqualand Tours: 011-394 9192/3/4
- Landscape Tours: 021-851 7706; www.landscapetours.co.za
- Namaqua Tours: 027-219 1377; www.namakwatoere.com
- Namaqualand Flora Tours: 011-973 5248; www.bushireservice.co.za
- Rand Coach Tours: 011-674 1818/9; www.randcoach.co.za
- Redwood Tours: 021-886 8138
- Specialised Tours: 021-434 1144; www.specialtours.co.za
- Springbok Atlas: 021-460 4700; www.springbokatlas.co.za
- Tours and Trails: www.toursandtrails.co.za
- Transworld Tours: 021-551 7187
- Travel in Africa: 021-782 6793; www.safricatours.co.za
- VIP & Executive Tours: 021-794 7355; www.viptours.info

Flower-watching tips

Okay, so you've booked into your accommodation and you're ready to see some flowers. What do you do next? Here are a couple of tips:

- *Ask questions, speak to people, get recommendations.* Conditions change almost daily so chat to local residents and fellow travellers to get feedback on where they've been and what they've seen. The staff at the local tourism offices can also give you the latest info on promising flower-spotting roads and sites.
- *Don't go out too early.* The flowers respond to the sun and only open as the day gets warmer. They will also

close when the sun starts going down. So, plan to do your viewing between 10:00 and 15:00—depending on how brightly the sun is shining that day. And do note that many flowers will not open up at all if it is too rainy, too overcast or too windy.

- *The flowers face and follow the sun.* Place yourself between the sun and the flowers to see them at their best. In the mornings, for example, the flowers on the left-hand side of the road may be open and vice versa in the afternoon. When driving, try to keep the sun at your back.
- *Look at your feet.* There is a vast diversity of flower species in Namaqualand, so don't just gaze out at the floral masses from a distance. Some of the rarer and smaller plants are much more interesting than the more common daisies that form the 'carpets'. So go down on your hands and knees and get up close.
- *Don't drive too fast.* Many of the most interesting species are hard to spot, so slow down and smell the flowers. It's also important that you drive considerately as people will be pulling over constantly for photographs and walkabouts. Remember that many of the flower roads are gravel and the dust kicked up by a speeding vehicle can make it unpleasant for plants and humans alike.
- *Do some homework.* Get a flower-spotting book, such as the relevant volume of the National Botanical Society's *Wild Flower Guide* series, and familiarize yourself with the plants you will be seeing. As one harried hotel manager told me, the local people are too busy to hold your hand. And don't pick any flowers to show your mates at the bar.
- *Come with the right attitude.* The flowers are disobedient and no one can (or should) offer you any guarantees. So, do not arrive with a sense of entitlement or arrogance in this regard. And don't

blame your service provider if the display is less impressive than you had hoped.

- *Be conservation-minded.* The plants are very delicate so be very careful where you step and always keep to demarcated roads.
- *Bundle up.* Take warm clothes as temperatures can drop below zero at night. If you're camping, an extra sleeping bag is a good idea.
- *Keep it local.* Since there is a paucity of guest houses and hotels, many residents open their homes and farms to overnight guests during the peak season. Ask at one of the tourist information centres for a list of private accommodation options.
- *Get a personal flower guide.* Some towns in Namaqualand have specialized guides who are available to usher you around the various sites. This will greatly add to your appreciation of the 'daisies'. Several organizations are also working to train local community members as guides—an initiative that is well worth supporting. Ask at the local tourist office for details.

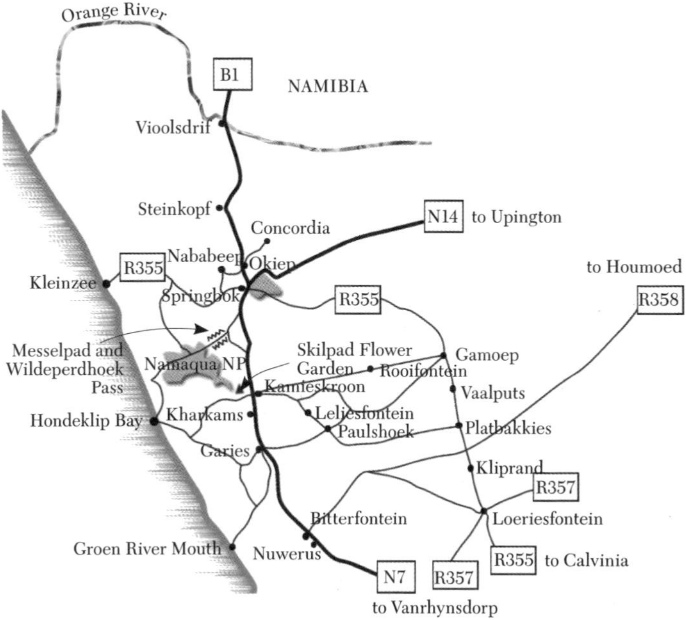

Springbok and surrounds

At first glance, there's not much to recommend Springbok. It is a hot and dusty place, surrounded by granite outcrops that are covered with dark vegetation. There are a couple of attractive sandstone churches and a pretty little rock garden built on a boulder in the centre of the town. But that's about it.

Nevertheless, Springbok has a subtle charm and a laid-back atmosphere, and there are several very worthwhile attractions nearby which make it a good place to spend a couple of days. It also offers easy access to a number of excellent flower-spotting sites, a wide range of accommodation options and an excellent tourist info centre with well-informed staff. So, all in all, it should rank quite high up on your Namaqualand itinerary.

In terms of food, there isn't much fine-dining to be had, but most of the hotels and guest houses have a restaurant attached. You will find plenty of fast-food outlets, though, including a very popular KFC, a Wimpy and a couple of dodgy hamburger joints on the main road. There are also several independent restaurants including the Godfather and the blatantly named El Dago Café.

The architecture of Springbok tends towards the utilitarian; low buildings with corrugated-tin roofs that beat back the summer heat. The main church is very attractive, however, and the Edwardian-style Springbok Hotel and art-deco façade of the Masonic Hotel are also notable.

While you're in town, check out the local museum housed in the old Jewish synagogue, located next to the Springbok Hotel. This was the centre of Namaqualand's once-influential Jewish community, most of whom came into the area after fleeing the pogroms in central Russia. Initially, they earned their living as 'smouses'—travelling salesmen who sold pots, pans, cloth and other useful merchandise from the back of their ox-wagons. A number of these itinerant peddlers eventually settled in Springbok to service the mines in the area. Now, however, the last Jewish families have left for greener pastures in the bigger cities of South Africa and abroad.

The museum contains an appealing clutter of artefacts, including old books, typewriters, documents and dresses, and fading info boards take you through the town's history. Next door, the old Jewish festival hall contains a newly established community-run art gallery and herbal tea shop, where you can buy paintings and embroidery made by local artists and craft-workers—an initiative that is well worth supporting. The museum is open Monday to Friday 08:00 to 17:00, Saturday 09:00 to 14:00 and Sunday 10:00 to 14:00.

Another good place to visit is the Springbok Lodge and Café. This unlikely looking establishment stocks an excellent selection of books on Namaqualand and Namibia, some of which are out of print and hard to find. They also have an extensive gem stone collection and a fun semi-precious scratch patch for the kids. The knowledgeable staff at the lodge can arrange trips to the old Blue Mine, the first commercial copper mine in the region, and other interesting sites in the area. The burgers from the attached restaurant are popular too.

Contacts:

- Springbok Tourism Info: 027-712 8035/6
- www.namakhoi.org.za
- Blue Mine Hiking Trail: 027-712 1321; www.springboklodge.com

Accommodation:

- Annie's Cottage****: 027-712 1451; www.spingbokinfo.com
- Blue Diamond Lodge****: 027-718 2624
- Boesmanland Guest House**: 027-712 1757; www.boesmanlandgh.co.za
- Cat Nap Accommodation***: 027-718 1905
- Daisy Country Lodge****: 027-712 3335/7; www.daisylodge.co.za
- Desert Rose Guest House***: 027-712 2330; www.desertroses.co.za
- Elkoweru Guest House***: 027-718 1202
- Harmony Estate Guest Lodge***: 027-718 1779
- Kings B&B***: 027-712 3063
- Kleinplasie Guest House****: 027-712 1141; www.kleinplasie.com
- Kokerboom Motel and Caravan Park**: 027-712 2685; www.namaqualandflowers.co.za
- Masonic Hotel***: 027-712 1505;

www.namaqualandflowers.co.za

- Mountain View Guest House****: 027-712 1438; www.mountview.co.za
- Namakwa Chalets: 027-718 1738
- Namaqua Game Lodge***: 027-718 1268; www.ngl.co.za
- Naries Namaqua Retreat*****: 021-930 4564; www.naries.co.za (photographic workshops)
- Old Mill Lodge****: 027-718 1705; www.oldmilllodge.com
- Olive Tree Guest House***: 027-718 1808; www.tot.co.za
- Rendezvous Overnight Rooms*: 027-712 1328
- Springbok Caravan Park***: 027-718 1584
- Springbok Hotel**: 027-712 1161; www.namaqualandflowers.co.za
- Springbok Lodge & Café**/***: 027-712 1321; www.springboklodge.com

Flower routes

The flowers in Springbok burst out of the most unlikely places. The verges along the N7 highway usually contain a bright spray of daisies, while the townships north of town are veritable wild flower extravaganzas with all sorts of colourful blooms transforming the plots into impromptu gardens. The people in the township are usually welcoming, as long as you approach with respect and ask permission before traipsing through their homes.

Outside of town, several farms also have large flower fields. Just remember that these are on private property, so respect closed gates and 'no trespassers' signs. The gravel roads around the Kokerboom Motel (about 5km south on the N7) are usually quite reliable in this regard. Another good oldfield display can be found about 12km down the Messelpad road towards Hondeklip Bay (accessed by turning off the N7 about 15km south of Springbok).

Goegap Nature Reserve (including the Hester Malan Wildflower Garden)

One of the most popular flower destinations in Springbok is the Goegap Nature Reserve, a conservation area covering about 15,000ha. It was first established when the Okiep Copper Company donated 4,600ha of agricultural land to the Cape provincial administration for the development of a wild flower reserve. This was duly opened in 1966, and named by Nico Malan in honour of his wife (which must have scored him some points at home). Later, the farm 'Goegap' (meaning 'waterhole') was bought by the CapeNature and Environmental Directorate and added to the reserve.

Today, this well-established facility has a tea garden and a nicely laid out succulent nursery with interpretive signs and attractive rock gardens. There is also a 13–17km gravel road which leads through a lovely landscape of boulders and koppies. It is easily accessible for most cars and is highly recommended. When the flowers are in bloom, the plains along this road are swathed in orange and yellow cloaks, making it very popular with photographers and TV crews. A total of 581 plant species have been recorded in the reserve, plus 45 mammal, 25 reptile, three amphibian and 94 bird species.

If you wish to explore further, the reserve has about 65km of rougher 4x4 roads for those with appropriate vehicles. There are also a couple of walking trails and mountain bike routes. Tourist facilities are rounded out by a picnic spot, campsites and a very reasonable self-catering guest house (R240pp for the first two people and R60 for each additional person).

To reach Goegap, head out of Springbok towards Pofadder. Just after you cross the N7, you'll find a turn-off for the tarred R355, which is marked for the reserve, the airport and the Springbok caravan park. A short distance later, you'll pass the golf course and country club. During flower season, the greens and fairways of this establishment are surrounded by delightful dollops of daisies. About 10km from Springbok, you'll see a turn-off for the Goegap Reserve. Head through the entrance gates and then keep going for another 5km on gravel to reach the reception. Entrance to the reserve is R15 per person and it's open from 08:00 to 16:00. If you keep going on the R355, the road turns to gravel and continues in a south-easterly direction to Platbakkies and, eventually, Loeriesfontein on the Bokkeveld plateau—*see* page 230.

Contacts:

- Goegap Nature Reserve 4x4 trails, hiking, camping and guest house***: 027-718 9906

Spektakel Pass and Kleinzee

From the centre of Springbok, follow signs for Kleinzee. This tarred road (R355) climbs a ridge, which offers great views over Springbok, before levelling out and heading west across the plateau. Here you'll see several large stands of flowers, especially in the township of Matjieskloof where the wild flowers bloom indiscriminately among the shacks and little houses. People here are very friendly and I took many pictures of the locals playing appreciatively in their flower gardens. It's good to see that the flowers are very egalitarian. They bloom everywhere and add a welcome dose of visual splendour to what would otherwise be a rather dull landscape.

From Matjieskloof, you can continue down the Spektakel Pass, which offers expansive views out over the hilly plains that lead to the sea. About 40km from

Springbok, there is a turn-off to the settlement of Kommagas. A beautiful drive of about 20km will bring you to this pleasant village with its colourful houses and friendly residents, most of whom work on the mine at Kleinzee. The road is tarred up to the village, before switching to gravel.

If you forsake Kommagas and continue straight on the R355 you will arrive at the De Beer's-owned mining town of Kleinzee (about 100km from Springbok). Please note that access to the town is restricted and, if you want to visit, you must arrange a permit through the Kleinzee Museum or the Houthoop Guest House. These should be organized several days in advance.

Once you have secured access to Kleinzee, you can go on a group tour through their mining operation, but no children or pregnant women are allowed due to the various security requirements. De Beers also offers several exciting 4x4 trails through their restricted territory, which take in pristine coastal scenery, shipwrecks and other 'natural' delights. These too must be booked in advance. Local birding guides are also available.

Please note that the tarred road along the coast between Kleinzee and Koningaas (which is marked on most road atlases) is restricted and not open to the public without prior permission.

Contacts:

- Kleinzee Museum, mine tours and 4x4 trails: 027-807 2999; www.coastofdiamonds.co.za
- Diamond Birding Routes: 011-789 1122; www.diamondroute.co.za
- Die Houthoop restaurant and guest house: 027-821 1669; www.houthoop.co.za
- Melkbospunt self-catering units and campsite: 027-807 2999; www.coastofdiamonds.co.za

The Messelpad and Wildeperdhoek Pass

From Springbok, drive about 15km south on the N7 and then take the turn-off marked for Hondeklip Bay and Soebatsfontein. This is the old Messelpad (Mason's road), which was once the main thoroughfare for the copper riders who transported ore from the Springbok mines to the harbour at Hondeklip. Today, this neglected gravel road cuts a tawny-coloured strip through the majestic mountains, and the extensive dry-stone retaining walls, which gave the road its name, can still be seen. It's a breathtaking drive, but you probably won't see many daisies, apart from a particularly impressive display on a farm about 12km from the highway. The succulent displays, however, are excellent.

After about 35km from Springbok, you'll see a small turn-off that leads back to the N7. This will return you to Springbok in a round trip of about 100km. However, the best part of the Messelpad is still to come, so continue driving until the road starts winding down a steep valley covered in succulents and aloes. This breathtaking stretch of gravel track then leads along the banks of the muddy Buffels River, which is lined with deep green trees, before rising up again and wending its way through the mountains once more. On this part of the road, you'll see a sign for the 'historic prison' that indicates the location of the old prisoners' compound, where the convict labour that built the pass was housed. Park your car in the demarcated area if you want to walk down to the prison and wander about the ruins.

The road then continues as the Wildeperdhoek Pass (pass of the wild horses) until it reaches a large cleft in the mountains. From here, there is an amazing view out over the Namaqua National Park below. Keep following the road as it clings to the sheer edge of the cliff face, with a precipitous drop-off to your left. The track now swoops along through the mountainous contours and descends to reach the shrub-covered plains. From here (about 55km from Springbok), you can either follow signs to the National Park reception area (which eventually connects to the N7 at Kamieskroon), or you can follow signs for Koningaas/Soebatsfontein and then turn north towards Kommagas to return to Springbok via Spektakel Pass. Either way, it's a worthwhile round trip of about 160km.

Okiep to Concordia

Head north from Springbok on the N7 for about 7km and then turn off towards Okiep. The name is Nama in origin and is said to mean either 'the place of the big tree', 'the little fountain' or 'brackish spring where copper occurs'. Either way, this was once the location of the richest copper mine in the world.

Okiep's mining heritage is still clearly in evidence. The old smelter smoke stack and Cornish pump are both extant and will interest those with a mineralogical bent. There are also the remnants of old ore bins, mine houses, granaries and stone-built churches built by the many Cornish tin miners and masons who came to Namaqualand during the copper boom.

Today, however, the mine is closed and the town is experiencing a dearth of employment opportunities. Nevertheless, the flowers bloom cheerfully along the roadsides and the school kids stroll amiably through the orange fields on their way home. Spend some time taking in the scene, then continue on the road out of town towards Concordia.

A short distance outside of Okiep, the road rises over a low saddle between two koppies and then dips across a shallow valley. The fields on either side of this road are often covered with swatches of yellow, white, purple and orange flowers. Unfortunately, a wire fence will prevent you from walking through the floral wonderland, but it's beautiful nonetheless.

Keep going for another 8km or so until you reach Concordia. This section of the road was once fortified by a row of block houses that were intended to keep the Boer forces at bay during the Anglo–Boer War of 1899–1902. However, they all fell to the Boers in 1902 and the invaders set themselves up at Concordia, from where they mounted the siege on Okiep. The remains of some of these block houses, as well as Fort Shelton, can still be seen.

Concordia is another former mission station and mine which has now become a humble settlement, made glorious for a few months each year by the spontaneous bounty of wild flowers. It is also the location of an outcrop of orbicular diorite—a rare rock texture that "is the result of granitoid magmas separating while in a fluid state, with one granite type forming ovoid 'orbs' showing concentric internal banding, within a ground mass of slightly different composition"—whatever that means …

From Concordia, you can continue on gravel roads to Carolusberg, the location of Simon van der Stel's original Copper Mountain mine shafts. Or just retrace your steps to Springbok via Okiep.

Contacts:

- Donkey cart rides: 083-945 6946
- Ferreira's B&B: 027-744 1427
- Narap Lodge**: 027-744 1000; www.okiep.co.za
- Okiep Country Hotel***: 027-744 1000; www.okiep.co.za
- Undulata Lodge***: 027-744 1000; www.okiep.co.za

Nababeep

From Springbok, head north on the N7 for about 7km then take the turn-off and drive for another 12km until you reach Nababeep. The name is Nama in origin, although the precise meaning is obscure. Depending on your pronunciation and your source, it is said to translate as 'the place where the giraffe drinks', 'the water behind the little hump or hill', 'where the rock is carried', 'rhinoceros place' or 'bad road'. Take your pick.

The main attraction here is the mining museum, an interesting facility with installations on the old copper mines that were once the lifeblood of the region. It also has photographic displays of the siege of Okiep and other documents from the period. A rusting old steam locomotive named Clara, which once plied the narrow-gauge railway between Okiep and Port Nolloth, has pride of place in the courtyard, along with several other bits of mining equipment. The museum's open Monday to Friday from 09:00 to 13:00, and every day until 17:00 during flower season.

Sadly, this once-prosperous mining village is now largely moribund. The houses are neat, however, and the hard, dry mountains that surround the town are starkly beautiful. And there are several eye-catching flower sites in the area, including one great location on the outskirts of town that combines kokerbooms and daisies to create a floral landscape with a uniquely local flavour. The nearby country club and golf course have been known to boast some truly overwhelming flower displays.

Contacts:

- Nababeep Mining Museum: 027-712 1321; www.springboklodge.com
- Skaaprivier Hiking Trail: 027-712 8035/6

Vioolsdrif and the Orange River

If you want to take a plunge into the Orange River, there are a number of riverside camps at Vioolsdrif (115km north of Springbok on the N7). You can also rent canoes or embark on a white-water rafting trip from here. If you have a 4x4, you can drive from Vioolsdrif, through the Helskloof Nature Reserve and into the Richtersveld Community Conservancy—*see* page 141.

Contacts:

- Amanzi Trails: 021-559 1573; www.amanzitrails.co.za
- Aquacade Camp: 027-761 8777; www.aquacade.co.za
- Aquatrails: 021-782 7982; www.aquatrails.co.za
- Bushwacked Adventures: 027-761 8953; www.bushwacked.co.za
- Dreamscape Restaurant: 027-761 8055
- Felix Unite: 021-404 1830; www.felixunite.com
- Fiddler's Creek Camp: 027-761 8953; www.bushwacked.co.za
- Ingwenya Tours: 082-773 8656; www.ingwenyatours.co.za
- Peace of Paradise Camp: 027-761 8968
- River Rafters: 021-975 9727; www.riverrafters.co.za
- Riverside Camp: 027-761 8677
- Ruff Overland Tours: 021-761 5222; www.ruffoverland.co.za
- Umkulu Tours: 021-853 7952; www.umkulu.co.za
- Water Wanderers: 021-976 3924; www.africanwaterwanderers.co.za
- Wild Thing Adventures: 021-556 1917; www.wildthing.co.za

Kamieskroon and surrounds

Once you've done your time at Springbok, head south on the N7 and drive for about 68km until you reach the little town of Kamieskroon. This is the centre of the Kamiesberg biome and offers access to several fascinating destinations. It is also the heart of the newly developed !Kimmies ('to gather') Route, a community-driven tourist initiative. An excellent brochure on the route and the region is available.

Kamieskroon itself is a rather messy little dorp consisting of about 100 unassuming homes arranged along a rough grid of gravel roads. It's a dozy, dreamy place and the enveloping mountains seem to cradle the town in a granitic embrace. In season, the gardens, yards and even the drainage ditches are made beautiful by sprays of wild flowers that poke up carelessly from the ground. I also found an adorable group of baby goats gambolling in an open plot next to one of the houses. But be careful—they nip!

In terms of tourist facilities, the town has an attractive church that's worth a look, a convenience store that sells petrol, and a couple of coffee shops (which may or may not be open when you visit). There is also a caravan park and campsite, and the local hotel offers photographic workshops that will teach you how to take better pics.

The first settlement in the Kamiesberg began in the 1860s on the farm Wilgenhoutskloof, located in a narrow valley about 8km north of present-day Kamieskroon. It was named Bowesdorp, after the local district surgeon Henry Bowe. Apparently, Bowe's son, Allan, went on to become a partner in the Fabergé jewellery firm—not bad for a country boy.

The Dutch Reformed congregation chose Bowesdorp as its Namaqualand headquarters in 1870, and a school, hostel, post office, hotel, shops and houses soon grew up around the small church. By 1924, however, the water supply had become insufficient for the growing population and the church was relocated to the nearby village of Kamieskroon. The eerie ruins of Bowesdorp can still be seen, slowly collapsing in their beautiful valley.

Contacts:

- Municipal office: 027-672 1627
- Hiking guide: 027-672 1762

- Cosy Mountain B&B: 027-672 1113
- De Hoek Guest House: 027-672 1632
- Gousblom B&B**: 027-672 1004
- Harry's Place***: 027-672 1856
- Kamieskroon B&B and Farm Accommodation: ** 027-672 1652
- Kamieskroom Hotel** and Caravan Park: 027-672 1614; www.kamieskroonhotel.com
- Rand Spaar Guest House**: 027-672 1604
- Verbé Farm Accommodation and Caravan Park: 027-672 1776

The Namaqua National Park
(including the Skilpad Wild Flower Garden)

A very popular stop on the flower-spotting route, the Namaqua National Park is a very special place indeed. The main entrance is located about 22km to the west of Kamieskroon, on good-quality gravel roads. Alternatively, it can be accessed from the slightly rougher Messelpad leading down from Springbok (follow signs for Kanariesfontein, or keep on the Messelpad and drive over the spectacular Wildeperdhoek Pass to enter the park from the rear).

The well-known Skilpad (Tortoise) Wild Flower Garden is situated next to the main gate. Originally established by the World Wildlife Fund for Nature in 1988, this is a reliable place to view some flower 'carpets' since it is located in a topographical bowl that effectively captures the moisture blowing in off the sea. The park works to keep this garden blooming by bringing in sheep and goats to graze away the secondary vegetation every couple of years.

A nice circular driving route around the Skilpad section has been laid out, which is suitable for all vehicles, and the park manager posts regular flower updates on the park website. Several walking trails through the flowers have also been established. The park contains about 3,000 recorded plant species and 1,500 of these can be found in the Skilpad section alone, so it's well worth a visit.

There is currently no camping in the park, and the only overnight accommodation is at the stunning Skilpad rest camp. This consists of four newly built chalets (one of which is wheelchair friendly) that look out over a breathtaking valley. It's an amazing location that offers unforgettable views in any season. The chalets are fully equipped for self-catering and can sleep up to four people (two single beds and a double sleeper couch).

There are no restaurants within the park, but there is a little hut called the 'Pannekoek Paleis' (Pancake Palace) on the road leading up to the main gate. The operating hours of this facility are somewhat erratic, however. There is also a private farm that abuts the main reception area with a farm stall which sells curios and snacks. In season, the local community sometimes operates a traditional *kookskerm* at the reception area that offers visitors a taste of traditional Nama-style cooking. Otherwise, bring along your own food and enjoy an al-fresco meal in the picnic area.

Educationally speaking, the park has a resource centre with good displays on the reserve's flora and fauna. Dormitory accommodation for school groups is available and this facility is used to educate local people about the park's conservation initiatives. Community outreach programmes are an integral part of the park's activities, and considerable progress has been made in this regard despite the scattered nature of the park's far-flung constituents.

Although the park is not rich in big game species, there are several iconic animals to be spotted within the reserve. These include the Namaqua speckled padloper (the world's smallest tortoise), the Namaqua dune molerat, the Bat-eared fox and the elusive caracal. Birders will be in their element with over 100 species recorded, and a breeding pair of Booted eagles which nest in the tall trees opposite the main reception block every year.

All in all, this beautiful reserve is one to watch. It is classed as a 'developing' park and, as such, there are lots of projects on the go. The first, and most important, task at hand is expanding the size of the current conservation area. This has been a relatively easy process as there are no land claims in the region and the land is reasonably cheap.

Accordingly, a large number of private farms have already been bought by SANParks and several others are under negotiation. De Beers, who own a huge chunk of un-mined territory along the coast between the Spoeg River mouth and the Groen River mouth, are also about to sell their land to the park, which will extend the reserve from the mountains all the way to the ocean.

So, from an original conservation area of just under 1,000ha, the park has grown to over 100,000ha. Soon, it will cover about 150,000ha and, when it's all done, it will be around 200,000ha, making it the third or fourth largest park in the country. The boundaries of the park will also be extended into the sea to create a large marine reserve of around one million hectares.

In the coming years, the park will be developing additional rest camps, campsites, walking trails and a five-day hiking trail along the coast. The establishment of horse-riding trails, mountain-bike trails and a multi-day 4x4 trail along the untouched shoreline are also being investigated. There are already a number of rough and ready 4x4 roads that lead through the park and these can be used, with permission, to visit the settlements of Soebatsfontein, Kommagas or the Wildeperdhoek Pass.

Bernard van Lente, the enthusiastic park manager,

is visibly excited by the park's potential. As he told me, the bio-diversity within the reserve is unequalled, the landscape is gorgeous and the local community is supportive. Here's hoping the park goes from strength to strength.

Contacts and details:

- www.SANParks.org/parks/namaqua
- Namaqua NP office: 027-672 1948
- SANParks central reservations: 012-428 9111
- Gates open from 08:00 to 17:00.
- No shop, restaurant or fuel is currently available in the NNP. Overnight guests must take along their own firewood.
- Skilpad Rest Camp rates (valid from Nov '08 to Oct '09, incl. VAT):
  - o Low season (1 November to 30 June)—R350 for first two people. R124 for each additional adult; R62 for each additional child under 12 (maximum of four people per unit)
  - o High season (1 July to 31 October)—R490 for first two people; R116 for each additional adult; R58 for each additional child under 12 (maximum of four people per unit)
- Daily conservation fee (valid from Nov '08 to Oct '09, incl. VAT):
  - o South African citizens and residents (with ID): R16 per person per day
  - o SADC nationals (with passport): R32 per adult; R16 per child under 12, per day
  - o Standard conservation fee: R64 per adult; R32 per child under 12, per day
  - o Holders of a valid Wild Card do not pay conservation fees

Leliefontein, Gamoep, Kharkams, Paulshoek and Rooifontein

To the east and south of Kamieskroon, there are a series of gravel roads that lead through the mountains. These make for an excellent day trip with great scenery, interesting towns and several good flower sites (at the right time of year). Many of the local farms also offer fantastic hiking and mountain-bike trails for those with the energy.

You can use these back roads to travel north to Springbok (via Gamoep and the gravel R355), south to Garies (via Leliefontein), or south-east to Loeriesfontein and Nieuwoudtville (via Platbakkies and the R355).

The town of Leliefontein, located in the middle of this under-explored area, is an interesting place to spend an hour or two. It was originally the kraal of a Nama chief, named Wildschut (wild shot) by the colonials. Unusually, the land was granted to the chief by Governor van Plettenberg in 1771, who turned down an application from a white farmer named Hermanus Engelbrecht in favour of the indigenous people.

Missionary work began here under the London Missionary Society in 1809, but an attack by the troublesome Jonker Afrikaner caused the station to be abandoned in 1811. In 1816, the chief asked for another station to be established and this challenge was taken up by Rev. Barnabas Shaw of the Wesleyan Missionary Society. Several church buildings were subsequently built and remain in use today, and the ceremonial sundial donated by Rev. Shaw still passes away the hours in the parsonage garden. Leliefontein is about 30km away from Kamieskroon.

But it wasn't all peace and light. During the Anglo–Boer war, the Afrikaner general Manie Maritz reputedly killed 35 Basters at Leliefontein, because he thought they were conspiring with the British. This massacre is little known today, but there is a plaque with the victims' names displayed in the Leliefontein church hall.

Paulshoek, a settlement high up in the heights of the Kamiesberg, is another nice place to visit. It has a cultural camp where visitors can enjoy traditional meals and spend the night in a *matjieshuis*, but prior booking is required. Paulshoek is about 70km away from Kamieskroon.

Rooifontein, about 50km away from Kamieskroon, offers hiking trails and a quiver tree forest with several unusual kokerboom houses. Hiking trails are also available at the nearby towns of Tweerivier, Klipfontein and Spoegrivier.

If you are so inclined, you can also visit the nearby town of Vaalputs, near Gamoep, which is South Africa's main nuclear waste disposal site. As the official website confidently proclaims, "in this area the annual evaporation exceeds the annual rainfall, which means that even if radioactivity should escape, it could not contaminate ground water". Well, that's reassuring.

The site goes on to allay fears by saying that "the Vaalputs site, allocated for the disposal of our low and intermediate-level waste, was chosen for its extreme isolation and dryness. This area is sufficient for storing the nuclear waste of three power stations the size of Koeberg for 40 years. The waste is stored in trenches 10m deep and radiation at the surface is almost at natural levels and does not constitute a health hazard. However, for safety reasons, the site is fenced off and monitored. On average 500 steel drums and 100 concrete drums are shipped to Vaalputs every year". Amazingly, visits to the site can be arranged—it sounds like a great place to take the kids.

The settlement of Kharkams, 25km to the south of Kamieskroon on the N7, is an excellent flower-spotting site. The name means 'gathering place of the Nama near abundant water' and was part of the old stock farmers' route between Leliefontein and Bethelsklip (an archaeological site which shows evidence of human occupation dating back over 800 years). The huge boulders at Bethelsklip were also used as a pulpit from where Rev. Shaw gave sermons to the local Khoikhoi. This has given the site its alternative name, 'Preacher's Rock'.

Contacts:

- Leliefontein municipal office: 027-672 1808
- Leliefontein info (Vera Engelbrecht): 027-672 1972
- Paulshoek municipal office: 027-541 1077
- Paulshoek info (Marianna Lot): 027-514 1540
- Paulshoek Cultural Camp and Sonop Guest House: 027-652 1014 or 027-541-1341
- Paulshoek Kliphoek campsite and Nama huts: 027-541 1048/55
- Pedroskloof B&B and hiking trails (Gamoep): 027-672 1666
- Rooifontein municipal office: 027-672 1221
- Rooifontein info (Cornelius Beukes): 027-672 1090
- Vaalputs Nuclear Waste Disposal Site: 027-712 2882; www.radwaste.co.za/vaalputs

Hondeklip Bay to Groen River mouth

The gravel roads that lead west from Kamieskroon to the coast give the adventurous traveller an opportunity to visit some remote and unusual places. This area can be accessed by following signs to Soebatsfontein and Hondeklip Bay from various points along the N7. Alternatively, for a more dramatic experience, drive through the Namaqua National Park towards Soebatsfontein and then wind your way along obscure back roads towards the sea.

The roads through the NNP are quite rough for a non-4x4, but it is a magnificent journey that trundles through several uninhabited river valleys before reaching the little dorp of Soebatsfontein (50km from Kamieskroon). The name translates as 'the spring of pleading', apparently because a shepherd was captured by Bushmen while drinking at the spring and had to beg for his life (which he lost).

Despite its rather melancholy name, this small cluster of houses exudes a gentle appeal. It has a post office, a couple of stores (where you can buy a refreshing cold drink to wash the dust from your throat) and a deeply abiding sense of peace and quiet. The short Boesman's Uitkyk (Bushman's Lookout) and Panorama hiking trails are close to the town. Permits and maps are available from the post office.

From here, continue south and east to Hondeklip Bay (although you will need to speak Afrikaans if you want to ask for directions). The road now leads through an undulating landscape, dotted with koppies and rocky outcrops. Occasional farmsteads offer the only visible reminder of human occupation, while herds of goats and sheep can be seen grazing gracefully on the shrubby slopes.

About 30km south of Soebatsfontein, you'll come to the Spoeg River (Spittle or Saliva River) which bubbles between small islands, covered with bright spurts of spring flowers. You'll now head east, past the ruins of the briefly-prosperous village of Wallekraal, towards Hondeklip Bay. The river soon veers off to the left where it enters the sea near the Spoeg River Caves, but this area can only be reached as part of a 4x4 trail (ask for details at the Namaqua National Park or Die Honnehok guest house).

As you continue on the main road towards Hondeklip Bay, you'll pass a turn-off for the De Beer's controlled mining area of Koningaas. The presence of mine dumps and high fences indicate that this is a restricted area, and you should watch out for the heavy industrial vehicles that lumber along this part of the road. Finally, about 90km from Kamieskroon, you'll reach the sea at Hondeklip Bay.

Maybe it was the grey, inclement weather, but my first impressions of Hondeklip Bay were not good. The sea was angry, the sky was brooding and the ramshackle collection of houses, plonked haphazardly in the sandy plain, were singularly unlovely. But then the sun came out and the atmospheric surroundings slowly won me over.

Hondeklip Bay (Dog Stone Bay) gets its name from a small, canine-shaped rock that looks out to sea. The 'ear' of this formation was chopped off in the 1850s and sent to Cape Town as the emblem of the spurious 'Dog's Ear Copper Company', which only succeeded in fleecing investors of their money before closing down. The rock was further damaged in 1970 when lightning struck off the 'nose', leaving behind a rather amorphous blob of gneiss. The rock is situated behind the police station on the edge of town.

Although this was once a bustling copper port, Hondeklip Bay is now a rather desolate place that is notable mainly for its wild, rocky coastline, excellent fishing and rusting shipwrecks that sprawl across the boulders like enormous steel carcasses. However, the best reason to visit Hondeklip Bay is to meet 'The Villain'. Allow me to explain …

The Villain is a local artist who paints 'oils, portraits, seascapes, landscapes, flowers, animals, others'. His real name is Dion and he describes himself as an adrenalin junkie. Unfortunately, this penchant for excitement got him involved in armed robbery and he was sent to jail for ten years. In prison, he started painting as a hobby and, when he got out, he and his wife packed everything they owned into an old Ford Sapphire station wagon and travelled around the country, looking for a place they could call home. One day, a couple of years ago, they arrived at Hondeklip Bay and decided to stay.

Now, the self-effacing Villain lives in a tiny shack in what he calls the *plakkerkamp* (squatter camp) on the outskirts of town. An adjacent caravan serves as his studio where he paints compulsively, either from memory or by copying images from the pages of magazines and newspapers. It must be a very meagre and difficult life, but he has embraced his destiny with an honesty and enthusiasm that is quite inspiring.

So, as you drive along the dusty road on the edge of town, keep an eye out for the rows of brightly coloured paintings that are neatly displayed on the sandy ground in front of his home. The Villain's subjects range from attractive flower-themed landscapes to wildlife scenes to gothic hard-rock icons to portraits of celebrities (which include an eclectic collection of luminaries such as Cher, Sophia Loren, Catherine Zeta-Jones and Amor Vittone). Oh, and he also likes to paint nude women, who pose provocatively as they gaze out into the veld.

The residents of Hondeklip Bay seem quite bemused by the Villain and his art, especially his nudes. Some of the people I spoke to said that he doesn't cause any trouble and has become a valuable part of the community. This is certainly true—he is becoming something of a local celebrity, attracting tourists to this out-of-the-way town.

In return, the Villain loves Hondeklip Bay. He said he could live here for 20 years and still see new things. He loves the sunrises, he loves the landscape, and he loves the flowers that bloom every spring. So, drop in on the unlikely art gallery and pick up a painting or two. Prices range from R50 to R100 for his pretty miniatures, while his larger images and 'masterpieces' go for several hundred rand.

I was fascinated by the Villain. He is so open, passionate and positive about his work and his life that it made my prosaic neuroses seem petty and irrelevant by comparison. Incidentally, he calls himself the Villain not because of his jail sentence per se, but because he wasn't allowed out for his mother's funeral. This, he says, made him feel like a real criminal and his pseudonym is intended as a tribute to his departed mum. But it's his tangible sense of pride that makes him such a profound character. Living in his tiny shack, painting in his little dark studio, the Villain doesn't have it easy, but he's happy with his considerable accomplishments.

In terms of accommodation, there are a couple of private guest houses in Hondeklip Bay and the local council is busy establishing a community-run facility. I would recommend Die Honnehok as a good place to stay. Run by Attie and Elise, a wonderful couple who know the area well, it's a friendly establishment and their well-stocked bar is enlivened by an ice-eating parrot which likes to play with a metallic beaker. And their jaffles filled with springbok meat are delicious.

Hondeklip Bay is also a rich fossil site and several teeth from the prehistoric Megalodon shark have been unearthed along the beach. Crayfishing is popular in season (if you have a permit) and there are a number of 4x4 roads along the untouched coastline. So, check out this wind-tossed little settlement and experience the Namaqualand coast at its most unusual.

As you leave Hondeklip, you can either head back towards the N7, or you can turn off to the south and head for the farms of Sarriesam and Soutfontein. This road is blocked by an interminable series of farm gates, but the route offers a truly unembellished insight into the life of this rural community. Sparks of wild flowers tickle the eyes, with shrubs and succulents doing their utmost to attract their respective pollinators.

This part of the country is associated with the strange and sinister story of Robey Leibbrandt. He was a South

African boxing champ who fell under Hilter's spell during the 1936 Olympic Games in Berlin. After the competition was over, Leibbrandt returned to Germany for training in espionage. He was then sent back to SA to assassinate General Jan Smuts and establish a new regime that was sympathetic to the Nazis. He secretly put ashore somewhere in the vicinity of Hondeklip Bay and slowly worked his way down to Cape Town before moving to Pretoria. Amazingly, Leibbrandt came very close to achieving his goals but was brought down by his arrogance and stubborn refusal to follow the orders of his German masters.

Anyway, after about 70km, the obscure farm roads reach an intersection with the 'main' gravel road to Groen (Green) River mouth. This part of the road has some fantastic wild flower displays, but watch out for the deep cracks that creep across the roadway. If you hit one of these crevices at speed, you could flip the car or twist an axle—neither of which would be pleasant.

The Groen River mouth itself is apparently beautiful but I didn't see it for myself because, when I was there, the Groen River was running very high over a low-level causeway and I chickened out from making the crossing. There are no facilities at Groen River mouth, but you can camp here if you are self-sufficient. Apparently, there is a long-standing community of hippie squatters living at the mouth, but the local municipality is currently trying to move them out.

When you are all done exploring this remote and fascinating part of the world, turn to the east and head back towards Garies and the N7.

Contacts:

- Hondeklip Bay Municipal Office: 027-692 3066
- Die Honnehok: 027-692 3041; www.hondeklip.co.za
- The Megalodon Self Catering: 083-286 7080

- Visbeen Lodge: 027-692 3993; www.visbeenlodge.co.za
- Noup Guest House and Koningaas Caravan Park: 027-807 7510; www.coastofdiamonds.co.za
- Flower Power Farm: 021-854 7417; www.flowerpowerfarm.co.za
- Groen River info: 027-531 1014

Garies

The little town of Garies (pronounced with a hard 'g') is another popular stop on the Kamiesberg flower route. It is named from the Nama word for 'couch-grass' *(Cynodon dactylon)*, which grows in the river. The town was first established in 1845 when the land was given to the Dutch Reformed Church by the owner of the farm Goedeverwagting.

Apart from flower-spotting, visitors can occupy themselves by tackling a number of walking and hiking trails in the area. The nearby Letterklip on the Studers Pass gravel road is another place to visit. This collection of boulders is famous for some very old graffiti that was made when Simon van der Stel wrote his name on the rocks, way back in 1685. Other travellers continued the tradition and, during the Anglo–Boer War, British soldiers carved their names and regimental insignia into the walls while they were hiding out from the Boer commandos.

Contacts:

- Municipal office: 027-652 8000
- Tourism info (flower season only): 027-652 1220
- Agama Tented Camp: 082-770 2955; www.agamacamp.co.za
- Garies Hotel & Restaurant*: 027-652 1042
- Garies municipal campsite: 027-652 8000
- Sophie's Guest House**: 027-652 1069

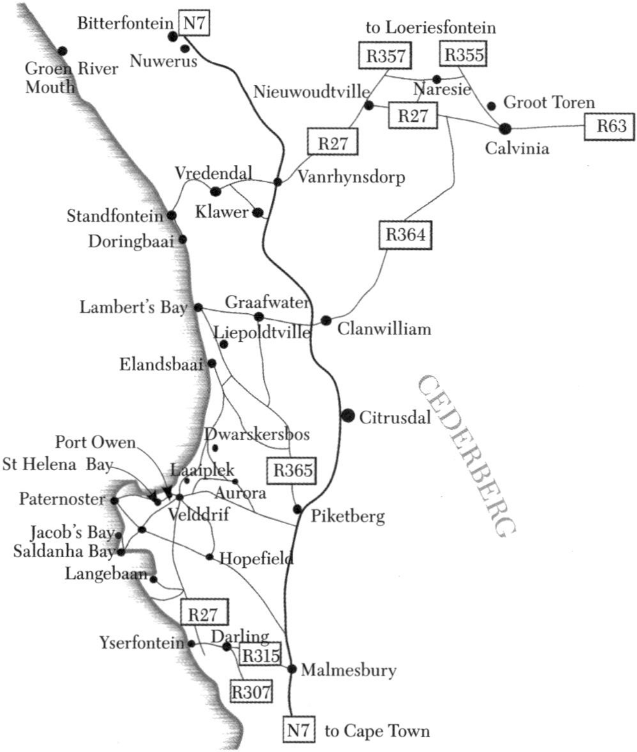

Vanrhynsdorp

From Garies, the N7 leads south, past the huge shunting yard at Bitterfontein, where the railway from Cape Town terminates. Bitterfontein is also the centre of the little-known Hardeveld tourist route, which takes you through the small villages of Stofkraal, Molsvlei, Rietpoort, Putsekloof, Kliprand and Nuwerus. For more information call the Bitterfontein tourism office on 027-642 7335 or see the website, www.south-north.co.za.

Continuing south into the pebbly plains of the Knersvlakte, you'll finally reach Vanrhynsdorp (150km from Garies). This is the centre of the Matzikama

Municipal District and tourist region, which stretches down to the coast and incorporates the towns of Doringbaai, Ebenhaezer, Klawer, Lutzville, Papendorp, Strandfontein, Vanrhynsdorp and Vredendal. The Olifants River Wine Route runs through this area, which should entertain bibulous visitors. Vanrhynsdorp is also the gateway to the Bokkeveld plateau and Nieuwoudtville, which lie to the east—*see* page 221.

But before you rush up the pass to see the famous flowers of Nieuwoudtville, spend some time in Vanrhynsdorp. It is a pretty town built around a relatively grand church. There's a good tourist info centre and a well-appointed museum that's worth a wander through. And next door is the Old Gaol complex, which has a couple of enticing coffee and craft shops. The succulent nursery, just out of town, is another popular attraction.

Lovers of retro-electronics should also pop into the Latsky Radio Museum—a private collection of old valve radios that is lovingly curated by a loquacious ex-school teacher. It's open every day except Sundays during flower season, and by appointment only during the rest of the year. It's the kind of place my eccentric Uncle Morris would love, but he doesn't like to leave his house.

Do note, during flower season this entire region is full, full, full. Every room for miles around is booked up and there's a mania in the air, with all the people frantically asking, "Where're the flowers? Where're the flowers?" Book ahead or face sleeping in the car.

But it's not just about the flowers. There are several important wetlands along the coast and nature-lovers can spend many happy days driving through the Matzikama. Accordingly, there are several conservation initiatives underway, which include the Knersvlakte Biosphere Reserve and the emerging Matzikama Eco-Park. For more information, check out the excellent tourist brochures, which also contain details about various cultural and historical sites, 4x4 routes, local guides and dining options in the Matzikama. And don't forget about the big annual events such as the succulent show at Vanrhynsdorp, the Maskam Rally, the West Coast Air Carnival, the cultural 'Rittelfees' and the agricultural show.

There are two highly rated multi-day hikes in the area. These are the Swart Tobie Hiking Trail along the coast and the Crayfish Hiking Trail.

Contacts:

- Vanrhynsdorp Tourist Info: 027-219 1552
- Vredendal Tourism Info: 027-201 3376
- www.olifantsriverwineroute.com
- www.matzikamamun.co.za
- Kokerboom Succulent Nursery: 027-219 1062
- Old Gaol arts and crafts: 072-149 7716
- Latsky Radio Museum: 027-219 1032
- Swart Tobie Hiking Trail: 0861-522 262; www.jacanacollection.co.za
- Crayfish Hiking Trail: www.south-north.co.za

Doringbaai accommodation:

- Benguela Lodge: 027-215 1539; www.south-north.co.za
- Die Anker Guest House and Restaurant: 027-215 1016; www.doringbaai.com
- Doringbaai Guest House: 083-632 2205
- Thornbay Accommodation: 027-215 1333; http://home.telkomsa.net/thornbay

Klawer accommodation:

- Africa Accommodation: 027-216 1513; www.matzikamamun.co.za
- Idma@Kapel wedding venue: 027-216 1419; www.idma.co.za
- Klawer B&B: 027-216 1544
- Oasis Country Lodge: 027-216 1520; www.oasiscountrylodge.co.za

Lutzville/Koekenaap accommodation:

- 22 Nama Karoo: 027-217 2223; www.22namakaroo.co.za
- Flowerland: 027-217 2130
- Hanzu: 027-217 1571
- Komkans Guest Farm: 027-644 4015; www.matzikamamun.co.za
- Lutzville Hotel: 027-217 1513
- The Golden Grape: 027-217 1099; www.thegoldengrape.co.za

Strandfontein accommodation:

- Ebenhaeser Guest House: 084-710 7970; www.south-north.co.za
- Jeanrienette: 027-215 1522; www.matzikamamun.co.za
- Papendorp Guest House: 027-215 1404; www.south-north.co.za
- Sol-Y-Mar: 082-718 2104
- Strandfontein Resort: 027-215 1169
- Strandfontein Self Catering Units: 027-219 1810
- VCSV Youth Camp: 027-215 1666
- West Coast Eco Tours & Accommodation: 027-215 1727; www.strandfontein.co.za

Vanrhynsdorp accommodation:

- Asbos Lapa: 027-219 1510
- Bo-tuin: 027-219 2721
- Gifberg Holiday Farm: 027-219 1555
- Griekwa Ratelgat: 027-213 5472; www.ratelgat.co.za
- Heldervue: 072-453 6766
- La Rochelle: 027-219 2578; www.matzikamamun.co.za
- Lombards: 027-219 1424
- Matzikamma Backpackers: 027-219 2817; www.matzikamamun.co.za
- Namaqualand Country Lodge: 027-219 1633; www.namaqualodge.co.za
- Nouroe: 027-219 1051; www.matzikamamun.co.za

- Suttridge Guest Farm: 027-219 1889
- Uitvlug: 027-219 1513
- Van Rhyn Guest House***: 027-219 1429; www.vanrhyngh.co.za
- Vanrhynsdorp Caravan Park: 027-219 1287; www.matzikamamun.co.za
- Vanrhynsdorp Self Catering: 027-219 1810
- Waterval Resort: 027-219 1005; www.watervalresort.co.za

Vredendal accommodation:

- Alfalfa: 082-801 3730
- Anna-Marie se Plek: 027-213 1942; www.matzikamamun.co.za
- Bergkraal 4x4: 027-213 2500; www.bergkraal4x4.co.za
- Chris-Mar Accommodation: 027-213 1594; www.matzikamamun.co.za
- In Weer: 027-213 1734; www.matzikamamun.co.za
- Kat-ma-koep: 027-213 4458; www.katmakoep.co.za
- Klein Aber Mein: 027-213 3354; www.matzikamamun.co.za
- Melkboomsdrift Lodge****: 027-217 2624; www.westcoaststay.co.za
- Onderhoek: 027-213 2326; www.matzikamamun.co.za
- River Lodge***: 027-213 1695; www.riverlodge.rsa.nu
- Ruanda Guest House: 027-213 1125; www.ruandaguesthouse.co.za
- Schreuder Accommodation: 027-213 1432
- Tharrakamma****: 027-213 5709; www.tharrakamma.co.za
- The Manor: 072-511 1893; www.themanor.rsa.nu
- Voorsorg Guest House: 027-213 2243; www.voorsorg.co.za
- Vredendal Caravan Park: 027-213 2924
- Westhouse: 027-213 2912; www.matzikamamun.co.za

Nieuwoudtville

As you head east on the R27 out of Vanrhynsdorp, the road runs dead-straight over the Knersvlakte towards the sheer wall of the Bokkeveld mountains. At the foot of the massif, you'll start to climb up the steep Van Rhyn's Pass, built by the legendary road builder Thomas Bain in 1880.

This short but dramatic pass offers fantastic views out over the scarred plains below, especially if you are stuck behind a slow-moving truck and have the time to look around. A couple of sharp hairpin bends at the top of the pass will take you over the summit and onto the Bokkeveld plateau. Unfortunately, at the time of writing the spectacular viewpoint at the top of the pass was closed for unspecified reasons, but one hopes that it will be re-opened soon.

From here, it is a short drive into the beautiful village of Nieuwoudtville (50km from Vanrhynsdorp). This is considered to be the heartland of the Namaqualand flower route and, in a good year, the displays in town and on the surrounding farms are nothing short of miraculous.

The town itself was established in 1897 on a piece of land bought from a farmer named Nieuwoudt. This part of the plateau had been used by white settlers since the mid-1700s because the sandstone rock layers make for good drainage during the wet winter months and allow life-giving springs to bubble up to the surface. The sandstone also provided excellent building material for the charming collection of small houses that began to spring up in the settlement. The gorgeous neo-gothic church in the centre of town dates back to 1906 and farmers from all over the plateau used to gather in the large piece of open ground around the church for their regular *nagmaal* (communion) ceremonies.

Many of the old sandstone homes that once housed traders and townsfolk have now been converted into charming B&Bs or self-catering units for tourists—the new lifeblood of the region. Accommodation is also offered on various farms in the area, and there are two campsites in town. But book ahead as things get very busy over the spring season.

Indeed, during this peak time, Nieuwoudtville throws off its sleepy demeanour and turns into a bustling little metropolis. Tour buses chug up and down the main streets, hundreds of people flit in and out of the tourism info centre, and visitors from all over the country meet in the coffee shops and restaurants to compare notes. There are also regular talks by experts, hosted by the local Eco-group, while the Indigo Development organization offers bio-diversity activities for groups and individuals. They also train up local community members as flower guides and, if you're a novice flower spotter, hiring one of these guides is highly recommended as they will make the experience so much more rewarding.

If you can't make it here for the big spring event, don't despair. Apart from the annual, short-lived displays of daisies and succulents, Nieuwoudtville is the self-proclaimed 'bulb capital of the world'. This is because it has an amazingly high number of different geophyte species, which bloom at various times of the year starting in March. The renowned bulb and clivia nursery, run by local enthusiast and regional boffin, Hendrik van Zijl, can be found on the outskirts of town. In the evenings, Mr van Zijl can usually be found at his Smidswinkel Restaurant, which offers delicious meals and interesting botanical displays to divert diners. Otherwise, check out his Nieuwoudtville.co.za website for more details.

But, despite the appeal of bulbs and Brunsvigias, most of us still want to know, "Where can we see the daisies?" Well, the small (150ha) wild flower reserve to the west of town is an obvious spot. This was established in 1974 to protect the district's flora, and it contains several endemic species, but the displays are somewhat erratic. Nevertheless, an unstaffed info centre does have educational display boards that describe the complex combination of climate, soil, rock and vegetation types that are present on the Bokkeveld plateau, creating the unique conditions that support the region's unparalleled botanical diversity.

Nearby, the 4,776ha Oorlogskloof Nature Reserve is another popular natural attraction, with a campsite, chalets and 146km of fantastic hiking trails that run along the edge of the mountains and down into the valleys. But bear in mind that this reserve is dominated by fynbos which grows in the poor quality soil that is found along the dry rim of the escarpment. So, not too many daisies here …

The good news is that, depending on the rains, patches of spring flowers can be seen just about everywhere. Farm fields, roadside verges and open plots in the town often boast beautiful splotches of colour, so all you have to do is keep your eyes open. Nevertheless, there are a few special places where you really do get to see the full grandeur of the annual flower 'carpets'. But remember, it's not just about the number of flowers, it's also about the number of species. So seek out the rarer endemics and look beyond the fields of *gous blomme* (marigolds), *katsterte* (cat's tails) and *pietsnot* (roughly translated as Pete's boogers, a singularly unlovely name that might refer to the plant's slimy sap).

A self-drive flower tour

Although conditions change all the time, here is a reasonably reliable two-day itinerary that should take you to most of the important sites. Before you set out, however, get a detailed map from the info office and ask around to find out where the flowers are blooming at the moment.

First, drive south out of town on the gravel road towards Matjieskloof farm. En route, you will see the newly established 6,300ha Hantam Wild Flower Reserve, which opened in January 2008. This is the ninth botanical garden in South Africa and operates under the auspices of the National Biodiversity Institute.

The garden is located on Glenlyon farm and currently offers walks and guided bus tours in season. Future developments include a gift shop, a research library and a coffee shop. Admission is R10 per person in season and free during the rest of the year.

A bit further on, you'll see a sign for the glacial pavement. Park your car and walk about 200m to see the grooves and striations carved into the rock floor by grinding glaciers that passed over this region 300 million years ago. Then continue on the road until you come to Matjieskloof (about 20km from Nieuwoudtville).

Matjieskloof is a marvel. In a good year, the fields are literally blanketed in flowers of every shape, size, colour and description. Apart from the sheer number of plants in bloom, get close to the ground and see how many different species you can identify. It's a mind-boggling display of bio-diversity at its most rampant.

To facilitate your exploration, the farm owners have established a series of gravel roads that lead through the property. This circular route is suitable for all types of vehicles and you will happily spend several hours driving slowly through the fields, stopping constantly to take pictures. Unfortunately, you won't be alone and the road can get quite congested with all the rubber-necking going on.

Just be patient and be careful where you drive. There aren't too many places where you can pull over and you don't want your tyres to crush the flowers (or a crouching photographer). If it's been raining, be especially cautious as the gravel tracks get churned up by the heavy traffic and it's easy to get stuck in the muddy patches. I volunteered to tow out one driver in a VW Polo, and all I got for my heroics was a burnt-out clutch.

Entrance to the Matjieskloof farm is about R10 per person. They also have a farm stall and a restaurant, which is housed in the historic thatched buildings at the entrance gate. Charming tractor-drawn wagon trips through the farm are also on offer.

When you're done, turn around and head back to town. I would suggest that you chill for the rest of the day as the flowers start to close around 15:00 and it's pointless to try and cram too much into a single outing. So, wander the village streets, check out the church, grab a bite to eat, enjoy sundowners on the stoep of your guest house—that sort of thing.

Around 10:00 the next morning, once the flowers have started opening, leave town and drive north towards Loeriesfontein on the tarred R357. About 7km along this road, you'll see the turn-off for the Nieuwoudtville waterfall. This is a spectacular sight, where the Doring River cuts through a sandstone rim to drop 100m into a huge natural amphitheatre.

Then, continue north until you see the sign for Gannabos (about 20km from Nieuwoudtville). Turn right onto this gravel road and drive for about a kilometre until you reach the Quiver Tree Forest. This is a remarkable colony of kokerbooms that cover the craggy, north-facing slopes of a koppie. The farmer who owns this land says he doesn't mind the tourists coming to visit, but does ask that they stick to the demarcated roads and clean up after themselves.

You can now either turn back or keep driving on this gravel road for another 20km until you see the turn-off to the left marked for 'Loeriesfontein and Cavinia oor Naressie' (going straight will take you back to Nieuwoudtville via Nuweplaas). Follow the Naressie road and try not to gawp at the millions of flowers that you'll see sprouting from the roadside and blooming up the mountain sides.

About 15km further along, you'll come to an intersection with the gravel R355. Left will take you up to Loeriesfontein; right will take you down to Calvinia. Turn right and drive for about 5km until you see the turn-off for the AP2286 to Toren. This is quite a long detour that leads through some very rugged mountains to the farm of Groot Toren, which often has excellent flower displays. A road has been laid out around this farm, and I found the setting to be superb. You will then have to turn around and drive back to the R355. The entire detour, including a drive around the farm, is about 45km but allow for a couple of hours.

Once you're back on the R355, drive for another 20km to reach the lovely Hantam Karoo town of Calvinia. Do note that there is nowhere to get food or drinks between Nieuwoudtville and Calvinia, so stock up before you leave on your trip or prepare to arrive in Calvinia parched and hungry. When you're done exploring this historic town, turn right on the tarred R27 and return to Nieuwoudtville (a distance of about 70km).

The total distance of this round trip is about 200km and the route will take you most of the day, but you won't be disappointed. So grab your camera and all the memory cards you can find, and get out there. If your timing is good, I can quite confidently predict that your flabber will be well and truly gasted.

Contacts:

- Nieuwoudtville Tourism Info: 027-218 1336
- www.nieuwoudtville.co.za
- www.nieuwoudtville.com
- Indigo Development and Change: 027-218 1148; www.indigo-dc.org
- Matjieskloof farm: 027-218 1217

- Glen Lyon Botanical Garden: 027-218 1200; www.sanbi.org

Accommodation:
- A La Belle Étoile: 027-218 1274
- Boereplaas: 027-218 1217
- Bokmakierie: 027-218 1285
- Cloudskraal: 082-789 0310
- Elmarie Spangenberg: 083-234 7503
- Greylingshof Guest House: 027-218 1182
- Griet Farm Accommodation: 027-268 1277
- Groenrivier Guest House: 027-218 1122/1265
- Hantamsdrift: 027-482 2807
- Helena's Self-catering Units: 027-218 1078
- Kleinplaas Farm: 027-218 1270; www.kleinplaas.com
- Kliprivier Farm: 027-218 1204
- Leeuriet Farm: 027-218 1131
- Lokenburg Farm: 027-218 1317
- Mensieskraal Farm: 083-626 6033
- Nieuwoudtville Hotel 027-218 1046
- Nieverderrie: 083-650 9914
- Nuweplaas Farm: 027-218 1248
- Olive Caravan Park: 027-218 1535
- Oorlogskloof Farm: 027-218 1214
- Oorlogskloof Nature Reserve and hiking trails: 027-2181 1159
- Ouma Khan se plaas: 027-218 1061
- Papkuilsfontein: 027-218 1246; www.papkuilsfontein.co.za
- Pepper Tree Cottage: 027-218 1125
- Piet se plek: 083-650 9914
- Rabe: 027-218 1139
- Rooidakhuis: 027-218 1061/1125
- Roosmaryn Guest House: 027-218 1056
- Sandra: 027-218 1277
- Sewefontein Farm: 027-218 1501

- Sonweelde Guest House: 027-218 1338
- Swiss Villa: 027-218 1347
- Trekpad Farm: 027-218 1205
- Twin Gecko: 027-218 1159
- Uncle Tom's Cabin: 083-609 8448
- Van Zijl Guest Houses and Smidswinkel Restaurant: 027-218 1535; www.nieuwoudtville.co.za
- Vlekkie se plekkie: 082-770 5438
- Wa-pad Gastehuis: 027-218 1387
- Willemsrivier Farm: 027-218 1205
- Ystervark Farm: 027-218 1522

Calvinia

Ecologically speaking, Calvinia is at the far eastern edge of the Namaqualand flower route. Nevertheless, it forms one corner of the triangle between the towns of Nieuwoudtville and Loeriesfontein and, as such, is drawn into the tourism sphere of the Bokkeveld plateau.

Besides, it's a lovely little place. Lying at the foot of the Hantam mountains, this is a classic Karoo dorp with tin-roofed houses, stoeps dripping with broekie-lace metalwork, and an impressive neo-gothic sandstone church. The town was founded in 1851 and named after John Calvin, the protestant reformer who set the puritanical tone for South Africa's dominant religious discourse during the apartheid years.

Today, Calvinia is one of SA's largest wool-producing centres. It also has one of the country's biggest post boxes, converted from an old water tower by the Chamber of Commerce in 1995. Mail that is posted in the box gets franked with a special flower stamp. This kind of quirky humour is similarly evident in the joyous Calvinia Vleisfees (meat festival) which takes place every year towards the end of August. So, if you like boerewors, chops and *langarm* dancing, don't miss this celebration of all things carnivorous.

In terms of activities, the nearby Akkerdam Nature Reserve is the place to go if you want to do some hiking, and several farms offer 4x4 routes. For those who are historically minded, a visit to the Calvinia museum is a must. This well-run facility is located in the old Jewish synagogue, which was built in 1920 and donated to the town in 1967 when the once-prominent Jewish community had dwindled. The museum can give you a good walking-tour map that will guide you on a pleasant stroll past all the important sites in town, including several of the original town houses that were built over 150 years ago.

Contacts:

- Calvinia Tourism Info: 027-341 1043/8100
- www.calvinia.co.za
- www.vleisfees.co.za

Accommodation:

- Berghaven Farm: 027-341 2220
- Biesra: 027-341 1076
- Brakfontein Farm: 027-341 1651
- Calvinia Caravan Park: 027-341 1871
- Calvinia Hotel: 027-341 2579
- Carmel Villa B&B: 027-341 1446
- Cobussegat (4x4 routes): 027-341 2326
- Commercial Hotel: 027-341 1020
- Groenewald Guest House: 027-341 1188
- Hantamhof and Rebunie: 027-341 1242
- Hantam Hotel**: 027-341 1512
- Hantam Huis****: 027-341 1606
- Huis van Rhyn: 027-341 1067
- Jo's Guest Rooms: 027-341 2247
- Katryns B&B: 027-341 1506
- Die Kliphuis Backpackers: 027-341 2154
- Klipwerf Guest House: 027-341 1126

- Maku-tuis: 083-227 1062
- Matjiesfontein Farm: 027-341 2203
- Middelpos Hotel: 027-341 2507
- NDM Woonstel: 027-341 8100 027
- Pella Karee: 027-341 2850
- Pionierslot Guest House and Die Blou Naartjie restaurant: 027-341 1263
- Rolbos B&B: 027-341 1666
- Rosa Villa: 027-571 2798
- Steenkamp Guest House: 027-341 1110
- Toekoms (4x4 routes): 027-341 2201

Loeriesfontein

The other town on the Bokkeveld plateau is Loeriesfontein, a peaceful place that is well known for its wild flower displays. It also has an unusual windmill museum—one of only two in the world (the other one is in America).

A good day trip for 4x4 enthusiasts leads from Nieuwoudtville to Loeriesfontein (64km) and down 'The Hell' pass. This rough track descends the escarpment and then runs south along the Knersvlakte to rejoin the tarred R27 at the foot of Van Rhyn's Pass. The journey will take you through some dramatic scenery and three distinct vegetation zones: Fynbos, Renosterveld and Succulent Karoo. It's a round trip of roughly 150km.

Contacts:

- Loeriesfontein Tourism Info: 027-662 1115/1159
- Windmill Museum: 027-662 1023
- Boesmanland Pub & Grill 027-662 1119
- Jobskraal Farm: 027-662 1069
- Loeriesfontein Hotel 027-662 1001
- Noute Farm: 027-662 1069
- Tinktinkie: 027-662 1204
- Viooltjie Guest House: 083-218 4846

The Cederberg

Continuing south from Nieuwoudtville, you will finally leave the Northern Cape and Namaqualand to enter the province of the Western Cape. Here, the displays of flowering succulents and annuals are supplemented by the restios (reeds), ericas and proteas that characterize the Fynbos biome. This latter vegetation type can be roughly divided into the dunefields of the Strandveld along the west coast, the endangered Renosterveld of the Swartland around Darling and the mountain Fynbos of the Cederberg.

We'll start with the unsurpassed visual drama of the Cederberg. To enter this mountainous wonderland from the Bokkeveld plateau, you can drive to Vanrhynsdorp and pick up the N7 highway south to the town of Clanwilliam—the gateway to the Cederberg. This route is about 130km. Alternatively, you can drive south from Nieuwoudtville on the gravel R364 over the lovely Botterkloof Pass to gain direct access into the sandstone fastness of these amazing mountains. This road eventually reaches the town of Clanwilliam after 150km, and you'll find the turn-off to the flower-rich Biedouw valley en route.

The weird, wind-blown rock formations of the Cederberg are beautiful in any season. Nature lovers will be entranced and could spend many days hiking through the cliffs, swimming in the rivers or exploring the exhilarating landscape in a 4x4. The birding is excellent, the campsites are stunning and there is even a winery (the highest in South Africa) for your viticultural delight. Stargazers may also want to check out the privately owned Cederberg Astronomical Observatory. Other highlights include the Wolfberg Cracks and Arch, the Maltese Cross, the Stadsaal caves, the Bushman paintings, and jumping off the precipitous rocks into the deep river at Malgat.

Unfortunately, in previous decades, much of the land in this wilderness region was degraded by unsustainable farming practices. The indigenous Clanwilliam cedar tree, which gives the mountains their name, was particularly hard hit and is currently a threatened species. Thankfully, these unique uplands are now under the protection of the Cederberg Conservancy, a collaborative organization that is working with private land owners and CapeNature to protect and restore the Cederberg's natural splendour.

In terms of flowers, the most reliable place to see them in bloom is the Biedouw valley, close to the picturesque mission station of Wupperthal. But do note that a hot Berg wind could wither this colony within a couple of days, so try to check ahead before you go.

Even though it generally blooms in the summer months, the rare Snow protea *(Protea cryophila)* is also worth a brief mention. This narrowly endemic plant is found only along the snow line of the Cederberg in a small belt, about 25km in length. It grows in the cracks between bare rocks and can survive in extreme cold and blistering heat, sometimes living for up to 70 years. The white, furry flowers take a full year to open and spotting one of these floral gems is a mega-tick for flower spotters.

If you are coming from the N7, the Biedouw valley can be accessed from the town of Clanwilliam by taking the gravel R364 over the jaw-dropping Pakhuis Pass. After about 40km on this road, you'll see a turn-off to the right marked for Wupperthal and the Biedouw valley. About 13km after this, you'll reach an intersection. To your left is the Biedouw valley route, which extends for about 30km up to the little settlement of Uitspankraal. You will then have to retrace your steps to Clanwilliam or continue northwards to the R355, which leads up to Calvinia (an additional distance of 100km from

Uitspankraal). To your right is the white-washed Rhenish mission station of Wupperthal (17km from the intersection). The village has changed little since it was established in 1830 and is an unusual destination.

Contacts:

- Cederberg Conservancy: www.cederberg.co.za
- www.cederbergtosea.co.za
- Cederberg Heritage Route: www.cedheroute.co.za
- Cederberg Observatory: www.cederbergobs.org.za
- www.wupperthal.co.za
- Wupperthal Tourism Info: 027-492 3410/3017/3317
- Cederberg Wine Cellar: 027-482 2827
- Cederberg 4x4 Tours: 021-913 4632; www.cederberg4x4.co.za

Accommodation:

- Algeria Cederberg Wilderness Area: 022-931 2088; www.capenature.co.za
- Boskloof Swemgat Cottages: 027-482 2522; www.boskloofswemgat.co.za
- Bushman's Kloof Wilderness Reserve: 021-685 2598; www.bushmanskloof.co.za
- Cederberg Bed and Breakfast: 022-921 3209; www.citrusdal.info/olivier
- Cederberg Chalets: 021-531 8212; www.cederbergchalets.co.za
- Cederberg Farm Cottages: 022-921 3209; www.citrusdal.info/olivier
- Cederberg Oasis and Backpackers: 027-482 2819; www.cederbergoasis.co.za
- Enjolife Farm (Biedouw Valley): 027-482 2869; www.soulcountry.info
- Kromrivier Tourist Park: 027-482 2807
- De Pakhuys: 027-482 1879; www.depakhuys.com
- Driehoek Tourist Farm: 027-482 2828

- Grootkloof Camping Site and Chalet: 027-482 2759
- Jamaka Organic Farm Cottages and Campsite: 027-482 2801; www.jamaka.co.za
- Kagga Kamma: 021-872 4343; www.kaggakamma.co.za
- Karookop Cottage: 027-482 2610; www.clanwilliam.info/karookop
- Karukareb Wildernis Reservaat: 027-482 1675; www.karukareb.co.za
- Keurbos Holiday Cottages: 027-482 2610; www.citrusdal.info/keurbos
- Keurbosfontein/Bakkrans/Mooiberg Wilderness Area: 021-871 1715
- Klein Boschkloof Chalets****: 027-482 2441; www.clanwilliam.info/kleinboschkloof
- Matjiesrivier Nature Reserve: 022-931 2088; www.capenature.co.za
- Mertenhof Guest Farm (Biedouw Valley): 027-482 2845
- Mount Ceder: 023-317 0848; www.mountceder.co.za
- Nuwerust Rest Camp: 027-482 2813; www.cederbergexperience.co.za
- Oudrif Farm: 022-921 3209; www.oudrif.co.za
- Sanddrif Campsite and Malgat Swimming Hole: 027-482 2825
- Traveller's Rest Cottages and Sevilla Hiking Trail: 027-482 1824; www.travellersrest.co.za

Clanwilliam

Originally established in 1725 as Jan Disselsvalleij, Clanwilliam is one of the ten oldest towns in South Africa. The name was changed to its current Celtic-sounding title by Sir John Cradock in 1814, who was trying to curry favour with his father-in-law, the Earl of Clanwilliam.

This once-sleepy farming town is the centre of South Africa's 'rooibos' (red bush) tea industry. A fragrantly tasty brew, rooibos is actually a species of fynbos that is endemic to the area and there are several farms in the vicinity that offer tours of their facilities.

Clanwilliam is the gateway to the northern Cederberg, as has been described above, but it is also an increasingly popular tourist destination in its own right with lots of shops, restaurants, guest houses and a large dam that is highly favoured by watersport enthusiasts.

It's no slouch in the flower department either. The Ramskop Nature Reserve and Wildflower Garden on the outskirts of town contains more than 350 species of 'cultivated' wild flowers. There are several paths that lead through this little slice of botanical heaven and the reserve offers great views out over the mountains. During peak season, the local women's organization runs a small tea shop in the garden. Opening times do vary, however, and you should contact the tourist info centre in town for more details.

The big flower event is the annual Wild Flower Show, held in the old Dutch Reformed Church on the main road. Hosted by the Clanwilliam Wild Flower Association, this ten-day extravaganza features a variety of enormous arrangements that sees farmers from the surrounding districts display their best flowers for the edification of townsfolk and visitors. The dates of the show vary, depending on the seasonal conditions, but it usually takes place towards the end of August and the beginning of September. All in all, about 360 different species can be seen inside the small church, and the associated festivities include concerts, art and food stalls and a street carnival.

Contacts:

- Clanwilliam Tourism Bureau: Tel: 027-482 2024
- Clanwilliam Tourism Info: 027-482 1777
- Cederberg Municipality: 027-422 1108
- Ramskop Wildflower Garden: 027-482 8000
- Wildflower Show: 027-482 2541

- www.clanwilliam.info
- www.tourismclanwilliam.co.za
- Pakhuys Country Winery: 027-482 2700; www.alphaexcelsior.co.za
- The Big Five Rooibos Tea Estate: 027-482 2640; www.africandawn.com
- Red T Company (farm & factory tours): 027-482 2862
- Carmien Organic Rooibos: www.carmientea.co.za
- Rooibos Ltd.: 027-482 2155; www.rooibosltd.co.za
- Strassberger Veldskoen Factory: 027-482 2140; www.strassberger.co.za
- Bushman's Cave Rock Theatre: 027-482 2918; www.bushmanscave.co.za

Accommodation:

- 11 Freezia Guest House: 083-454 3754
- Agama: 027-482 1892
- Alpha Excelsior Guest Farm: 027-482 2700; www.alphaexcelsior.co.za
- Augsburg Accommodation: 027-482 2120
- Beefwood***: 027-482 2249; www.beefwoodcorner.co.za
- Bergsig 3 Self-Catering: 027-482 1508
- Biedouw's guest room: 027-482 2833
- Blommenberg Guest House***: 027-482 1851; www.blommenberg.co.za
- Brannewijnkop: 027-482 2882
- Bushman's Cave: 027-482 2918
- Cedar Inn Motel: 027-482 2185
- Cederberg B&B: 022-921 3904
- Clan Court****: 027-482 1143; www.clancourt.co.za
- Clanvilla: 027-482 1042
- Clanwilliam Hotel: 027-482 1101; www.clanwilliamhotel.co.za
- Clanwilliam Dam Holiday House: 027-482 1083
- Clanwilliam Dam Resort: 027-482 8000

- Clanwilliam Lodge: 027-482 1777; www.clanwilliamlodge.co.za
- Daisy Cottage: 027-482 1603
- Elandsberg: 027-482 2022
- Elephant River: 027-482 1455; www.clanwilliam.info/elephantriver
- Freezialaan 10: 027-482 1743
- Freezialaan 22: 027-482 1344
- Freezialaan 24: 027-482 1491
- Freezialaan 32: 027-482 1497
- Gantouw: 027-482 2605
- Gecko Creek Wilderness Lodge: 027-482 1300
- Jakkalsvlei: 027-482 2729
- Klein Kliphuis: 027-482 2564
- Krakadouw Mountain Cottages: 027-482 2507; www.krakadouw.co.za
- Lebanon Citrus; 027-482 2508
- Little White Schoolhouse: 027-482 2832
- Marg-Will Barnhouse**: 027-482 2537; www.clanwilliam.info/marg-will
- Ndedema Lodge****: 027-482 1314; www.ndedemalodge.co.za
- Oppiedam Vakansiehuis: 027-482 1571
- Oudrif: 027-482 2397
- Owl's Hoot: 027-482 2509
- Rectory Guest House***: 027-482 1629; www.clanwilliam.info/rectory
- Reënblomstraat 3: 027-482 1894
- Rondegat Cottages on Clanwilliam Dam: 027-482 2527; www.clanwilliam.info/rondegat
- Saint du Barrys****: 027-482 1537; www.saintdubarrys.com
- Shikoko Cottage: 072-212 8181
- Skoolstraat 13: 027-482 1138
- Strassberger Hotel: 027-482 1090
- The Longhouse: 027-482 1240;

www.thelonghouse.co.za

- The Outhouse: 027-482 2040
- The Waenhuis: 027-482 2613; www.clanwilliam.info/waenhuis
- Tophouse B&B: 027-482 2537
- UCT Living Landscape Centre: 027-482 1191; www.cllp.uct.ac.za
- Vrede-oord: 027-482 1333
- Yellow Aloe: 027-482 2018
- Ysterfontein Guest Farm: 027-482 2512; www.ysterfontein.co.za
- Zeekoevlei: 027-482 2062

Citrusdal

At the southern end of the Cederberg mountains, about 60km south of Clanwilliam on the N7, is the attractive riverside town of Citrusdal. As the name implies, there are several large citrus farms in the area and tours can be arranged during the harvest season.

Citrusdal offers visitors the usual array of shops, accommodation, restaurants and a wide range of leisure activities. These include hiking trails, 4x4 trails, quad biking, canoeing in the Olifants River, rock climbing, a golf course and mountain biking. The popular CapeNature campsites in the Cederberg can be accessed via the gravelled Nieuwoudt's Pass, which winds up into the mountains about 20km north of town.

There are several good wild flower routes around Citrusdal, including the Bo-Rivier road that runs between the banks of the Olifants River and the steep flanks of the Cederberg. The road up to The Baths hot springs resort is another popular route for spotters. You can also try the road to Paleisheuwel, which can be reached from the top of Pikenierskloof Pass (Ravine of the Pike Men, who were soldiers armed with long spears who used to protect this important route to the north).

From Citrusdal, you can either head off to the Strandveld region along the West Coast, or you can continue south, over the majestic Piekenierskloof Pass to Cape Town, which is 170km away.

Contacts:

- Citrusdal Tourism Bureau: 022-921 3210
- www.citrusdal.info
- Museum: 022-931 3686
- Goede Hoop Citrus Farm Tours: 022-921 2085
- Citrusdal Cellars: 022-921 2233; www.gouevallei.co.za
- Johann Van Zyl Wines: 022-921 3328.
- Reality 4x4 hire: 022-921 3295; www.reality4x4hire.co.za
- Ihlathi Adventures: 082-974 9701; www.ihlathi.co.za

Accommodation:

- Aan d' Oewer: 022-921 2085; www.citrusdal.info/oewer
- Allandale Guest Farm: 022-921 3305; www.allandalefarm.co.za
- Appel se Riviergat Cottage***: 022-921 2255; www.wheretostay.co.za/vuurgat
- Boontjiesrivier Farm Accommodation: 022-921 3131; www.citrusdal.info/boontjiesrivier
- Boschkloof Farm Cottages: 022-921 3533; www.boschkloof.com
- Bosplaas Guest House: 022-921 2947
- Cedarberg Lodge: 022-921 2221; www.cedarberglodge.co.za
- Citrusdal Caravan Park & Chalets: 022-921 3145
- Citrusdal Gastekamers: 022-921 2033
- Petersfield Farm: 022-921 3316; www.petersfieldfarm.co.za
- De Eike: 022-921 2334
- Elephant Leisure Resort Conference Centre &

Chalets: 022-921 2884; www.elephantleisure.co.za

- Excelsior Guest Farm: 022-914 5853
- Gekko Getaways Backpackers Lodge: 022-921 3353; www.gekko.co.za
- Hazel's House, Farm B&B: 022-921 8012
- Hebron: 022-921 2595; www.hebron.co.za
- Kardoesie Self-catering: 022-921 2382
- Kardouw Farm House: 022-921 2474; www.citrusdal.info/kardouw
- Kleine Vallei Farm Accommodation: 022-921 3079; www.kleinevalleiguestfarm.co.za
- Koedoeskop Farm Accommodation: 022-921 2622; www.citrusdal.info/koedoeskop
- Kunje Guest House & Mountain Cottage: 022-921 3536
- Lungile Self-catering: 022-921 3288
- McGregor's Cottage and Camping: 022-921 3628
- Nuwedam Guest Cottage: 022-921 3431; www.citrusdal.info/nuwedam
- Olifantsrus Farm Guest House: 022-921 3528; www.olifantsrus.com
- Piekenierskloof Mountain Lodge: 011-267 8300; www.dreamvacs.com
- River Camp: 082-805 7973
- Rockwood Cottage: 022-921 3517; www.rockwoodfarm.co.za
- Sewefontein: 022-921 3301; www.citrusdal.info/sewefontein
- Sophia's Bed and Breakfast: 022-921 2866
- The Baths Hot Springs Resort and Camping: 022-921 8026; www.thebaths.co.za
- The Country House: 082-773 8310; www.citrusdalquadfarm.co.za
- Waterfall Farm: 021-790 2928
- Winkelshoek: 022-913 1092
- Wolfkop Nature Reserve***: 022-921 2255; www.wolfkopreserve.co.za

The West Coast

For the purposes of this book, we are going to say that the West Coast region runs along the sea from Lambert's Bay in the north to the Langebaan lagoon in the south. It's a lovely part of the world that offers visitors charming small towns, quiet gravel roads, bird-filled wetlands, excellent seafood and unpretentious hospitality.

Unfortunately, these delicate delights are also attracting ever-increasing numbers of property developers who are slowly spreading their particular blend of holiday-home horror up the shoreline. One only hopes that the region is able to strike a responsible balance between development, aesthetics and conservation.

It is beyond the scope of this book to discuss the West Coast in detail. Instead, I will briefly focus on the tourist hot-spots around Lambert's Bay, Elands Bay, Velddrif, Paternoster, Saldanha Bay and the West Coast National Park at Langebaan. Suffice it to say, however, that each town offers its own special combination of historical sites, hiking trails, fishing, whale-watching, boat trips, 4x4 routes, flower-spotting and other natural and cultural attractions.

Please note that many of the roads in this part of the world are gravel or sand, but there is a lot of construction going on and several thoroughfares are in the process of getting tarred. Ongoing roadworks may therefore cause traffic delays.

Contacts:

- West Coast Regional Tourism Office: 022-433 2380
- www.sawestcoast.com
- www.capewestcoast.org
- www.route27sa.com
- www.wideblue.co.za
- www.bokkom.co.za
- www.capebiosphere.co.za

Lambert's Bay, Graafwater, Leipoldtville

Known primarily as a fishing resort, Lambert's Bay is a nice seaside town with a well-developed tourism infrastructure. In terms of flowers, there are several farms in the area that sometimes have good displays, and the road to Leipoldtville is recommended by the locals.

For those who like a bit of history, check out the Heerenlogement (Gentleman's Lodging) cave near the town of Graafwater. This was a regular stop on the old wagon road to the north, and the walls of the cave are covered with historical graffiti made by travellers of old.

You can access Lambert's Bay by taking the tarred R364 from Clanwilliam. Alternatively, you can follow the gravel roads along the coast, either from Strandfontein in the north or Elands Bay in the south. You can also take the private Sishen–Saldanha toll road, which runs close to the sea along the railway line, to Elands Bay.

Lambert's Bay contacts:

- Tourism Bureau, museum and crayfishing permits: 027-432 1000
- www.lambertsbay.co.za
- Bird Island Nature Reserve: 021-659 3500; www.capenature.org.za
- HMS Sybille Room at Steenboksfontein: 027-432 2720
- Eco Boat Trips: 082-922 4334
- Panorama Park Game Reserve: 027-432 1722
- The Dunes (4x4, quad bikes, hiking trails): 027-432 1244
- Quad Bike Trips: 083-306 6684
- Brandwag (wild flowers): 027-432 1305
- Dassiepoort (wild flowers): 027-432 1017
- Van der Westhuizen (proteas): 027-422 1732
- Bosduifklip Open-air Restaurant: 027-432 2735; www.bosduifklip.co.za
- Muisbosskerm Open-air Restaurant: 027-432 1017;

www.muisbosskerm.co.za

- Rooidop Wines: 027-432 1325; www.rooidop.co.za

Accommodation:

- Albatros Akkommodasie: 027-432 1038
- Arendzicht: 027-432 1005
- By Die C: 083-633 0620
- De Villiers-kamers: 027-432 1401
- Die Pophuis: 027-432 1317
- Dolfyntjie: 027-432 1226
- Dollika: 027-432 2719
- Doorspring: 027-432 2235
- Du Preez—Wondersig: 027-432 2151
- Flaminkie: 027-432 2907
- Grietjie: 027-432 2301
- Happy-Ness: 083-475 8191
- Hello Fello: 082-732 0216
- Kehrwieder: 027-432 1305
- Komma Inn: 027-432 1433
- KommaWeer: 027-432 2140
- Kosmoshuisie: 027-432 1305
- Lafenis: 027-432 1719
- Lamberine Woonstelle: 027-432 1038
- Lambert's Bay Caravan Park: 027-432 2238
- Lamberts Bay Hotel: 027-432 1126
- Lapalouma: 027-432 2511
- Lekker Bly: 083-370 0400
- Lochner Huis: 082-926 7553
- Maki Tuis: 027-432 1240
- Malkopbaai Flats: 027-432 1530
- Meeuland: 027-432 1533
- Muller House: 027-432 2954
- Ou Skip: 027-432 2954
- Pediunker: 027-432 2954
- Pik & Pikkie: 027-432 2719
- Raston Guest House:073-143 2603

- Redelinghuys Cottage: 027-432 1806
- Redelinghuys Flats: 027-432 1234
- Rosebud: 027-432 1285
- Sir Lambert's***: 027-432 1117
- Sybille: 027-432 1844
- Van Puttens Vlei: 027-432 2508
- White Sands B&B: 027-432 1554
- Xamarin Guest Farm: 083-250 4706; www.xamarin.co.za

Graafwater and Leipoldtville contacts:

- Heerenlogement Cave and Four Winds Fynbos Farm: 027-422 1723
- Klipfontein Farm & Museum: 027-422 1108
- Elandsberg Eco-Tourism and Rooibos estate: 027-482 2022; www.africandawn.com
- Rock Art and Mountain Bike Routes: 027-482 2022
- Rooibos Tours: 027-482 2022
- Boschenbach Nature Reserve: 027-422 1100
- Sandsteen Mine and Boegoeberg 4x4: 027-482 2933
- Sandberg Game Camp and 4x4: 027-412 2662

Accommodation:

- Dorpstraat 2: 021-903 7089
- Graafwater Hotel: 027-422 1324
- Jakkalsvlei: 027-482 2729
- Lambertshoek: 027-482 2933
- Leipoldt's Country Retreat: 027-412 2116; www.leipoldts.co.za

Elands Bay

As soon as I drove into Elands Bay, I knew it was something special. A small resort town built around a magnificent bay, it's everything a West Coast seaside village should be. The beach is wide and pristine, the air is clean and the atmosphere is tranquil enough to soothe

the breast of even the most hard-core urbanite.

There are several accommodation choices in Elands Bay. Guest houses and the rather old-fashioned hotels offer traditional rooms with sea-views, but I would recommend staying at the local caravan park, which is quite literally on the beach.

Worth special mention is the Talm Langer restaurant, located on the main square, across from the hotel. This picture-perfect bistro has sea sand on the floor, a crackling fireplace and a varied menu offering all kinds of tempting fare. Although I was going to try their fresh calamari, the owners recommended the hamburger, a house speciality. Usually, I don't eat red meat, but I made an exception and, let me tell you, it was a revelation. The huge handmade patty, dressed with fresh salad, served between a crisp home-baked bun blew me away.

The flowers on the roads around Elands Bay aren't too shabby either. The displays begin shortly outside the town of Eendekuil, which can be accessed from the N7 at the foot of the Piekenierskloof Pass. From here, the road largely keeps to the north bank of the Verlorenvlei River as it flows towards the sea, about 80km away. You can also access this road from the Citrusdal side of the mountains.

In its later stretches, the river spreads out across a series of wetlands that harbour a wealth of avian and botanical life. The farm at Ventersklip has a particularly eye-popping location on the banks of a vlei, and boasts a dense display of wild flowers that bloom profusely around the headstones in their small family cemetery. The accommodation and restaurant at Ventersklip is also fantastic. The actual Verlorenvlei Reserve can be reached just outside the town of Redelingshuys.

From Elands Bay, you simply must do the short drive around the adjacent headland known as Baboon Point. The gravel road leads right along the sea, offering amazing views out over the ocean. It's also a good place to see the local strandveld flowers bloom in the fecund, green vegetation that grows right up to the water's edge.

The Sishen–Saldanha industrial railway line runs right past Elands Bay and, for a small fee, you can drive on the private road that runs along the railway line all the way up to Lambert's Bay. It's a very scenic route that lets you motor right along the coastline.

When you've done your time at Elands Bay, you either have to return to the N7 or continue south down the coast on the gravel roads that lead past the Rocherpan Wetland and Bird Reserve to Velddrif.

Contacts:

- Tourism info: 021-873 3474
- www.elandsbay.co.za
- Verlorenvlei RAMSAR wetlands: 022-962 1650
- Talm Langer Restaurant: 022-972 1551
- Jakkalskloof Castle Hiking Trail: 082-413 2011
- Sandveld Potato Festival and Road Race: 022-962 1602

Accommodation:

- Bottergat Vissermanshuisie: 082-457 8907
- De Vlei: 022-972 1387; www.wheretostay.co.za/devlei
- Die Kuierhuisie: 022-714 3605
- Eland's Bay Caravan Park: 022-972 1745
- Elands Bay Guest House: 022-972 1229; www.elandsbayguesthouse.co.za
- Elands Bay Community Guest House: 083-346 5394; www.south-north.co.za
- Eland's Bay Lodge and Backpackers: 022-972 1640
- Emma's Guest House: 022-972 1755
- Hotel Eland: 022-972 1640
- Kruisfontein Guest House: 022-962 1937
- Redelingshuys Manor: 022-962 1642; www.red.com
- Sandveld Cottages: 022-962 1665
- Sandveld Caravan Park: 022-962 1746

- Sandveld Dorpshuys: 022-962 1746
- Vensterklip: 022-972 1340; www.vensterklip.co.za

Velddrif, Port Owen, Laaiplek, Dwarskersbos, Hopefield, Aurora

The conurbation of Velddrif, Port Owen and Laaiplek are at the centre of this agglomeration of marinas, harbours and holiday homes at the mouth of the Berg River. It is a good place for fishermen and those who are keen on boat trips or whale-spotting. There is a full range of tourist facilities and several well-established resorts, but the area around the harbour stinks of fish.

The sea itself is rather muddy, as is often the case at river mouths, but I still spent a couple of happy hours sitting on the beach and chatting with some local fishermen who were enjoying the sunset over a box of wine. If you want a change of pace, the outlying towns of Dwarkersbos, Hopefield and Aurora offer some nature-based activities, including flower-spotting.

Contacts:

- Velddrif Tourism Bureau: 022-783 1821
- Rocherpan Nature Reserve: 021-659 3500; www.capenature.org.za
- Fish Factory Tour (bookings only): 022-783 1103
- Salt Processing Tour (Thursday mornings): 022-783 1133
- Velddrif Cheesemakers: 072-415 7997
- Berg River Boat Trips: 022-783 0698
- Pelican Harbour Charters: 083-225 4292
- Canoeing & Mini Golf: 022-783 1137
- Fishing at Swartjiesbaai: 022-783 0818
- Klein Tafelberg (4x4, quad bike & hiking routes): 083-429 9313
- Port Owen Yacht Club: 083-701 9434
- Sunset Adventures (quad bikes, etc): 022-783 2763

- Velddrif Yacht Club (dinghies): 022-783 0942

Accommodation:

- Aflaaiplek: 082-809 6813
- Berg River Accommodation: 022-783 0294
- Berg River Lodge***: 022-783 0686
- Biebie at Kingfisher Heads: 041-992 2395
- Celba's C-Cottage***: 073-475 9482
- Cloeteskraal Chalets: 022-783 1414
- Cynni: 022-783 0303
- Draaihoek Lodge****: 022-952 1170; www.draaihoek.com
- Duinerosie: 082-562 9753
- Dwarskersbos Beach Resort: 022-784 0110
- Dwarskersbos Holiday Accommodation: 022-783 2109
- El Shaddai: 083-290 3424
- Fairfields Guest Farm: 022-783 0939; www.fairfieldsguestfarm.co.za
- Fish Eagle's Nest: 082-897 7522/1
- Harbour Lights***: 022-783 2099; www.harbourlights.mrinfo.co.za
- Kliphoek Guest Farm Chalets: 022-783 0822
- Kom Dudu B&B: 022-784 0121
- Kopereend: 021-887 1917
- Koraal Vakansiewoonstel: 082-748 6082
- Kuifkopvisvanger B&B*: 022-783 0818; www.kuifkop.co.za
- La Amour B&B****: 022-783 1550
- Laaiplek Hotel**: 022-783 1116; www.eigevis.com
- Langrietvlei Cottages**: 022-783 0856
- Marina Accommodation: 082-852 8295
- Mossienes: 022-912 4861
- Pelican Post Cottage: 022-713 4151; www.pelicanpost-velddrif.com
- Pelikaan Beach Resort: 022-783 0383
- Pelikaan Lodge: 022-783 2055

- Piet-my-vrou B&B: 022-783 0775
- Port Owen Holiday Accommodation: 022-783 2466
- Port Owen Marina Resort: 022-783 1144
- River Cottage: 022-783 1865
- Riverside B & B: 022-783 1865; www.riversidebb.co.za
- Riverside Sunset: 022-783 0946
- Riverwalk Self Catering: 082-515 9495
- Riviera Hotel and Chalets**: 022-783 1137; www.eigevis.com
- Sandvelder****: 022-783 0385
- Seafront Flat, Dwarskersbos: 022-783 0867
- Seefontein Cottage: 022-784 0097
- Seemeeu Nes, Dwarskersbos: 022-912 4862
- Skilpadjies: 082-901 2440
- Stywelyne Beach Resort: 022-783 0408
- The Den: 022-783 2627
- The Waterfront****: 082-330 9777
- Weskus Huisie: 082-361 5526
- Willow Place: 022-783 2936
- Wonderzee: 022-783 2232

Aurora contacts:

- Gousblom B&B: 022-952 1577
- Kliphout Krans Cottage: 022-952 1864
- L'aurore Guest House: 022-952 1755
- Mountain Mist Cottages: 022-952 1750
- Sun Mountain: 022-952 1870
- Aurora Women's Network (handmade paper): 022-952 1577
- Basie Jantjies (handmade toys): 022-952 1577

Hopefield contacts:

- Tourism Bureau and Fynbos Garden: 022-723 0500
- Flower Show: 022-783 1720
- Hopefield Lodge: 022-723 0530

- Kersefontein B&B: 022-783 0850
- Savico Game Lodge: 022-723 2000
- Yahweh Yireh: 022-723 1844

Paternoster, St Helena Bay

For me, one of the highlights of the West Coast is at Paternoster. Not the town itself, you understand. This once-quaint fishing village has been destroyed by rampant and uncontrolled development. Instead, you should drive straight through the village and explore the transcendent Cape Columbine Nature Reserve.

This small, municipal reserve of 263ha was declared in 1973 and it is a real gem. Consisting of a series of rocky bays, surrounded by grey boulders, Cape Columbine is a stunning juxtaposition of sea and stone. The waves smash themselves into salty spray on the rocks, as sea birds wheel and screech in the skies above. During spring, the green dunes of the reserve are full of wild flowers, many of which are rare or narrowly endemic.

Several campsites have been established in the various coves and crannies of the headland and, although there are few facilities, they offer intrepid campers an unsurpassed seaside location. You can also camp at the cheekily named Tietiesbaai beach, where there is a cold-water ablution block. This famous bowl-shaped bay is indeed shaped like a boobie, but the appellation is probably a corruption of a person's name, one Mr Titus, who used to own a farm in the area.

Overlooking the scene is the Cape Columbine lighthouse. This was the last manned lighthouse built in South Africa, in 1936. It is still manned today, and tours to the top of the tower can be arranged. The lighthouse also offers comfortable overnight accommodation in two adjacent chalets.

The other place to overnight in the reserve is the extraordinary Beach Camp and Backpackers. This isn't a luxury establishment. Accommodation is in simple A-frame canvas huts. There's no electricity, the ablution facilities are nothing more than functional, and the bar seems to be made of driftwood. But you can't beat the location, right on the lip of a small beach, and I can't think of any other place where you can sleep so close to the sea.

During the day, the Beach Camp is lovely. You can take walks through the reserve or do one of their sea-kayaking excursions, weather permitting. You can even try out their giant catapult and shoot stones at the specially marked barrel on the other side of the beach. At night, however, it's a dream. Candles offer the only illumination, apart from the braai and a coal-burning Aga stove that keeps the chilly sea breeze at bay. Then, when you go to sleep, there's nothing like closing your eyes and hearing the waves break only metres from your head. Lovely.

And despite what I said earlier, the town of Paternoster isn't a total write-off. The iconic white-washed fishermen's houses are still in evidence, as is the famous 'Winkel op Paternoster'—a nicely cluttered general dealers with an old row-boat stranded in the sand outside. The beach itself is beautiful, with a wide, golden shingle, and there are plenty of pottery studios, art galleries and craft shops through which you can browse.

For those who want a bit of pampering, the upmarket guest houses and wellness centres in the area are more than happy to oblige, and there are several well-regarded restaurants. I tried out the Noisy Oyster, on the main road, and I was blown away by the quality of the food. I even went back for lunch the following day.

Oh, and while you're in the area, check out the Vasco da Gama memorial at nearby St Helena Bay. This is the location where the Portuguese navigator dropped anchor way back in 1497, thereby starting the whole colonial adventure in southern Africa. The burgeoning towns at St Helena Bay, Britannia Bay and Stompneus Bay also offer an ever-increasing range of tourist facilities. In fact, this entire part of the peninsula is full of activity. The number of holiday homes is soaring and developments are springing up like, well, wild flowers. I suppose it's to be expected. The 'sea-nery' and beaches are fantastic and Cape Town is only two hours away. What can you do?

Paternoster contacts:

- Cape Columbine and Tietiesbaai Nature Reserve: 022-752 2718
- The Beach Camp @ Cape Columbine: 082-962 2267; www.ratrace.co.za
- Cape Columbine Lighthouse and Guest House: 022-752 2705; www.npa.co.za
- Noisy Oyster Restaurant: 022-752 2196
- Die Winkel op Paternoster: 022-752 2105
- Angling, Diving and Crayfish Trips: 083-480 4930; www.seafish.co.za
- Hiking Trails from Tietiesbaai: 022-701 7000
- Sea Kayaking and Mountain Biking: 082-926 2267; www.kayaktrails.com
- Drikus Horse Trails: 082-748 5596

Accommodation:

- Ahoy Guest House: 072-639 0727
- Baywatch Villa: 022-752 2039
- Beachwalker's Cottage: 022-752 2150
- Blue Dolphin: 022-752 2001; www.bluedolphin.co.za
- Cape Columbine: 021-449 2400
- Casa Nostra house: 083-601 0568; www.wheretostay.co.za/casanostra.htm
- Die Inkommers: 011-753 2869
- Die Opstal: 022-752 2648; www.paternoster.co.za
- Far Out: 022-752 2222; www.madeinpaternoster.co.za

- Fisherman's Cottage: 022-752 2632
- Hoekie: 022-752 2077
- J'aime la mer: 083-701 2650
- Mosselbank B&B: 022-752 2632; www.weskus.com
- Paljas: 083-988 4645
- Paternoster Beach Cottage: 022-715 3034
- Paternoster Hotel: 022-752 2773; www.paternosterhotel.co.za
- Paternoster Lodge: 022-752 2023
- Paternoster on C: 022-752 2207; www.paternosteronc.com
- Paternoster Village Backpackers: 082-777 6680
- Paternoster Villas: 083-988 4645; www.paternoster-villas.co.za
- Salt Coast: 022-752 2063; www.saltcoast.co.za
- Stay in Paternoster Booking Agency: 022-752 2186; www.stayinpaternoster.co.za
- The Oystercatcher's Haven: 022-752 2193
- Voorstrand: 022-752 2038

St Helena Bay contacts:

- Vasco da Gama Nautical Museum: 022-741 1906
- Fishing (snoek in season): 083-480 4930
- Surfing and windsurfing: 022-742 1944
- Whale watching: 083-425 7678
- Elandskloof 4x4 trails: 022-736 1071

Accommodation:

- Blue Berry Hill Self-catering: 022-742 1045; www.cape-venues.co.za/blueberry.htm
- Britannia Beach Self-catering: 022-742 1964
- Dolphin B&B: 022-742 1944; www.dolphinza.com
- Elm Tree Farm: 022-736 1159
- Goblins Creek Manor House: 022-742 1331
- Grenache Self-Catering: 022-921 2904
- La Hoya B&B: 022-742 1682

- Laingville Holiday Resort: 022-736 1684
- Midwest Caravan Park: 022-736 1518
- Shell Self-Catering Cottage: 022-742 1224
- St Helena Hotel**: 022-736 1160
- Steenbrasbay Guest House: 021-976 7556
- The Oystercatcher Lodge: 022-742 1202; www.oystercatcherlodge.co.za
- The Sunfish: 022-742 1916
- Villa Dauphine: 022-742 1926; www.villadauphine.com

Saldanha Bay, Vredenburg, Jacob's Bay

The Saldanha–Sishen railway line, which stretches for over 1,000km through Namaqualand and Bushmanland, terminates at the huge industrial complexes of Saldanha Bay. This is said to be the only really good natural harbour in South Africa, as all our other ports have required extensive dredging and re-working. Despite the heavy industry, it is not a dirty or polluted port. The boats bobbing in the blue bay are very picturesque and there is a full range of accommodation and dining options.

The nearby town of Vredenburg offers more of the same, while the nearby seaside village of Jacob's Bay is an up-and-coming destination that sometimes offers good flower-spotting.

The West Coast Fossil Park can be found in the vicinity, a few kilometres down the road to Langebaan. This 14ha site was once part of a phosphate mining operation, which uncovered one of the richest animal fossil sites in the world. Two hundred different kinds of prehistoric creatures have been found here and these are now displayed at the park's interpretation centre.

Saldanha Bay contacts:

- Tourism info: 022-714 2088; 022-701 7000

- www.saldanhabay.co.za
- www.cape-whaleroute.co.za
- Saldanha Nature Reserve: 022-702 3523
- Hoedjieskoppie Nature Reserve: 022-714 2088
- Sishen-Saldanha Iron-ore Project (tours by appointment) : 022-703 4204; www.portnet.co.za
- Sea Harvest Fish Shop: 022-701 4100; www.seaharvest.co.za
- Birdwatching: 022-713 1930
- Benguela Stratos Fishing Charters: 022-714 2511
- Saldanha Beach Sailing Club: 022-714 3922
- Weskus Half Marathon (August): 022-706 2911
- West Coast Fossil Park: 022-766 1606; www.iziko.org.za, click on 'our partners' link

Accommodation:
- Hoedjiesbaai Hotel**: 022-714 1271
- Avondrust Guest House: 022-714 2369; www.capetourism.org/avondrust
- Bam se Plek: 022-714 2812
- Blouwaterbaai Holiday Resort: 022-714 1177; www.blouwaterbaai.com
- Blue Bay Lodge: 022-714 1177; www.blouwaterbaai.com
- Drop Anchor Beach Lodge: 022-714 1207; www.dropanchor.co.za
- Jane's Guest House: 022-714 3605; www.janes.co.za
- La Capitaine: 022-714 0106
- Oranjevlei Guest Farm and Nature Reserve: 022-714 2261
- Protea Hotel Saldanha Bay***: 022-714 1264 ; www.proteahotels.com
- Room with a View: 083-332 0247
- Saldanha Backpackers: 022-714 4234; www.packafrica.co.za
- Saldanha Holiday Resort: 022-714 2247;

www.saldanhabay.co.za

- Stone Castle: 082-552 7971; www.stone-castle.co.za
- Strandloper Guest House: 022-714 3099; www.strandloop.co.za

Vredenburg, Jacob's Bay contacts:

- Tourism office: 022-715 1142
- Diving & Angling: 083-480 4930
- Scott's Nursery: 022-715 3016

Accommodation:

- Baviana Beach Lodge: 022-715 3114
- Beach Front Resort: 022-715 3333; www.beachfrontresort.co.za
- Crayfish Creek: 021-975 9123; www.capecarol.com
- HR Farger Guest House: 022-715 3505
- Jacobsbaai Guest House: 022-715 3105; www.portfoliocollection.com
- Jacobsbaai Hotel: 022-715 3333
- Juffroushoogte Guest Farm: 022-715 3020; www.juffroushoogte.com
- Kuielekka Cottage: 082-446 5970
- Parc 10: 083-450 0884
- Swartriet Holiday Resort: 022-715 4044; www.wavesailing.co.za/swartriet.htm
- The Way House: 022-713 3134
- Villa Vita Nouva: 084-656 8263
- Vredenburg Lodge: 022-713 1181
- Windstone Lodge and Backpacker: 022-766 1645; www.windstone.co.za

Langebaan, Yserfontein

At the southern end of Saldanha Bay is the extensive Langebaan lagoon system. It's a broad waterway that supports a wide range of boating and watersport activities. The town is a popular destination for holiday makers and has all the facilities that you would expect, including a casino.

The main attraction here is the West Coast National Park, a beautiful conservation area that protects both sides of the lagoon from development. For flower-spotters, the Postberg Mountain is a well-known place to view the spring flowers that bloom on its slopes. It is the closest wild flower site to Cape Town (only 90km away) and makes for a good day trip from the Mother City. This can be supplemented by a stop-off at the nearby town of Yserfontein, at the southern edge of the reserve.

Langebaan contacts:

- Tourism info: 022-772 1515
- www.langebaaninfo.co.za
- West Coast National Park: 022 772-2144; www.SANParks.org/parks/west_coast
- Mykonos Casino: 022-707 7000; www.mykonoscasino.co.za
- West Coast Bird Club: 022-742 1944
- Angling Trips: 082-751 6267
- Islander Boat Trips: 082-556 6110
- Tropico Boat Trips: 082-556 5418
- Sunny Park Kiddies Fun Park: 022-772 2293
- Golfing: 022-772 2112; www.golf-langebaan.co.za
- Cape Sport Centre and Rentals: 022-772 1114; www.capesport.co.za
- Langebaan Yacht Club: 022-772 2466
- Boat trip to islands: 022-772 2144
- Binks Mackenzie Tours: 072-243 9122
- Brian's Tours: 083-456 2345
- Offtrac Trails & Tagalongs: 083-452 6931; www.offtrac.com

Accommodation:

- A House to Rest: 022-772 1741;

www.langebaanaccommodation.com

- Accommodation Bureau: 080-026 2000
- Amazana: 022-772 1792; www.lockers.co.za/amazana
- Bavaria Haus: 022-772 1640; www.langebaaninfo.com/bavaria
- Bayview: 022-772 2431
- Calypso Villas: 022-772 2920; www.calypsovillas.co.za
- Casa Carita: 082-410 6453
- Club Mykonos Resort: 022-707 7000: www.clubmykonos.co.za
- Croeso Welcome***: 022-772 1725:
- Duinepos Chalets: 022-707 9900
- Falcon's Rest Guest Lodge ****: 022-772 1112; www.falconsrest.co.za
- Feathers Campsite: 022-772 1527
- Friday Island: 022-772 2506; www.fridayisland.co.za
- Glenfinnan: 022-772 1341
- Horizon Guest House: 022-772 2459; www.horizonghouse.co.za
- House of Penquin: 082-924 5951
- Langebaan Beach House: 022-772 2625; www.langebaanbeachhouse.com
- Langebaan Guest House: 022-772 1610
- Leentjiesklip Caravan Park: 022-772 2461
- Martinique: 082-340 2991
- Mossienes: 082-556 7325
- Oliphantskop: 022-772 2326; www.oliphantskop.snowball.co.za
- Oostewal Caravan Park: 022-772 2442
- Point Guest Lodge: 083-464 9318; www.pointguestlodge.co.za
- Primary Colours: 082-772 1073
- Rest for Sure: 082-566 2416
- Sandra's Guest House: 022-772 2034; www.sandras.co.za
- Seagulls Guest House: 022-772 1017;

www.gocco.co.za/seagulls.htm

- Seawinds: 022-772 1612
- Seeduiker: 082-977 4439
- Souvenir Holiday: 082-928 8848
- Stonehaven: 084-864 6275
- The Farmhouse Hotel: 022-772 2062; www.thefarmhouselangebaan.co.za
- Tjailatyd: 082-565 6255
- Van Breda Cottage: 022-772 2134; www.geelbek.com
- Villa Verano: 022-772 2884; www.villaverano.co.za
- Westlantic Lodge: 022-772 2167; www.westcoastsa.co.za/pts/westlantic
- Windstone Backpackers: 022-766 1645; www.sawestcoast.com/windstone
- Zizi's Cottages: 022-772 1073

Yserfontein contacts:

- Tourism Bureau (hiking, birding, flowers, kite surfing, mountain biking): 022-451 2366/2211
- www.tourismyzerfontein.co.za
- Blombos 4x4 and nature trail: 022-451 2790
- Angling Club: 082-468 1466
- Boat Club: 082-932 5202
- Fishing/crayfishing/slipway available: 022-451 2344
- Mountain Biking: 082-722 7809
- Bokbaaivygie Route: 022-451 2263
- Whales in Season: 022-451 2615
- Dieu Donné Tours: 082-955 8047

Accommodation:

- 134 Dassen Island: 082-719 3117
- 14 On Beach: 022-451 2783
- 19 Main Road: 023-614 2280
- 34 On De Jongh: 022-451 2876
- 38 Versveld: 083-261 9010
- Albatros Villa: 083-288 5991

- Ammi: 022-451 2907
- Blombos Hideaway Lodge: 022-451 2790
- Cam-E-lot: 022-451 2254
- Cape Villa: 021-715 2045
- Casa del Mare: 022-451 2757
- Dassenview B&B: 022-451 2253
- Deo Gloria: 022-451 2405
- Die Rondawel: 022-451 2217
- Elbé @ The Waves: 022-451 2760
- Emmaus-on-Sea: 022-451 2650
- Ganzekraal Camping: 022-492 2752
- Gilbert's Gift: 022-451 2229
- Harbour View: 022-451 2615
- Huis Nemesia: 022-451 2470
- Igley: 022-451 2663
- Jenni's Ama Do-doo: 022-451 2771
- Kaijaiki: 022-451 2858
- Kiewiet: 022-451 2995
- Lewens Essens: 022-451 2390
- Like Home: 022-451 2998
- Liza View Guest House: 083-500 0768
- Michadri: 022-451 2725
- Mount Royal: 022-451 2229
- Ocean View House: 022-451 2882
- One Couple: 022-492 2782
- Pasha's Place: 022-451 2757
- Sea-Esta: 022-451 2589
- Serenity: 022-451 2581
- Spearchukka: 022-451 2662
- Stonechat: 022-451 2762
- Strändhus: 022-451 2523
- Surfsong: 022-451 2761
- Swept Away: 022-451 2556
- The Gulls B&B: 022-451 2264
- Time Out: 022-451 2879
- Tobi House: 082-377 0634

- Villa Pescatori: 022-451 2422
- Y-Worry Homes: 022-451 2966
- Yzerfontein Caravan Park: 022-451 2211

Darling

Whether you are heading down to Cape Town on the N7 from Citrusdal or coming in from the West Coast, the Swartland town of Darling is worth a visit. This lovely little place has a range of art galleries, antique shops, wine farms and other cultural activities. It is also the home of the invaluable Pieter Dirk Uys and his alter-ego, the unstoppable Evita Bezuidenhout. Together, they hold court at Evita se Perron (platform), a converted train station which is now painted pink and surrounded by an unusual sculpture garden known as Boerassic Park.

Darling also has several wild flower reserves and an annual wild flower show, usually held in September. These reserves, which include the Tienie Verster wild flower site, protect the highly endangered veld type known as Renosterveld and boast impressive displays during the season.

From Darling, it is a short trip back to Cape Town (75km) through the bright yellow flowers that bloom in the Canola fields (which are cultivated as opposed to wild). And there, in the shadow of The Mountain, we must leave you. The flower-spotting adventure that began all the way up in Springbok, 600km to the north, has finally come to an end.

Contacts:

- Tourism Bureau and museum: 022-492 3361;
- www.darlingtourism.co.za
- www.darlingflowers.co.za
- Evita se Perron: 022-492 2831; www.evita.co.za
- !Khwa ttu San Culture & Education Centre: 022-492 2998; www.khwattu.org
- Duckitt's Nurseries: 022-492 2606

- Orchid Shop at Oudepost Farm: 022-492 2368
- Darling Cellars: 022-492 2276; www.darlingcellars.co.za
- Cloof Cellars: 022-492 2839; www.cloof.co.za
- Groote Post Cellars: 022-492 2825; www.grootepost.com
- Ormonde Vineyards: 022-492 3540; www.ormondevineyards.co.za
- Tukulu Cellars: 021-809 7000; www.tukulu.co.za
- West Coast Ostrich Ranch: 021-972 1955; www.wcor-av.co.za

Accommodation:

- Aloe Cottage: 083-400 1666
- Beds @ Bistro 7: 022-492 3626
- Buffelsfontein Game Nature Reserve and 4x4: 022-451 2824; www.buffelsfontein.co.za
- Corazon B&B: 022-492 3554
- Darling Hotel: 022-492 2263
- Darling Lodge: 022-492 3062
- De Gans Gastehuis: 022-492 2576
- Droërug Guest House: 022-486 5822
- Jacaranda Moon B&B: 022-492 3633
- Kalimera Holiday Home: 076-705 0085; www.kalimera.co.za
- Maison Amnesia: 022-492 3875
- Rondeberg Reserve: 022-492 3435; www.rondeberg.co.za
- Sonquasfontein Cottages: 082-378 1180
- Strathnaver B&B: 022-492 3810
- The Granary: 022-492 3155
- Trinity Lodge: 022-492 3430
- Tuinhuis Cottage: 022-492 2268; www.tuinhuissouthafrica.com
- Waylands Guest House: 022-492 2873
- Ye Olde School: 022-492 2816

References/further reading

- Boonzaier, Emile; Berens, Penny; Malherbe, Candy; Smith, Andy. 1996. *The Cape Herders—a history of the Khoikhoi in southern Africa.* David Philip, Ohio University Press.
- Cowling, Richard and Pierce, Shirley. 1999. *Namaqualand—a succulent desert.* Fernwood Press.
- Fleminger, David. 2005. *Back Roads of the Cape.* Jacana Media.
- Forbes, V. S. 1965. *Pioneer Travellers in South Africa.* A. A. Balkema.
- Jowell, Phyllis and Folb, Adrienne. 2004. *Into Kokerboom Country—Namaqualand's Jewish Pioneers.* Fernwood Press.
- Joyce, Peter. 2004. *Flower Watching in the Cape—scenic routes throughout the year.* Struik.
- Le Roux, Annelise. 2005. *South African Wild Flower Guide 1—Namaqualand.* Botanical Society of South Africa.
- Manning, John and Goldblatt, Peter. 2007. *South African Wild Flower Guide 9—Nieuwoudtville, Bokkeveld Plateau & Hantam.* Botanical Society of South Africa.
- Manning, John and Goldblatt, Peter. 2007. *South African Wild Flower Guide 7—West Coast.* Botanical Society of South Africa.
- Manning, John. 2003. *Photographic Guide to the Wildflowers of South Africa.* Briza Publications.
- Manning, John. 2004. *Southern African Wild Flowers—jewels of the veld.* Struik.
- Norman, Nick and Whitfield, Gavin. 2006. *Geological Journeys.* Struik.
- Odendaal, Francois and Suich, Helen. 2007. *Richtersveld—the land and its people.* Struik.
- Raper, Peter E. 2004. *New Dictionary of South African Place Names.* Jonathan Ball Publishers.

- Ross, Graham. 1998. *The Interactive Role of Transportation and the Economy of Namaqualand.* Unpublished PhD thesis.
- Ross, Graham. 2002. *The Romance of Cape Mountain Passes.* David Philip.
- Smalberger, John M. 1975 (reprinted 2000). *A History of Copper Mining in Namaqualand.* Struik/Scholtz Trust.
- Smith, Gideon. 2003. *Sasol First Field Guide to Aloes of Southern Africa.* Struik.
- Smith, G. F.; Chesselet, P.; Van Jaarsveld, E.; Hartmann, H.; Hammer, S.; Van Wyk, B-E.; Burgoyne, P.; Klak, C. and Kurzweil H. 1998. *Mesembs of the World—a complete field guide to the Mesembryanthemaceae.* Briza Publications.
- Smith, G. F.; Van Jaarsveld, E. J.; Arnold, T. H.; Steffins, F. E.; Dixon, R. D. and Retief, J. A. (eds). 1997. *List of Southern African Succulent Plants.* Umdaus Press.
- South African National Parks. 2006. *|Ai-|Ais|Richtersveld Transfrontier Park—official information guide.* SANParks.
- Steenkamp, Willem. 1975. *Land of the Thirst King.* Howard Timmins.
- Truter, Cornel. 1998. *West Coast Tourist Guide.* UCT Press.
- Van Rooyen, Gretel & Steyn, Hester. 1999. *South African Wild Flower Guide 10—Cederberg: Clanwilliam & Biedouw Valley.* Botanical Society of South Africa.
- Van Wyk, Braam. 2000. *A Photographic Guide to Wild Flowers of South Africa.* Struik.
- Viljoen, M. J. and Reimold, W. U. 1999. *An Introduction to South Africa's Geological and Mining Heritage.* Mintek.
- Williamson, Graham. 2000. *Richtersveld—the enchanted wilderness.* Umdaus Press.

Useful websites

General info and accommodation

- www.northerncape.org.za
- www.south-north.co.za
- www.capetowntourism.co.za
- www.capewestcoast.org
- www.southafrica.net
- www.tourismregions.co.za
- www.northcape-venues.co.za
- www.wheretostay.co.za
- www.routes.co.za
- www.countryroads.co.za
- www.places.co.za
- www.encounter.co.za
- www.caravanning.co.za

Special interest

- Succulent Karoo Ecosystem Programme: www.skep.org
- www.succulents.co.za
- www.diamondbirdingroute.co.za
- www.plantzafrica.com
- SA National Biodiversity Institute: www.sanbi.org
- www.dlist-benguela.org